Multiverse Analysis

There are many ways of conducting an analysis, but most studies show only a few carefully curated estimates. Applied research involves a complex array of analytical decisions, often leading to a "garden of forking paths" where each choice can lead to different results. By systematically exploring how alternative analytical choices affect the findings, *Multiverse Analysis* reveals the full range of estimates that the data can support and uncovers insights that single-path analyses often miss. It shows which modeling decisions are most critical to the results and reveals how data and assumptions work together to produce empirical estimates. Focusing on intuitive understanding rather than complex mathematics and drawing on real-world datasets, this book provides a step-by-step guide to comprehensive multiverse analysis. Go beyond traditional, single-path methods and discover how multiverse analysis can lead to more transparent, illuminating, and persuasive empirical contributions to science.

Cristobal Young is Associate Professor of Sociology at Cornell University. He received his PhD from Princeton University in 2010. His first book, *The Myth of Millionaire Tax Flight: How Place Still Matters for the Rich*, was published by Stanford University Press in 2017.

Erin Cumberworth is a researcher in the Department of Sociology at Cornell University. She received her PhD from Stanford University in 2017. Her work has been published in journals such as *Sociological Methods & Research* and the *ANNALS of the American Academy of Political and Social Science*.

ANALYTICAL METHODS FOR SOCIAL RESEARCH

Analytical Methods for Social Research presents texts on empirical and formal methods for the social sciences. Volumes in the series address both the theoretical underpinnings of analytical techniques as well as their application in social research. Some series volumes are broad in scope, cutting across a number of disciplines. Others focus mainly on methodological applications within specific fields such as political science, sociology, demography, and public health. The series serves a mix of students and researchers in the social sciences and statistics.

Series Editors

R. Michael Alvarez, *California Institute of Technology*
Nathaniel L. Beck, *New York University*
Stephen L. Morgan, *Johns Hopkins University*
Lawrence L. Wu, *New York University*

Other Titles in the Series

Maximum Likelihood for Social Science, by Michael D. Ward and John S. Ahlquist
Computational Social Science, by R. Michael Alvarez
Spatial Analysis for the Social Sciences, by David Darmofal
Time Series Analysis for the Social Sciences, by Janet M. Box-Steffensmeier, John R. Freeman, Matthew P. Hitt, and Jon C. W. Pevehouse
Counterfactuals and Causal Inference, Second Edition, by Stephen L. Morgan and Christopher Winship
Statistical Modeling and Inference for Social Science, by Sean Gailmard
Counterfactuals and Causal Inference: Methods and Principles for Social Research, by Stephen L. Morgan and Christopher Winship
Data Analysis Using Regression and Multilevel/Hierarchical Models, by Andrew Gelman and Jennifer Hill
Political Game Theory: An Introduction, by Nolan McCarty and Adam Meirowitz
Essential Mathematics for Political and Social Research, by Jeff Gill
Spatial Models of Parliamentary Voting, by Keith T. Poole
Event History Modeling: A Guide for Social Scientists, by Janet M. Box-Steffensmeier and Bradford S. Jones
Ecological Inference: New Methodological Strategies, edited by Gary King, Ori Rosen, and Martin A. Tanner
Regression and Other Stories, by Andrew Gelman, Jennifer Hill, and Aki Vehtari
Inferential Network Analysis, by Skyler J. Cranmer, Bruce A. Desmarais, and Jason W. Morgan
Formal Models of Domestic Politics, Second Edition, by Scott Gehlbach

Multiverse Analysis

Computational Methods for Robust Results

CRISTOBAL YOUNG
Cornell University

ERIN CUMBERWORTH
Cornell University

CAMBRIDGE
UNIVERSITY PRESS

Shaftesbury Road, Cambridge CB2 8EA, United Kingdom

One Liberty Plaza, 20th Floor, New York, NY 10006, USA

477 Williamstown Road, Port Melbourne, VIC 3207, Australia

314–321, 3rd Floor, Plot 3, Splendor Forum, Jasola District Centre, New Delhi – 110025, India

103 Penang Road, #05–06/07, Visioncrest Commercial, Singapore 238467

Cambridge University Press is part of Cambridge University Press & Assessment, a department of the University of Cambridge.

We share the University's mission to contribute to society through the pursuit of education, learning and research at the highest international levels of excellence.

www.cambridge.org
Information on this title: www.cambridge.org/9781316518786
DOI: 10.1017/9781009003391

© Cristobal Young and Erin Cumberworth 2025

This publication is in copyright. Subject to statutory exception and to the provisions of relevant collective licensing agreements, no reproduction of any part may take place without the written permission of Cambridge University Press & Assessment.

When citing this work, please include a reference to the DOI 10.1017/9781009003391

First published 2025

A catalogue record for this publication is available from the British Library

A Cataloging-in-Publication data record for this book is available from the Library of Congress

ISBN 978-1-316-51878-6 Hardback
ISBN 978-1-009-00996-6 Paperback

Cambridge University Press & Assessment has no responsibility for the persistence or accuracy of URLs for external or third-party internet websites referred to in this publication and does not guarantee that any content on such websites is, or will remain, accurate or appropriate.

Contents

List of Figures	*page* vii
List of Tables	ix
Acknowledgments	xi

PART I INTRODUCTION

1	The Many Worlds of Analysis	3
2	The Multiverse as a Philosophy of Science	13

PART II THE COMPUTATIONAL MULTIVERSE

3	Hurricane Names: An Applied Introduction	37
4	The Multiverse Algorithm	43
5	Empirical Multiverses	59
6	Influence Analysis and Scope Conditions	70
7	Good and Bad Controls	98
8	Some Alternative Approaches	115

PART III EXPANDING THE MULTIVERSE

9	Functional Form Robustness *Coauthored with Sheridan A. Stewart*	125
10	Data Processing: Invisible Decisions That Matter	154
11	Data Processing Multiverse Analysis of Regnerus and Critics	177
12	Retractions in Social Science: Misadventures in Data Processing	199
13	Weighting the Multiverse	208
14	Conclusion	226

Appendix: Coding with MULTIVRS in Stata	235
References	253
Index	269

Figures

3.1	Modeling distribution of hurricane name effects	page 39
5.1	Output from Stata MULTIVRS command	62
5.2	Modeling distribution of race effect on mortgage lending	63
5.3	Modeling distribution of gender effect on mortgage lending	65
5.4	Modeling distribution of job training program effect	68
6.1	Influence effects for race effect on mortgage lending	78
6.2	Influence effects for gender effect on mortgage lending	80
6.3	Average size of race and gender effects on mortgage lending, by number of control variables	83
6.4	Influence effects, experimental data versus cross-sectional data	88
6.5	Average size of job training program effect, by number of control variables	90
7.1	Causal diagram of a confounder (C)	100
7.2	Causal diagram of a mediator (C)	101
7.3	Causal diagram of a collider (C)	103
7.4	Simulation of a collider (C)	104
7.5	Diagram of marriage as a collider	106
7.6	Marriage as a collider between age and happiness	107
7.7	Causal diagram of a proxy variable (C)	108
8.1	Density graphs of modeling distributions versus specification curve graphs	116
9.1	Modeling distributions: effect of job loss on subjective wellbeing	138
9.2	Effect size of job loss by number of control variables	139
9.3	Modeling distributions: effect of college degree on voting for Donald Trump in 2016	141

9.4	Effect size by number of control variables, voting data	143
9.5	Multiverse results: effect of skin tone on red cards	146
10.1	Effects of peak fertility on the religiosity of women in relationships	161
11.1	Distribution of gay/lesbian parenting effects in control variable multiverse	180
11.2	Distribution of gay/lesbian parenting effects in full multiverse	187
11.3	Distribution of gay/lesbian parenting effects in Regnerus multiverse versus Rosenfeld multiverse	194
13.1	Weighted modeling distributions, air pollution effect on student reaction time	222
A1	Basic multiverse output: union hours example	236
A2	Density graph produced with MULTIVRS command	237
A3	Model results saved to data file using "saveas" option	238
A4	Do file produced with "saveas" option	238
A5	Grouping control variables	239
A6	Either|or syntax to specify alternative estimation commands	241
A7	Allowing sample to vary across models with "nolistwise" option	242
A8	Including a preferred estimate	243
A9	Modeling distribution with normal distribution and preferred estimate	244
A10	Options for reducing size of model space	246
A11	Full modeling distribution versus 1 percent sample, Regnerus multiverse from Chapter 11	247
A12	Unweighted modeling distribution (uniform weights) versus exponential BIC weights, R^2 weights, and influence weights	249

Tables

2.1	Robustness footnotes in top sociology journals, 2010	page 18
3.1	Negative binomial regression models predicting hurricane deaths	38
3.2	Multiverse options and influence analysis for the effect of female hurricane names on deaths	41
4.1	Estimates of model variance and sampling variance in meta-analysis and many-analysts studies	49
5.1	Baseline regression models for race effect on mortgage lending	60
5.2	Model robustness of race effect on mortgage lending	62
5.3	Model robustness of gender effect on mortgage lending	65
5.4	Model robustness of the effect of job training programs, field experiment versus cross-sectional analysis	67
6.1	Influence statistics for race effect on mortgage lending	77
6.2	Influence statistics for gender effect on mortgage lending	79
6.3	Model influence regressions for race and gender effects on mortgage lending	81
6.4	Mortgage approval rates by gender, race, and marital status	85
6.5	Model influence regressions for effect of job training programs, CPS dataset	89
7.1	Simulation of a collider: regression models predicting Y	105
9.1	Comparison of coefficient magnitudes	136
9.2	Functional form robustness of effect of job loss on wellbeing	138
9.3	Functional form robustness of effect of college degree on voting for Donald Trump in 2016	142
9.4	Functional form robustness of effect of skin tone on receiving red cards	146

A9.1	Influence effects for effect of job loss on subjective wellbeing	151
A9.2	Influence effects for effect of college degree on voting for Trump	152
10.1	Multiverse options and influence analysis, Durante et al. study	163
11.1	Regression models for effect of family structure on positive outcomes index, Regnerus versus Rosenfeld definitions	185
11.2	Multiverse results, gay/lesbian parenting effect	189
11.3	Influence effects for gay/lesbian parenting effect	190
13.1	Single and double lasso demonstration	216
13.2	Regression models of student reaction time on in-school air pollution, with three types of model weights	218

Acknowledgments

We are grateful to so many friends and colleagues for their feedback, enthusiasm, criticism, and encouragement over many years of working on multiverse analysis. We first thank Katherine Holsteen, John Muñoz, and Sheridan Stewart (who coauthored Chapter 9 of this book), who have been essential collaborators on the path of turning initial ideas into working software, tested methods, and applied results.

We have benefited from conversation and correspondence with many sociologists and methodologists, including Jeremy Freese, Scott Long, Michelle Jackson, Matt Salganik, Gary King, Michael Rosenfeld, Tom Stanley, Per Engzell, Felix Elwert, Chris Wildeman, Garrett Baker, Kim Weeden, Scott Lynch, Simon Cheng, Nate Breznau, Cassie Short, Claudia Neuendorf, and Bruce Western, as well as an anonymous reviewer. We thank many cohorts of sociology graduate students at Cornell and Stanford who studied these working materials with patience and scrutiny. This book is in conversation with all of these scholars who have shared their thoughts and questions with us.

We thank the editorial team at Cambridge University Press for their confidence in this project and their support in bringing it to fruition.

Cristobal dedicates this work to Patricia, his wife and brilliant companion in life for these last twenty-four years. Erin dedicates this work to her husband, Jack, and her daughter, Eleanor.

PART I

INTRODUCTION

I

The Many Worlds of Analysis

A fragile inference is not worth taking seriously.
—Edward Leamer (1985)

The best defense against subjectivity in science is to expose it.
—Silberzahn et al. (2018: 354)

Statistical models are, at best, only approximations of reality. Econometric theory is built on imperfect assumptions and provides only "inexact … guidance about how to do empirical research" (Solon, Haider, and Wooldridge 2015: 311). The link between social theories and statistical models is often vague, open to debate, and dependent on many auxiliary assumptions (Western 1996; Strevens 2020). Testing a hypothesis – estimating a coefficient – requires taking many approximate inputs from social and statistical theory and turning them into a single, exact regression model. Out of many fuzzy things, one.

There are many ways of conducting an analysis, but most studies report only a few carefully curated estimates. Behind the curtain, in the backstage realm of research, lie many worlds of alternative analyses that could have been conducted: alternative models and alternative results. Multiverse analysis explores and reports on this often-hidden world between theory and data. From one published analysis, we can imagine many feasible alternatives.

The principle of robustness is central to modern science. In the most general sense, robustness refers to "situations in which something is stable under variations of something else" (Basso 2017: 57). This book is about model robustness: where an estimate – a regression coefficient of interest – is (or is not) stable under different variations of the model. And model robustness is fundamental to the credibility of research.

Researchers want to be able to say: "This is not my opinion, this is what the evidence says." Multiverse analysis gives us a tool to *show* how much results are driven by the evidence rather than by subjective researcher choices and assumptions. Statistical models involve so many unique decisions that they become a "garden of forking paths" (Borges 1941; Gelman and Loken 2014). In theory, there is a single "true" model of the data generation process, but that model is almost never known. In practice, a single-path analysis represents a bundle of assumptions: ideas about the correct choice of controls, functional form, estimation command, variable definitions, and more, which are not yet proven to be true. A single-path point estimate reflects just one ad hoc route through the forking paths world. Different researchers studying the same question almost never use the same models (Breznau et al. 2022). Sometimes a different model would give a similar answer, but other times it might diverge dramatically. It can be difficult for readers to know if a result is driven more by the data or by the author's model assumptions. The raw data are often external to a researcher and must be accepted as given, but the model assumptions are not. Typically, researchers decide on their model assumptions with the data in hand, and they can see which assumptions favor their hypothesis. This is a problem of asymmetric information between analyst and reader: Analysts with data in hand know much more about the sensitivity of results than do readers, who have access only to the curated results published in the paper.

The inspiration and language of the multiverse come from quantum physics and cosmology (Gribbin 2009; Carroll 2019a). In a multiverse, there is more universe and there are more worlds than we can currently see. We know the universe extends beyond the cosmic horizon of our best telescopes and instruments, but we can only guess what might be out there. The universe is what we can *see*, while the multiverse is everything that *exists*. When applied to methodology, the multiverse means there are many more ways of estimating a parameter than what any one study shows. Individual papers tend to offer only a narrow horizon into the plausible model space. But scholars are awash with computational power and can easily estimate a vast number of models prior to selecting a careful few for publication. The multiverse software we used in preparing this book can estimate 1,000 unique model specifications in a matter of seconds using a normal computer. In an hour, one can see typically results from 100,000 model variations. The most ambitious multiverse analysis on record ran more than nine billion regressions (Muñoz and Young 2018). With such staggering computational power in the hands of analysts, thinking in terms of one estimate is anachronistic at best.

There are many ways of thinking about model robustness, and including some version of robustness analysis has become increasingly common in quantitative research papers. Social scientists often publish tables with only a few specifications but also have "robustness footnotes" mentioning other models that, inevitably, are said to "show the same results" (Young and Holsteen 2017). These footnotes are weakly transparent, but they at least acknowledge the existence of other plausible model assumptions. In meta-analysis studies of the existing literature, we see a kind of multiverse of models that have been used in past research. And meta-analysis routinely reports that individual studies are a poor guide to the true range of results that multiple studies show (Stanley and Doucouliagos 2012). Each individual study reports a point estimate and a confidence interval, and in theory that confidence interval shows the range of results that should occur 95 percent of the time. But it is very common for the next study to show an estimate entirely outside that interval. Compared to the wide range of results seen in most social science literatures, the individual studies making up the literature all seem very *overconfident*. This is because confidence intervals do not take into account *model error* or the possibility that other studies will make different assumptions and use different methods.

One response to the troubling range of results in the published literature is to organize an adversarial collaboration: Researchers with rival views and prior beliefs agree to jointly analyze one dataset (Mellers, Hertwig, and Kahneman 2001; Clark et al. 2022). The resulting publication shows the strongest possible results from each side in the debate. This elegantly shows (1) how much *common support* the data provide to each side of a debate and (2) how much the modeling assumptions shape what each side can claim. Often, adversarial collaborations do not result in agreement between the different sides, but rather they help clarify which auxiliary assumptions drive their disagreement and help build a future research agenda for new data collection and new empirical testing.

Many-analysts studies expand on this approach by drawing in modeling expertise from larger and more diverse groups of researchers, all studying the same question with the same raw dataset. An emerging consensus from these many-analysts trials is that no two researchers ever use the same model specification nor ever get exactly the same results (Silberzahn et al. 2018; Schweinsberg et al. 2021; Breznau et al. 2022). Participants are routinely surprised by the variation across other participants' estimates. A number of studies have asked researchers, after they completed their own analysis of the data, to predict the range of results from other research teams. Researchers almost uniformly underestimate the range of models that other intelligent people will think of. "Individual scientists do not appreciate how different their peers' analytical choices are and how much results will be affected" (Camerer 2022: 3). When you consider a model specification but eventually decide "nobody would run that model," you are likely wrong. In crowdsourcing studies, knowledgeable scholars as a collective seem willing to run almost any plausible model – and the diversity of methods and results is not explained by researcher training, experience, publication record, or even peer evaluations of quality. This is not a world where "bad scholars" use "bad models," while "good scholars" use "good models." Scholars should embrace thinking in the gray – the gray zone between one's own first-choice method and alternative methods that could be defended by others. Between those two points are a range of methodological strategies that deserve attention.

WHERE DO "MANY MODELS" COME FROM?

Ideal-Type Approaches

There are two ideal-type illustrations of how to develop a large set of plausible models that define the model space. The first approach is what we call the "super log file" approach, which captures any model a researcher ever estimated or looked at in a project. The second approach uses a task force of experts representing theory competition and adversarial collaboration. Neither of these approaches are practical for day-to-day work, but computational methods aim to approximate their best features.

The Super Log File Approach

An interesting feature of Excel files is that they remember every computation that was ever conducted, with or without the author knowing or wanting it.[1] In contrast, when researchers use Stata or R, they have to choose what parts of their work get recorded and saved for others to see.

---

[1] This feature of Excel has been used to identify evidence of manually tampering with data to generate supporting evidence in social science publications (https://datacolada.org/109).

There is an unknown selection process to what researchers chose to publish. However, imagine that statistical software kept a super log file that automatically captured the results of every unique regression a researcher ever ran in the course of studying their data and preparing an article. Once the project is finalized, the log program generates a graph showing every unique regression result an author ever looked at.

The philosophy here is that any model a researcher considered worth running is also worth reporting (even if the model could be criticized – as all can be). This is full disclosure of all results the author has ever seen. If an author chooses to run a model specification, it becomes part of a permanent record available to all readers. We like this thought experiment for two reasons: (1) It allows authors to disclose the many ways they a priori think a model could be credibly specified and (2) it equalizes the information asymmetry between authors and readers – authors can see an estimate only if they are also willing to show it to their readers.

The Task Force Approach

Another ideal-type way to develop the model space is to convene a task force of specialists to study an important social question. The task force would reflect on a range of disciplinary and political perspectives, ensuring a healthy dose of theory competition and adversarial collaboration (Mellers et al. 2001; Doucouliagos and Stanley 2013). Any model specification that a task force member credibly argues for becomes part of the model space. There might be one model and estimate that gets the most votes by the majority of the task force, but a graphical display shows what results can be found by serious scholars using credible alternative methods. Dissenting votes and rejected model specifications are part of the public record. The final report might include any number of different specifications that best reflect the methodological views among the task force. One example is the American Psychological Association task force on the relationships between race, genetics, and intelligence, published as "Intelligence: Knowns and Unknowns" (Neisser et al. 1996). The task force sought to "make clear what has been scientifically established, what is presently in dispute, and what is still unknown" (Neisser et al. 1996: 77). These kinds of prestige task forces are rare, but they provide an ideal of how to elicit a wide range of analytical views from top scholars in a field. In recent years, crowdsourcing studies have sought to emulate the task force approach, recruiting many scholars to analyze a specific question using a shared dataset, with each participant sending back their preferred specification, code, and estimate.

The Computational Multiverse

Both of the aforementioned approaches involve running many unique models and reporting a distribution of results in graphical form. Computational model robustness aims to incorporate features of both the super log file and the task force approaches. The objective is to reduce the discretion of authors to pick an exactly preferred model and result (the strength of the super log file approach) while expanding the range of models and results that any one author considers (the merit of the task force approach). The method involves specifying a set of plausible model ingredients (including possible controls, variable definitions, estimation commands, and standard error calculations) and estimating all possible combinations of those model ingredients. The principle is to use only vetted, credible model inputs, as any author would do when selecting a single estimate, but then report back every estimate that can be obtained from those inputs. It perturbates the model using a combinations algorithm while also reporting how much each modeling input (or assumption) matters for the results.

To be clear, a computational approach can only *aspire to* the breadth of insight available in an expert task force assembled for adversarial collaboration. It requires users to specify credible alternatives for each model input. But the checklist is valuable for any author to work through. For each control variable, is the variable strictly necessary or is it possibly a bad or unnecessary control? What arguments could be made against including a control? For each equation, is there another credible functional form – another way to link the left- and right-hand sides of the model? For any variable in the system, could it be defined or coded in a different and possibly better way? After working through these questions, the resulting *modeling distribution* shows what estimates are possible, while *model influence* shows how these decisions affect the results. As we will see in Chapter 9, Figure 9.5, applying this set of questions to a project generates a multiverse of possible models that is at least similar to the range of models in a many-analysts study. And in a multiverse analysis of intergenerational mobility Engzell and Mood (2023) showed how this process is constructive, developmental, and informative and how working through the many decisions a researcher inevitably has to make can yield unexpected insight.

The Central Theorem of Multiverse Analysis

The core principles of multiverse analysis are as follows: Confidence intervals never show the true range of credible results. Every analysis depends on untested assumptions that are never exactly correct. Every analysis is a rough approximation of the true model. There is always model error; it is just rarely acknowledged.

The aim of multiverse methods is to reduce the discretion of authors to pick an exactly preferred model and result while expanding the range of models and results under consideration. The method involves specifying a set of plausible model ingredients (including possible controls, variable definitions, estimation commands, and standard error calculations) and estimating all possible combinations of those model ingredients. Acknowledging those other paths allows multiple plausible models and yields a modeling *distribution* of estimates. A single-path point estimate is a "best guess" starting place to enter the multiverse: a reference point from which to define alternative assumptions and to see how different the alternative estimates are from the author's *first choice* of model specification. From here, we leave the point estimate behind and think primarily in terms of distributions: What is the range of plausible estimates from alternative models? How many model assumptions can be relaxed without overturning an empirical conclusion? Which model assumptions affect the results the most?

The multiverse approach goes far beyond simply generating possible models; it demands careful thinking about model specifications and their underlying assumptions. It calls for prudent interpretation and highlights what methods, techniques, and assumptions need rigorous evaluation before they can be considered a credible part of the analysis. When a finding lacks robustness to model specification, this introduces a *methodological scope condition* that not only shows under what conditions a result holds but also serves as a guide to further deliberation and research.

Notes on the Multiverse Metaphor

The term "multiverse analysis" was first used by Steegen et al. (2016); we assume, but do not know for sure, that this imagery comes from Andrew Gelman, a coauthor of the study and a statistician who has a great gift for vivid writing. This language, in our work, now replaces less inspired but perhaps more descriptive terms like "multi-model analysis" or a framework for "model uncertainty and robustness" (e.g., Young and Holsteen

2017). The multiverse concept encapsulates the problem of uncertainty and the solution of robustness, all while being packaged in a metaphor that sparks the imagination.

At the same time, we must acknowledge that some scholars have reservations about the term due to its ascendance in popular culture, science fiction circles, and superhero movies. This can lead to misconceptions or oversimplifications of the idea when applied to scholarly discourse. We recognize the concern but push back in part because we welcome a newer style of methodological terminology. Classical statistics and econometrics have a dismal and stodgy record of naming new methods. In the formative years of statistics, new concepts were given intimidating, polysyllabic names derived from Greek and Latin: heteroskedasticity, autocorrelation, multicollinearity, nonparametric, kurtosis, and endogeneity. What is distinctive about these terms is that they have no common meaning in English and serve as purely technical constructs that intimidate outsiders. In this style, the problem of "small sample size" could be given more scientific gravitas by calling it "micro-numerosity."

With the rise of data science, developments in statistical methods are given more informal and vivid, often playful, names. Early examples are the bootstrap and the jackknife: resampling methods that invoked folk terminology to suggest their underlying logic (e.g., the jackknife uses a one-at-a-time resampling method, in analogy to how a Swiss army knife has many blades that can be taken out one at a time). More recent data science tools come with names like neural networks, decision trees, and random forests, which are all variants of machine learning. The spirit of data science naming conventions has been to make the language more vivid, approachable, and even fun to talk about.

The language and empirical imagery of the multiverse in social science is catching on fast. To illustrate, we list disciplines that have, following Steegen et al. (2016), published studies that embrace the language of multiverse analysis. The language and methods of multiverse analysis are experiencing rapid take-up in the social sciences.

RECENT ARTICLES USING MULTIVERSE LANGUAGE AND METHODS

Sociology: Engzell and Mood (2023); Young and Stewart (2021); Auspurg and Brüderl (2021)

Computer Science: Liu et al. (2021); Hall et al. (2022); Sarma et al. (2023)

Political Science: Saraceno, Hansen, and Treul (2021)
Psychology: Harder (2020); Modecki et al. (2020); Olsson-Collentine et al. (2023)
Public Policy: Breznau et al. (2022)
Education: Robitzsch (2022); Herrala (2023); Neuendorf and Jansen (2023)
Organizational Behavior: Schweinsberg et al. (2021)
Religion: Hanel and Zarzeczna (2023)
Health and Epidemiology: Cantone and Tomaselli (2023); Levitt, Zonta, and Ioannidis (2023); Rengasamy et al. (2023)

OUTLINE OF THE BOOK

This book walks readers through every aspect of a rigorous multiverse analysis, drawing on real-life datasets and providing code for others to use in their own work (and to replicate our work). In this process we believe that almost everyone's beliefs about modeling assumptions will be deeply challenged. The goal is to better understand how data and assumptions work together to produce empirical estimates. In Chapter 2, we round out the introduction of this book by discussing the multiverse as a philosophy of science.

As we move on to Part II, The Computational Multiverse, we start with a vivid empirical case: research claiming that female hurricanes are deadlier than male hurricanes (Chapter 3). We demonstrate multiverse analysis using analytical inputs from many scholars in a high-profile empirical debate. The original claims appear remarkably weak: 99.7 percent of alternative models show weaker results, and 88 percent of models report null findings. From here, we cover the core methodology of multiverse methods across five chapters (Chapters 4–8). First we aim at understanding that the modeling distribution is distinct from the sampling distribution and at applying the method to multiple datasets. Next we discuss the second pillar of multiverse methods: influence analysis, which documents how different features of model specification (such as individual controls) affect the results. Part II mostly builds the foundations of multiverse methods using assumptions about control variables and discusses in depth the complexity and difficulty of assuming that a control variable belongs or does not belong in a model (Chapter 7, "Good and Bad Controls").

Part III, Expanding the Multiverse, explores the next two dimensions of modeling assumptions: functional forms that link the left- and right-hand sides of a regression model and data processing choices such as cleaning, coding, and categorizing variables. In Chapter 9 (coauthored with Sheridan Stewart) we develop multiverse analyses that compare estimation commands such as OLS, logit, probit, inverse probability weighting, and two different matching algorithms. Does the use of these different link functions or algorithms lead to different empirical findings? Do some yield more stable and reliable estimates than others? In Chapters 10–12, we show that data processing is a large world of model uncertainty, where there is little clear guidance for practice and where researcher degrees of freedom are often nearly invisible to readers. Chapter 10 digs into theories of how data processing influences results. Chapter 11 illustrates a complex data processing multiverse with a reanalysis of a highly contentious work by Regnerus (2012a). Chapter 12 reviews a series of social science cases where articles were retracted due to errors in data processing that undermined their analyses – powerful lessons about the centrality of data processing in analytical work. Chapter 13 explores a frontier question of whether, or how well, one could weight models by their probability of being the true model. This is a challenging task and involves a fundamental tradeoff between transparency and model selection.

In Chapter 14, we revisit the key conclusions and insights from multiverse analysis we found along the way. We emphasize that computational power has transformed social science in both positive and negative ways: It has greatly expanded the capacity for empirical research but also created a large information asymmetry between analyst and reader that lies at the core of the crisis in science. Computational power makes multiverse analysis feasible and, we believe, inevitable. However, computational power does not replace the need for human knowledge and judgment. The best multiverse analyses will come from scholars with advanced statistical training, rich field-area knowledge about the research question, and a great capacity to understand and appreciate rival scientific views.

2

The Multiverse as a Philosophy of Science

> What are the ethics of telling people something that's wrong?
> —Erin Leahey (2008: 625)

Multiverse analysis is not simply a computational method but also a philosophy of science. The following are the core elements of that philosophy: (1) A raw dataset does not speak for itself, and subjective assumptions are an inherent part of research; (2) asymmetric information between analysts and readers deeply challenges the credibility of science – readers should know as much about the reliability of results as do analysts; and (3) theory competition and methodological transparency are central for science to operate as a self-correcting knowledge machine. In our view, the foundational principles of the multiverse are exciting and no less important than the technical details of how to conduct and interpret a "many worlds" vision of robust empirical research.

THE NEW WORLD: COMPUTATIONAL POWER AND ASYMMETRIC INFORMATION

The information age has greatly expanded the world of empirical science. If one reads the leading social science journals of the 1960s, 70s, and 80s, the work was far less evidence-based than today. In the past, two key ingredients of empirical science were very scarce resources: data were hard to access and the computational power required for analysis was limited. Today there is a vast reservoir of social data available online for anyone to download, and computational power is cheap and ubiquitous. The basic capacity of science to learn from evidence has never been greater. What have we done with all this data access and computational power? The information age was supposed to usher in "a renaissance of human knowledge," but it often seems more like "a tsunami of noise and misinformation" (Stanley and Doucouliagos 2012: 1). There has been a tremendous increase in empirical work, but also a new "crisis in science" in which there is declining confidence in the quality, objectivity, and robustness of empirical results.

In the early days of social science, calculating all the sums of squares needed to compute an "ordinary least squares" regression coefficient by hand was a daunting task. We doubt that any modern reader has ever attempted a paper-and-pencil calculation of a regression coefficient using nontrivial data. But if anyone did, they would not be inclined to do it again, just to try out a different specification. By the 1920s, statistical labs had expensive machines that helped to compute sums of squares mechanically; yet producing a regression coefficient could still take hundreds of hours of human labor. Running a second regression model was computationally unrealistic. In those days, researchers had to plan out their analysis entirely in advance, and they could only afford the time and effort to estimate one model. That one estimate was the only result the authors ever saw, and when published, authors and readers had exactly the same knowledge about possible results.

By the 1970s and early 1980s, university researchers were using time-shared mainframe computers with physical punch cards for data and code. Running multiple regression models was easier than in the 1920s but still comedically difficult by today's standards. The potential for p-hacking had emerged, but it was limited by computational constraints. It is the twenty-first-century advent of personal computers for statistical research that fundamentally changed the game of social science. Computations that used to take months of human labor now occur almost instantaneously. A multiverse analysis estimating 1,000 different models takes only minutes or even seconds. The computational cost of running an alternative model has gone from prohibitive to trivial. For this reason, we should assume that researchers today know a great deal about model dependence and sensitivity. Researchers have the time and resources, even without an algorithm, to run thousands of models while thinking about their analysis and its many possible variants. The only problem with this state of technology is that the capability of readers – consumers of research – to evaluate the research has not kept pace. In many ways, readers have lost ground relative to authors and are in a worse position to evaluate research quality than perhaps ever before.

The information age has created a fundamental asymmetry between analysts and readers – or between producers and consumers. Analysts can test thousands of plausible models, trying out different model assumptions. Consumers are still constrained to know only the handful of model specifications that are curated for publication. Technology created this problem, and technology will have to be part of the solution.

Some social science methodologists have argued that most published research findings today are false positives and that most empirical breakthroughs are actually dead-ends (Ioannidis 2005; Simmons, Nelson, and Simonsohn 2011). We hope this diagnosis is too pessimistic, but the problems in replication are by now undeniable. In fields where there have been intensive efforts to replicate published research, the results have been sobering.[1] This includes research into the causes of cancer (Prinz et al. 2011; Begley and Ellis 2012), genetics research on intelligence (Chabris et al. 2012), the social psychology of priming (Giolla et al. 2022), and the determinants of economic growth across countries (Sala-i-Martin et al. 2004). These research lines have at least at their peak represented some of the most exciting research in their fields, produced by leading scholars and published in the top journals. In each of these areas, large portions of exciting and even path breaking research have turned out to be nonrobust, false positive findings.

Primary medical research has been an area with especially detailed replication efforts. Private sector biotech labs closely follow the primary science literature for findings that could be developed into new medicines and treatments. However, industry labs that try to replicate published biomedical research are often unable to reproduce the findings. Enormous resources go into these replications. Biotech giant Amgen reported on ten years of efforts to replicate fifty-three "landmark" studies that pointed to new cancer treatments. With its team of 100 scientists, only 11 percent of these studies could be replicated (Begley and Ellis 2012). Other pharmaceutical companies have reported similarly disappointing results, and as an Amgen vice president noted, "on speaking with many investigators in academia and industry, we found widespread recognition" of replication failures in primary medical research (Begley and Ellis 2012: 532). While the rapid success of the COVID-19 vaccines shows that biomedical science can still deliver game-changing

---

[1] Much of sociology has not yet been subjected to large-scale replication, but we suspect replication in sociology would not go any more smoothly than it has in psychology or economics.

breakthroughs, no one should ignore the preponderance of false positives that make up so much of the published literature.

In psychology and behavioral genetics, a large accumulated literature has found evidence for genetic determinants of general intelligence, identifying at least thirteen specific genes linked to intelligence quotient (Payton 2009). However, in comprehensive replication, applying the same core model to multiple large-scale datasets, a major interdisciplinary research team found that virtually all of these associations appear to be false positives (Chabris et al. 2012). Across thirty-two replication tests, only one gene yielded barely nominal significance. This is just below the expected 5 percent rate of significant findings when there are no true associations in the data.

Replication has also been hard in an area of psychology known as social priming. This literature asserts that subtle, almost subconscious, cues and influences can have dramatic effects on behavior. Findings report, for example, that people primed with the word "professor" perform 13 percent better on tests than those primed with the term "soccer hooligan" (Giolla et al. 2022). Another study, titled "Analytical Thinking Promotes Religious Disbelief" and published in the journal *Science*, reported that showing a picture of the Rodin sculpture *The Thinker* caused people's belief in God to fall by a third – implying that religiosity is overturned by the mere suggestion of mental effort (Gervais and Norenzanyan 2012). In a meta-analysis of sixty-five replications of social priming research, results were stark: (1) Fewer than one in five replication attempts reported a significant effect in the same direction; (2) replications were successful only when an original author was also doing the replication; (3) when independent labs that did not include an original author were doing the replication, none (out of forty-nine) of the replication studies were successful (Giolla et al. 2022). This suggests that the entire field of social priming research is comprised of false positive results.

In macroeconomics, the literature on economic growth likewise appears thick with nonrobust results. In a set of now-classic robustness studies, Sala-i-Martin (1997; Sala-i-Martin, Doppelhofer, and Miller 2004) revisited sixty-seven "known" determinants of national economic growth – variables that had been previously shown to have a significant effect on gross domestic product. For example, studies have variously reported that distance from the equator, degree of capitalism, and dependence on natural resources have important effects on the wealth of nations. Testing their robustness against many sets of possible controls, only eighteen growth determinants (roughly 25 percent) showed consistent and nontrivial effects; forty-six of the variables were consistently weak and nonsignificant; some were significant in only 1 out of 1,000 regression models. There is now widespread doubt about how much was learned from the extensive literature on cross-country economic growth (Durlauf, Johnson, and Temple 2005; Ciccone and Jarociński 2010).

Rigorous science is in direct competition with misinformation, and its long-term survival depends on winning this competition. Literatures that continually produce research that fails to replicate are contributing to the declining confidence in science in general and diminishing their own fields in particular. Social science embraces the belief that our statistical tests differentiate truth from falsehood with 95 percent confidence. But we all know something has gone wrong when far more than 5 percent of studies fail to replicate.

Science is a set of principles, rules, and guardrails that bring to light new knowledge. The guardrails serve to prevent the personal beliefs and biases of researchers from coloring their results. When the guardrails work, *researchers* may have personal biases but their *results* do not; scholars with different values and beliefs can trust that evidence is transparent and reliable. With strong guardrails, the pressure to publish is tightly coupled with the goal of producing informative and cumulative research of lasting value. When the guardrails fail, whole literatures can drive off a cliff of unchecked prior belief, producing a long chain of nonreplicable results, each relying on one another for supportive citations and credibility. With failed guardrails, literatures get tilted toward "performative research aimed at like-minded colleagues," focusing on the business enterprise of adding up publications of little scientific value and avoiding serious intellectual competition with rival theories (Clark et al. 2022: 1).

THE WEAK ROBUSTNESS OF FOOTNOTES

One of the guardrails of science that lacks credibility today is the practice of reporting "robustness footnotes." There is tacit and widespread acknowledgment that research results may not be robust, and studies often provide footnotes about additional, unreported, models that are said to support the main findings – an informal and ad hoc approach to transparency.

A brief study illustrates how common and uninformative these robustness footnotes are in sociological research. Young and Holsteen

TABLE 2.1 *Robustness footnotes in top sociology journals, 2010*

	Total articles	Quantitative articles	Articles with 1+ robustness footnotes	Percentage of articles	Average robustness footnotes per article
American Sociological Review	39	32	26	81	3.0
American Journal of Sociology	35	28	25	89	3.5
Total	74	60	51	85	3.2

Source: Young and Holsteen (2017)

(2017: 7) recorded the average number of footnotes referring to additional, unreported, results in the 2010 editions of two top sociology journals: the *American Journal of Sociology* and *American Sociological Review*. Of the sixty quantitative articles published in 2010, the vast majority – 85 percent – contained at least one footnote referencing an additional, unreported, analysis purporting to confirm the robustness of the main results (see Table 2.1). The average article contained 3.2 robustness footnotes. The text of these notes is fairly standard: "We ran additional models X, Y, and Z, and the results were the same/substantially similar/support our conclusions." Not a single one of the 164 footnotes failed to support the main results. Authors are not, in these footnotes, ever disclosing models that qualify, weaken, or contradict their main findings. What credible purpose do these footnotes serve if they uniformly report perfect robustness? In our view, these footnotes acknowledge the importance of transparency without actually providing it – a failed guardrail in social science.

Scholars often wish the replication crisis would simply go away. But this cannot happen until our methods and practices of science improve – until the *trustworthiness* of social science improves. The guardrails of science need to be updated in light of the information age. This calls for greater transparency about how much authors can influence their empirical results. We assert two key principles: (1) Make it harder to publish dubious results and (2) make it easier to evaluate the robustness of results. The way to advance both goals is greater transparency.

ROBUSTNESS VERSUS THEORY INNOVATION

In our experience of discussing transparency with other sociologists, there is a commonly expressed view that science ought to nurture the possibility of new ideas. A vibrant discipline, in this view, favors publishing studies that *might be true* and fears that the demands of robust evidence stifles the process of idea formation and development. We agree that robustness is not the single standard for evaluating a study. New ideas often require new data and new measurement in order to be adequately tested – data which may not yet exist. Studies that can offer only partial, nonrobust, evidence can still justify investment in more and better data if the theory is not well measured in existing data. Indeed, new theories cannot be dismissed simply because the data needed for testing them do not yet exist. Robustness is a central criterion for a claim to become a high-visibility stylized fact, but it should not be a barrier to discussing new ideas. At the same time, scientific papers must always be clear about the scope of their claims: Are they holding up a new idea that might be true or are they claiming to establish strong empirical validity?

We value exploratory research that opens up new ideas, but science also needs a process for correcting wrong ideas and closing down mistaken leads, rather than letting them live on without accountability. The nature of science is that any idea or hypothesis, no matter how odd or exotic, can be submitted for empirical testing. But when the ideas are wrong, and fail to find strong empirical support, they should be jettisoned from the literature with the same enthusiasm with which they entered it.

Science was always meant to be a destroyer of false ideas. At the dawn of the scientific revolution, scholars believed that earth was the center of the universe, that animals could spontaneously generate, that humans would perish if they ventured too close to the equator, and that bathing was poisonous because water "opened the pores to infection and plague" (Dolnick 2011: xv). When science emerged out of medieval society, the stock of human knowledge about the world was not so much *limited* – there were no shortage of theories about how the world worked – as it was *wrong*. The task of science has not simply been discovery but just as much a process of refuting a vast body of wrong beliefs. Science did not fill in an *absence of beliefs* about the world but rather replaced wrong ideas with scientifically and empirically supported ideas.

In a sense, there is a rigor-versus-innovation tradeoff in social science that requires balance. But the ultimate standard of science is being right about the evidence, and no research line can put off this judgment for very long.

TRANSPARENCY IN THE HISTORY OF SCIENCE

Early science emerged sometime around 1500 AD, and looked very different from science today. It also existed in a very different social world and faced an enormous credibility problem: What is it about "science" that makes it believable? Why should anyone believe what scientists say? The scientific revolution emerged from a world of superstition, mystics, prophets, and doomsayers. Scientists needed to separate themselves from the age of dogma and superstition. Sir Francis Bacon had laid out the central tenets of the scientific method: skepticism, observation, careful reasoning, and the like. But science also had to be communicated, and it had to be more convincing than superstition. How could we know that the insights from science actually derived from scientific methods? For science to become knowledge that accumulates and builds on itself, we needed the principle of replication: "follow these methods and see for yourself."

In the history of science, replication was the foundation of discovery. When a scientist discovered something about the properties of light, magnetism, electricity, the body, or objects in the solar system, the task was then to explain to other scientists exactly how to replicate their research so that others could observe the same evidence and be persuaded by their own eyes. Replication meant transparency.

For early science to succeed, it had to overcome three basic problems: (1) the cultural authority of ancient knowledge, (2) the many bizarre ideas about the natural world in circulation, and (3) the dishonesty of many early scientists and their lack of integrity (Dolnick 2011; Wootton 2015; Strevens 2020).

First, the precursor to the scientific revolution was an age of absolute deference to ancient knowledge, much of it codified by Aristotle in the third century BC. It was deeply believed that the ancients had complete knowledge of God's world, and the role of mediaeval scholars was to understand and preserve that knowledge, not to question it. If one was to study astronomy, or physics, or geology, they would read and interpret what Aristotle wrote on the subject. There was nothing new to be discovered about the world that the ancients did not know, and medieval scholars and religious authorities were intolerant of any claims to the contrary. But when Columbus sailed across the Atlantic and found a continent unknown to Aristotle, it ruptured contemporary understanding of the nature of our planet.[2]

---

[2] Aristotle had posited that our planet was a sphere made of water with one landmass floating on top of it; this was inconsistent with the discovery of another landmass floating on

The scientific revolution was in large part a process of realizing that the ancient knowledge was more dogma than a body of truths – often wrong and wholly incomplete. Things could be learned that Aristotle and the ancients did not know: A new age of discovery was possible. Even more galling for the old guard, it was an uneducated sailor rather than a scholar that first broke the authority of the ancients.[3]

A second, albeit closely related, problem for science was that scholars in this age believed many bizarre ideas about the natural word, much of it passed down from the ancient writing. Mice are spontaneously generated in straw, and scorpions can form out of crushed basil (Wootton 2015: 266). Johannes Kepler, one of the great scholars of the scientific revolution, believed that geese came from barnacles (Wootton 2015: 268). Robert Boyle, the first modern chemist, advocated using powdered human feces as a treatment for cataracts (Dolnick 2011: 51).

Galileo revolutionized astronomy, but he was also an astrologer and wrote horoscopes for the Grand Duke of Tuscany (Wootton 2015: 258). In his day, most believed that the purpose of astronomy was to conduct astrology – to read the messages in the heavens and predict when the stars best aligned for marriages, military campaigns, and other endeavors. Isaac Newton, perhaps the greatest physicist who ever lived, was obsessed with alchemy and devoted much of his research to ancient myths about turning base metals into gold. Alchemy, astrology, and science were undifferentiated fields – new science comingled with mystical and magical beliefs.

The third problem for science was that many of the early scientists were "incorrigibly dishonest" (Wootton 2015: 272); despite making important contributions, they also made wild claims and gave personal testimony to observing them. Scholars documented phenomena like ghosts, virgin births, and babies born with animal fur or monster hybridity; they interviewed "witches," insisted that goat's blood softened diamonds, and wrote

---

the other side. Scholars soon after deduced, correctly, that the earth was instead more like solid rock with water on the surface – a complete inversion of ancient knowledge. Note that the idea of a flat earth was never, since Aristotle, taken seriously by scholars.

[3] It should be noted that Columbus was bad at math and had severely miscalculated the circumference of the earth. His goal was to sail around the world to reach Asia. Scholars of the day generally recognized that trip would be far too long to sail without resupplying and had warned against financing Columbus's voyage. Indeed, the only reason why he and his crew survived was sheer luck: there happened to be another continent halfway between Europe and Asia. Columbus never accepted that his math was wrong and for the remainder of his life believed he had made it all the way to Asia, rather than only half way.

about "natural magic" – such as healing cuts and wounds by applying an ointment, not to the wound itself but to the blade that caused the wound (Wootton 2015: 287, 291, 300). Gottfried Leibniz was a towering intellect who coinvented calculus; he also published a case report of a talking dog that could speak thirty words in French (Dolnick 2011: 237). Early scientists operated jointly in the realms of facts, fantasies, and fabrications. Science and nonsense liberally comingled. Among the early scientists, "for every genius there was a crank or a charlatan … [and] often the genius and the crank were the same person"; the "boundary that separates the possible from the impossible" was not well established (Dolnick 2011: 51), and there were many incentives for "men of science" to make fantastical claims.

Thus, science had three fundamental problems to solve: (1) overturning the oppressive authority of Aristotle and the ancients – thus unlocking the potential for new discoveries; (2) finding a new basis for belief that was distinct from superstition and mysticism (the alternative becoming known as "empirical evidence"); and (3) enforcing standards of honesty among scientists.

When Britain's academy of science, the Royal Society, was founded in 1660, its motto was *Nullius in Verba*: translated as "take no one's word for it" or "see for yourself." This doctrine of replication – seeing the evidence for oneself – was a war on "false rumor" and "opinions based on unreliable and untrustworthy foundations" (quoted, Wootton 2015: 283). A kindred community of scientists in Florence set their motto as "test and test again," equally asserting that replication was the pathway to truth. Members of these new societies wrote indictments of lesser scholars as "Traitors to Truth … plotting manifest falsehoods," while also criticizing naïve readers "as Ideots, for believing and admiring such fopperies" (quoted, Wootton 2015: 270). Establishing the credibility of science meant discarding "the old and useless luggage" or "the rubbish" of ancient authorities and contemporary peddlers of lies (quoted, Wootton 2015: 299).

The new framework of science had to start first from principles to establish "what is, and what is not." The entire basis of truth as opposed to error or falsehood was reinvented on the grounds of transparent, reproducible evidence.

This conviction in the power of replication stems from transformative successes in early science. In 1610, word of a new discovery by Galileo spread like fire, with rumors that he had found a new solar system with planets orbiting a distant star. This was shocking to human knowledge of the day, which held that everything in the heavens rotated around the earth as the center of the universe. If Galileo was right, he was pulling a thread that could unravel everything humans understood about the cosmos. The discovery was met with great skepticism, and many thought Galileo was simply spreading lies in pursuit of fame (Wootton 2015: 220). In fact, Galileo had found moons orbiting Jupiter – somewhat less fantastic than the early rumors but no less devastating to ancient wisdom. What happened next was a defining moment in the emergence of science: large-scale, independent replication. Scholars scrambled to acquire their own high-quality telescopes – technology that was previously only used for warfare and navigation – and within months, Galileo's discovery was widely confirmed throughout Europe. These shared observations about the moons of Jupiter formed the first in a series of "killer facts" that laid waste to eighteen centuries of deep belief in geocentrism – the view that the earth is the center of the universe.[4]

Early science had to fight for truth in a world of superstition and dogma. Science had no authority to rest on. Early scientists like Galileo, Newton, and the founders of the Royal Society desperately wanted their work to be replicated. Without replication, scientists had no way of distinguishing empirical evidence from the "fopperies" and "rubbish" in wide circulation. Replication was a central foundation of the scientific revolution – and it was central to distinguishing science from dogma. To have one's work replicated was to truly enter the discourse of science, as well as a chance to have one's discoveries demonstrated for the eyes of others. Without this, scientists were no more trustworthy than sailors returning from sea with tales of dragons.

Over the centuries, the principle of replication fell into disuse and lost its role as a mission statement in credible research. Replication came to be seen as either low-status grunt work – merely confirming the intelligence of others – or an incipient attack on another scholar, challenging their competence or integrity and risking a feud that diminishes everyone's credibility. For any given article, it became reasonable to assume that the work would never be replicated, and no one would ever "see for themselves" how the evidence was created.

Ironically, there has never been a time in history when technology has been so supportive of the Royal Society's belief in *Nullius in Verba* ("see

---

[4] For his contributions, Galileo was convicted of heresy by the Inquisition and spent his remaining years under house arrest. The church had formed a de facto alliance with the geocentric teachings of Aristotle, and an obscure passage in the Bible seemed to confirm the everyday perception that the sun rotates around the earth.

for yourself"). Today, it is very easy to distribute data and code along with an article, empowering readers to run alternative models when they are skeptical of an analysis. Readers can see a statistical analysis for themselves in ways that were never possible in the past. Many sociologists still resist the movement toward open data and code (and sometimes data cannot be shared for legal or ethical reasons), but the practices are now well established in economics and political science and we are optimistic about the future of open science.

Multiverse analysis is closely tied to transparency movements. The main reason scholars today are skeptical of published research, we believe, is due to the concern that authors have large influence over the results. When researchers see a result they disbelieve, they often think "if I had those data, I would get a different result." If this sentiment is common (we think it is) then researchers are often not convinced by empirical results unless they already agreed with the conclusions. That is the crisis in science, in short form: researchers not believing the empirical claims of other researchers unless they believed the claim before reading the article. From this perspective, the goal of multiverse is to include enough rival analyses that skeptics are left to say "well, I guess that result is *in the data*" (rather than just in the model assumptions). Skeptics can still raise objections about the underlying quality of the data in the study, but multiverse analysis aims to rule out idiosyncratic or debatable model assumptions as reasons to object to a study.

It is disappointing that modern versions of the "fopperies" and "rubbish" (to which we add good faith errors) that plagued early science have reappeared and now seem so common. But early scientists always argued that transparency must be fundamental to the scientific process.

THE INHERENT SUBJECTIVITY OF SCIENCE

Science cannot be taken for granted to always work as a well-oiled machine of knowledge. Every self-governing branch of science needs to continually earn its credibility and prove the soundness of its practices. The reason is that subjectivity is an inherent part of science. When you look at the very core of scientific work, what you see is subjectivity, researcher degrees of freedom, bias, motivated reasoning, fundamental errors, and commonplace skepticism among scholars over the validity of findings. Science goes wrong every day. What makes science so successful over time is not the avoidance of errors but rather a system of debate that channels all disagreements into empirical questions (Strevens 2020).

When two scholars disagree, the scientific solution is not to denounce the other as a heretic but rather to study the arguments and evidence more closely, to learn more, and to collect more and better data with more accurate measurements. As long as scholars are willing to continue debating a theory, the winning strategy in science is to produce better evidence with more refined analysis. It is through this kind of debate and theory competition that science becomes a self-correcting knowledge machine (Doucouliagos and Stanley 2013).

Science is inherently subjective because theories are always paired with auxiliary assumptions (Strevens 2020). In an empirical study, hypotheses are tested against data. But every empirical test involves auxiliary assumptions that are not themselves being directly tested. *Auxiliary assumptions tell us the conditions under which an empirical study constitutes a valid test of a theory.* If a hypothesis fails to find empirical support, one can always revisit a host of axillary assumptions about measurement and model specification and find fault with those assumptions rather than the theory itself: The measurement is wrong, the data are messy, the model is poorly specified. One can always say there was some failure in either the conception or the execution that renders the study uninformative about the theory it was meant to test. In any scientific debate, when a theory fails empirical testing, "the 'loser' will have a chance to save their theory by rejecting one auxiliary assumption in favor of another" (Strevens 2020: 95). As Strevens (2020: 71) elaborates:

> A theory, like a medieval knight, never fights alone, but rather rides into empirical combat with a retinue of assumptions. It is this formation as a whole – what you might call the theoretical cohort – that makes predictions about and gives explanation of the outcomes of experiments, measurements, and other observations. The theory gets all the attention. But it cannot engage the enemy without its coterie of men at arms. Consequently, when something goes wrong, a theory can be saved from refutation by blaming the assumptions.

Auxiliary assumptions can defend a theory from being wrong and similarly can be invoked discreetly to generate supporting evidence. They are a theory's best friend precisely because they get less attention than the headline hypothesis. Auxiliary assumptions are the backstage of a scientific study. They can be invoked with little effort: One can simply state, "I controlled for variable Z," and now the validity of that control variable is intrinsically tied to the conclusions of the study. Auxiliary assumptions can also be easily sacrificed: If a study yields a disbelieved result, critics can simply claim there is an omitted variable or some other problem with the model specification. At a moment in time, debates about auxiliary assumptions are often not informed by evidence but rather by prior beliefs. Debates over control variables can be turned into follow-up empirical questions, but often at the time of the debate, empirically informed answers are not available. Scholars often disagree simply because they *prefer* different auxiliary assumptions, not because they have good evidence favoring their assumptions.

In physics, for example, surprising results can always be explained as a result of poor measurement or malfunctions in the extremely sensitive test equipment used in applied research. At the CERN particle accelerator in Switzerland, for example, researchers in 2011 discovered neutrinos moving faster than the speed of light – something thought to be impossible. Einstein's theory of relativity posits a cosmic speed limit in which nothing can travel faster than light. But neutrinos are strange and scarcely understood particles. Some scholars were captivated by the faster-than-light neutrino observations as evidence of a new physics beyond Einstein. Others immediately dismissed the finding and all the excitement around it as surely some sort of error. Under intense scrutiny, the team replicated their results in repeated testing at CERN, and the findings were published as a game-changing violation of the known laws of physics. As a news story in the journal *Science* stated, it was potentially "the biggest discovery in physics in the past half-century" (Cho 2011). Alas, it was not. In time, the problem was discovered: A loose fiber-optic cable was causing an error in the measurement of time and speed.

Skeptics were right to disbelieve the result, but a priori no one could have known what, if anything, was going wrong with the CERN neutrino tests. The only indication of error was that a highly regarded theory failed an empirical test. These suspicions could have been wrong and invoked simply to save Einsteinian physics from contrary evidence. When a theory fails empirical testing, it means either the theory is wrong or one or more of the auxiliary assumptions of the test are wrong. Which of these two options seems more believable is a matter of subjective interpretation: How good is the theory, and how good is the testing? The interpretation of any one empirical test is inherently subjective and depends on one's prior beliefs – in no small part, the views one had prior to seeing the results.

In the CERN neutrino case, the critical auxiliary assumption was that all the testing equipment was telling the truth. Perhaps the social science analogy is an assumption that survey data have a reasonable correspondence to the theoretical constructs relevant to a hypothesis. We generally take for granted that respondents understand the questions they are being asked, know the answers, and are willing to answer them. That sentence contains three untested auxiliary assumptions that, if wrong, could be devastating to an empirical analysis. An even deeper auxiliary assumption might be that the minimum wage employees administering telephone surveys actually care about this work. Consider a famous sociological example. After a heated debate over the apparent decline of social capital in America (McPherson, Smith-Lovin, and Brashears 2006; Fischer 2009), data anomalies in the latest wave of the General Social Survey (GSS) were eventually identified (Paik and Sanchagrin 2013). A number of call center employees were evidently disregarding a portion of the survey that called for especially onerous work: collecting lists of respondents' close friends. Instead of working through the long set of follow-up questions in this "friends" module, workers were inputting zero close friends and calling the survey finished. Compared to past years when the survey was administered differently, these results looked like a disturbing decline in social connectedness. The problem took many years and a great deal of effort to sort out and understand – much like a loose fiber-optic cable in a particle accelerator.

These are examples of assumptions about data quality and data processing – which we will discuss in several chapters of this book. But these are simply vivid examples of auxiliary assumptions gone wrong. Many aspects of statistical research and modeling could suffer the same problems, and be equally fatal to the results. Since so many auxiliary assumptions are nearly invisible like this, it is always credible to invoke auxiliary assumptions when disputing a finding, and it is also a bit ideological to do so. Follow-up research and new data can always help test the auxiliary assumptions – as both the CERN and the GSS examples show. But in the moment, the evidence available never fully settles the matter; drawing a conclusion always involves making assumptions. Were the scholars who warned of declining social capital biased toward evidence of decay in American society? Was their leading critic trying to simply deflect criticism in the hope that nothing could be wrong? Or did these researchers simply have different prior beliefs about the underlying data quality?

MODEL ASSUMPTIONS AND VAGUE THEORY

Another way to understand auxiliary assumptions is to say that theory is inherently vague. There is often a large distance between sociological ideas and "their representation as statistical models" (Western 1996: 166). Max Weber argued that the protestant ethic played a key role in the development of modern capitalism, but it is not at all clear what regression equation he had in mind or how he thought new data should be collected (Young 2009). This makes it difficult to say that "Weber was wrong" since the underlying theory was itself vague and open to many interpretations. Theorists usually do not lay out a set of well-specified critical empirical tests that would definitively support or disprove their ideas once and for all. The work of making a theory concrete enough to be empirically tested is left to applied researchers to figure out: Those details are the auxiliary assumptions. Thus, assumptions are a central and unavoidable part of research. There is no assumption-free way of conducting an analysis, and a dataset never speaks for itself (Heckman 2005).

Empirical findings are a joint product of both data and analytical assumptions. Data never yield conclusions without researchers making choices about how best to analyze the data. Analytical choices may be informed by theory and applied diagnostic tests, but these provide only rough guidance, not a "single best" statistical model that is known to be correct. Indeed, modeling is sufficiently uncertain and complex that when two different researchers study the same problem with the same data, they never conduct the analysis in exactly the same way – and often do it in very different ways (Breznau et al. 2022).

How many specific modeling decisions do researchers make in the process of developing the statistical code that generates their empirical estimates? How many alternative and different decisions could have been made along the way? Any single model specification represents a complex bundle of modeling assumptions, representing analytical choices among the set of appropriate controls, data preprocessing decisions, variable operationalizations, standard error calculations, and possible estimation commands and functional form issues (Young and Holsteen 2017). This diversity of analytical approaches is a good thing for cumulative science: Different scholars draw on unique insights and imagination to explore the space of possible models.

In a given study, it is often unclear to what extent results are derived from the data rather than the model (Leamer 1983; Glaeser 2008; Young 2009). We generally think of research as "data analysis" and talk about what is found "when you look at the data," but this assumes that the data are the main ingredient that produces findings and conclusions. In reality, "the modeling assumptions can control the findings of an empirical exercise" (Durlauf, Fu, and Navarro 2013: 120). Relaxing these modeling assumptions makes results more empirical and less model dependent and focuses attention on the model inputs that are critical to the results.

LEAMER'S MAP

It is always possible that data can serve simply as a canvas on which authors use statistical assumptions to paint any empirical picture they wish. A classical hypothesis test assumes that the data and the model are independent of one another. Researchers are imagined as using prior knowledge, rather than the current dataset, to inform and specify the model. When this independence rule is violated – as almost all inferential research surely does – the meaning of a significance test is greatly diluted. Edward Leamer (1983: 40), a Bayesian econometrician who helped found the literature on model uncertainty, emphasized the circularity of such a process:

Suppose I think that a certain coefficient ought to be positive, and my reaction to the anomalous result of a *negative* estimate is to find another variable to include ... so that the estimate is positive. Have I found evidence that the coefficient is positive?

The answer is, "no." This researcher is trying to save a hypothesis from being refuted. If an initial result is regarded as wrong, and authors "fix" this result by searching for a new model that gives "more sensible" results, nobody should treat the result as *empirical* evidence. The model choices are doing all the work. If authors can do what Leamer describes – overturn initial results by adding a new control variable or changing an assumption – then the data are not the primary voice, and authors can write up whatever conclusion they like. Only naive readers would believe such results.

Leamer was not "anti-science"; on the contrary, he was defending the integrity of science against those who would abuse its trust and was warning readers about how misleading statistical results can be. In his day, the US Supreme Court was using social science research to inform rulings on capital punishment. In 1971, the Supreme Court imposed a mortarium on capital punishment, but it then reversed the judgment and restored executions in 1977. In the reversal, the Court cited high-profile research claiming that executions greatly deterred violent crime: For every convict put to death, ten or more innocent lives would be saved – an effect so large as to be a kind of moral imperative to execute (Ehrlich 1975; Angrist and Pischke 2010). Leamer (1983) issued a devastating reanalysis, showing these kinds of findings were driven by assumptions rather than the data. The data were readily consistent with any possible hypothesis, including no effect or even opposite results, that capital punishment leads to more homicide ("possibly by a brutalizing effect on society," Leamer 1983: 42). It was not the *data* that supported capital punishment; it was the authors' *model assumptions* that made the case for more executions. Leamer never said this, but one gets the sense he thought the Supreme Court judges were either fools or ideologues for believing the published research.[5]

Most strikingly, Leamer provided an *empirical map* starting from political beliefs, which drives the selection of a model, which in turn generates selective empirical results. It was a map or a cross-walk from ideology to specification to conclusion that anyone could use to claim empirical support. To show this, Leamer described five common political views about the causes of crime and then summarized the sets of control variables that best match those beliefs. An "eye-for-an eye" conservative, for example, believes that the only thing deterring homicide is capital punishment and thus the only control variable needed is the probability of execution. In contrast, a "bleeding-heart liberal" believes that crime is influenced by poverty and inequality in society and thus believes more variables are needed to condition on the social and economic environment. As it turns out, models that control only for the probability of execution find that capital punishment deters crime; models that control material and social conditions often yield null or opposite-signed results. In this way, different political beliefs lead researchers to favor different models and thereby obtain different empirical results: "a mapping from assumptions into inference" (Leamer 1983: 39). This is the foundation for influence analysis: documenting the influence of each model input. Leamer was able to go a step further, presenting political beliefs consistent with model specifications. But his map powerfully states why we need to reflect on the assumptions that drive modeling decisions.

There are analogies for this problem in journalism. Reporters can color a story by "speaking through sources": finding a source that agrees with their views and then quoting them. This can give reporters an air of objectivity – they are merely reporting what others said – while effectively writing their own opinion column. Social scientists can do the same thing by selecting modeling assumptions that best support their preferred result. Journalism and science face the same problems of objectivity and subjectivity – the challenge of separating evidence from editorial viewpoint – and they face the same long-term threats to their credibility.

---

[5] For what it is worth, modern research with better evidence and methods suggests that if there is a deterrent effect of capital punishment, it is small (Angrist and Pischke 2010).

VERSIONS OF THE MULTIVERSE

There is never just one estimate, but always many possible estimates. As we prepare to go deeper into multi-model analysis, we want to say a bit more about why we think the multiverse metaphor is compelling and deserves to "stick" in the concepts of statistical methodology. The idea of the multiverse comes from a long literature in physics and cosmology (Everett 1957; Gribbin 2009; Carroll 2019a). Key arguments from these fields make for strong analogies with the multiverse of methods. The physics of a real multiverse are complex and largely theoretical but are suggested by evidence and implied by standard theory to greater or lesser degrees. Let's dig into this literature for a more vivid and more grounded understanding of the multiverse concept.

One vision of the multiverse focuses on what lies beyond the cosmic horizon. We all have a limited perspective on the world, and there are many things outside our field of vision. The horizon is a radius around a viewer defined by how far they can possibly see. In astronomy, there is a cosmic horizon: There are places in the universe we cannot see, because the light from those distant stars has not yet had time to reach us. There is no reason to think the universe stops at the range of our vision, and the universe may well be infinite. From a different place in the universe, we would have a different cosmic horizon and a different portion of the heavens would be visible to our telescopes. From what we can see, the universe seems to be infinite, meaning that bubble universes the scale of our own visible universe (everything we can see and detect) probably continue out endlessly in every direction. What we call the universe is simply "a portion of the multiverse accessible to a particular set of observers"; the multiverse, in contrast, is everything that actually exists, regardless of whether we can observe it or not (Gribbin 2009: 11). In short, there is more universe out there than what we can perceive; each cosmic location has its own different observable universe.

This awareness of the cosmic horizon might be as far as anyone needs to go with the multiverse imagery. Most research articles open up only a narrow empirical horizon, showing readers just a few carefully selected estimates. The multiverse of methods is everything that exists – it is every statistical method that could reasonably be applied to a dataset. Different scholars come to a dataset with different toolkits and prior assumptions about the analysis. Standing in different locations, they have different methodological horizons and can only see or report a portion of the multiverse of credible methods. For this reason, different researchers inherently tend to produce different estimates.

There are also deeper ideas of the multiverse, drawing on quantum physics, that also serve as a vivid and compelling analogy for researchers. At the quantum level, in the world of very small things, particles have a bizarre ability to be in more than once place or state at the same time. Existing in "superposition," particles are essentially in multiple places at once – they are simultaneously in every place they could be. A quantum particle exists as a kind of cloud of states and locations until it is precisely observed, which forces the particle to somehow "choose" its definite properties. Prior to observing or measuring a quantum particle, it is in superposition. At the moment of measurement (imagine taking its picture with a camera), its distribution of locations collapses into one exact spot: one electron in one of its possible places. This is not a philosophical perspective but rather the known behavior of quantum particles that make up all matter. Quantum mechanics work very well, as demonstrated by technology such as nuclear reactors, magnetic resonance imaging machines, and lasers. But as the Nobel laureate Richard Feynman said, none of it makes intuitive sense and, in a way, "nobody really understands quantum mechanics" (Carroll 2019b).

One way of understanding the quantum puzzle of superposition is the "many worlds" interpretation (Everett 1957; Carroll 2019a). In this view, a quantum particle fills up all possible locations, and the act of measuring the particle does not make the particle choose its location but rather opens up a multiverse in which every possible location is realized in parallel worlds. In a sense, the superposition *is* the multiverse; when we observe a quantum particle, we enter into the multiverse with it; the multiverse is now *us observing the particle* in its every possible position. Only one version of these many worlds is visible to us, the others being branched into parallel worlds where a different quantum outcome occurred. For our purposes, this idea can be simplified to say "everything that can happen, does happen" but we only get to see one version. And that is an excellent metaphor for a research process where scholars, facing uncertainty, test many model specifications but report only one result.

A similar vision of many worlds inspired writer Jorge Luis Borges (1941) in a short story called "The Garden of Forking Paths." The story imagines a labyrinthine novel in which all narrative junctures are written out, creating "diverse futures ... which themselves also proliferate and fork" into an expanding "net of divergent, convergent, and parallel times" (Borges 1941: 13, 16). When a character in that novel faces a crossroad with several alternatives, they choose all of them simultaneously. Everything that can happen, does happen. Alternate histories and timeline divergences are now common literary devices; even if only one world actually exists, the branching of reality into many worlds is easy to imagine and tempting to ponder.

In conventional analysis, when researchers face a set of alternatives, they choose one and eliminate the others. How they make that choice is mostly unknown and unreported. In a multiverse analysis, the goal is to realize all plausible modeling strategies. As long as reasonable alternatives for a specification are available, there is more to know and understand. Unless a model is *prohibited by theory*, it is permitted; it exists in the multiverse, and until it is reported its existence is asymmetric: available to authors but not to readers. The modeling process generates not a single point estimate but rather a distribution of estimates showing what the data can support under different model assumptions.

To summarize, there are two big viewpoints in physics on the multiverse: the horizon perspective and the many-worlds interpretation. The "horizon" multiverse simply asserts there is more reality out there than can be seen from any given point – and the unknown space could extend very far and contain many surprises. The "many worlds" quantum interpretation goes further, positing that every allowable possibility of the universe is always realized but in alternate or parallel worlds that are hard to access. In our view, both of these views give rich intuition about model uncertainty and the inherent reality of other estimates. A model specification is a bundle of choices and assumptions driven partly by each author's methodological horizon, and the results of every reasonable alternative assumption can be understood as existing even if they are not yet shown to readers.

We aspire to capture all that can be known about model assumptions and their corresponding estimates. The entire multiverse of methods is never fully observable, but we aim to expand horizons and see more worlds of results from more assumptions and methods. Our goal is to show what estimates the data can support under as many different credible assumptions as possible.

With this introduction in place, let's continue to Part II, where we start building and analyzing a computational multiverse.

PART II

THE COMPUTATIONAL MULTIVERSE

3

Hurricane Names

An Applied Introduction

Are "female hurricanes ... deadlier than male hurricanes" (Jung et al. 2014a)?. According to a high-profile study, a hurricane named Charlie might be just as powerful as one named Eloise, but Eloise will likely kill more people. The reason, the study's authors argue, is that people tend to dismiss the destructive potential of feminine-sounding storms and take fewer precautions than when storms have masculine names.

The popular press had a field day with the story. Some news outlets liked the "vengeful female storm" angle. Other outlets favored the "gender bias can kill you" viewpoint. Independent scholars began downloading the data for themselves and were soon reporting the lack of robustness in the result. We draw on a lively empirical debate, published as comments and responses in the original journal, to create a multiverse of credible methods and assumptions in the analysis of these data (Bakkensen and Larson 2014; Christensen and Christensen 2014; Jung et al. 2014b, 2014c; Maley 2014; Malter 2014).[1]

How did the original analysis work? Table 3.1 shows three nested models, culminating in the authors' preferred specification. The outcome variable is the death count of a hurricane. Model 1 shows the simplest form of the analysis: Are death counts explained by the femininity of names? The coefficient is small and not statistically significant. The authors instead focus attention on an interaction model: It is not that female storms, per se, are deadlier; rather, when storms are highly destructive, female storms are deadlier than male storms. This interaction of femininity with the

---

[1] The replication package for all analyses presented in this chapter is available online at https://osf.io/45ft2/files/osfstorage.

TABLE 3.1 *Negative binomial regression models predicting hurricane deaths*

	1	2	3
Femininity index	0.22	0.10	0.17
	(0.15)	(0.12)	(0.12)
Damages (2013$)		1.27***	0.86***
		(0.22)	(0.21)
Damages × femininity index		0.36	0.71***
		(0.21)	(0.18)
Minimum pressure			−0.55***
			(0.15)
Minimum pressure × femininity index			0.40*
			(0.16)
Constant	3.00***	2.57***	2.48***
Sample size	92	92	92

***p < 0.001, **p < 0.01, *p < 0.05

financial damages of a storm is presented in Model 2, where the coefficients for femininity and its interaction with damages are still both nonsignificant. (Damages have a large and significant effect on deaths, meaning that destructive storms kill more people, as one would expect.) Model 3 shows Jung et al.'s (2014a) preferred model, which adds a measure of storm strength (minimum atmospheric pressure) as both a control and an interaction with the hurricane's name.[2] When these terms are added to the model, the interaction between damages and storm femininity becomes significant, and this is the result they show in the article.

The title of the article, "Female Hurricanes Are Deadlier than Male Hurricanes," is misleading, since the main effect of femininity has no effect on deaths; rather, it is an interaction effect with storm damages that is significant. Moreover, an additional control variable – storm severity – is required for the results to support the interactive hypothesis. While this control variable seems plausible for inclusion, it is not clear why that variable would be *necessary*, and the authors include it without justification. This is common in social science: Many articles rely on controls to obtain significant results (i.e., have null results without controls) and are not transparent in reporting how the results fundamentally depend on the

---

[2] Note that stronger storms have lower minimum pressure, so this variable would be expected to be negatively associated with the number of deaths.

controls (Lenz and Sahn 2021). Table 3.1 illustrates that this is the case in the hurricanes study: The coefficient of interest (for damages × femininity) is not significant until a control variable is introduced in Model 3.

We draw on debates published around this study, along with the contributions made by Muñoz and Young (2018a) and Simonsohn, Simmons, and Nelson (2020), to build a multiverse analysis and test the robustness of the original result. The multiverse includes a variety of different types of model ingredients: different ways of handling outlier storms, of adjusting for population growth, of dealing with the 1979 change in how storms are named, alternative ways of estimating the variance–covariance matrix, different combinations of controls, and different types of regression models (negative binomial or ordinary least squares [OLS] log-linear regression). Taking all possible combinations of the model ingredients yields 10,240 unique model specifications.

Figure 3.1 shows the distribution of estimates of the gender effect (× damages) across the many iterations of the model. The claim that

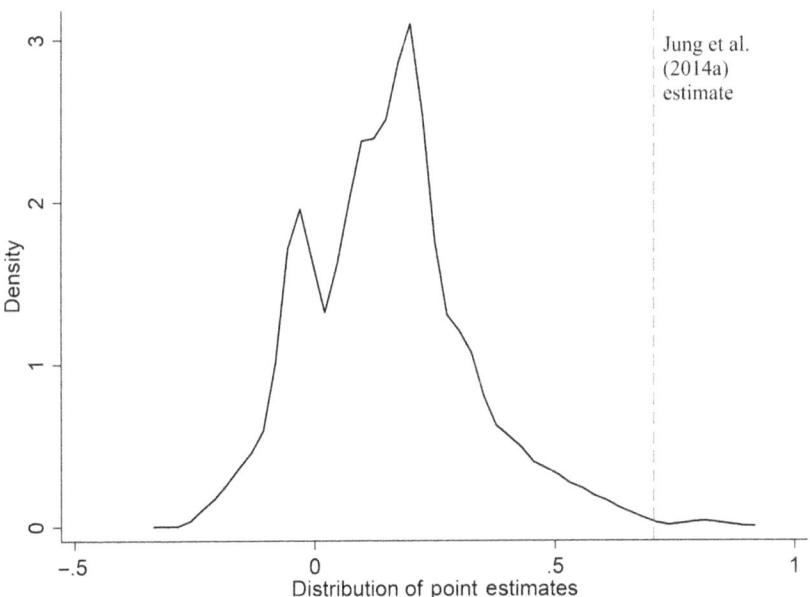

FIGURE 3.1 Modeling distribution of hurricane name effects
Note: Density graph of estimates of the gender × damages interaction effect from 10,240 models. The original estimate is indicated by a vertical line. Of these models, 80 percent are positive but only 12 percent are positive and statistically significant; 99.7 percent of the models yield a smaller estimate than reported in Jung et al. (2014a).

female hurricanes are deadlier, even in the interaction with storm damages, is clearly an extreme tail result. The authors reported an estimate that is among the 0.5 percent most favorable to their hypothesis; a full 99.7 percent of the estimates are less supportive. Some other models still support the claim but with much smaller effect sizes. Overall, only 12 percent of the estimates are statistically significant.

Clearly, the results depend a lot on how one specifies the model. For the authors' conclusion to be credible, readers need to believe nearly every modeling assumption they invoke and to regard most alternative modeling assumptions as wrong and misleading. The authors' set of modeling assumptions might well be true (see Jung et al. 2014c). However, nonrobust results require careful scrutiny to understand why the results depend so critically on certain model assumptions.

While robustness to a particular assumption can settle a question, nonrobustness inherently requires more investigation. We need to (1) know which modeling assumptions are necessary for the result to hold and (2) have compelling reasons to believe that those modeling assumptions are a priori more justifiable than the alternative assumptions. Multiverse analysis can show which assumptions matter – part (1) – but cannot provide theoretical justification for those assumptions – part (2). Multiverse analysis *describes* how results depend on assumptions, providing a kind of mapping from model assumption to empirical result (Leamer 1983).

To understand the influence of specific model assumptions, we conduct a meta-analysis of the multiverse. Table 3.2 lists all of the modeling options in the multiverse, along with the average regression coefficient for models that use that option. How much does the average estimate depend on each model ingredient? For clarity, we also show the percent difference from the overall mean estimate. We list options for each class of modeling assumptions together; the first option listed is the one that was used in the original analysis.

Hurricane damages and hurricane deaths are both highly skewed, and the decisions about how to treat the outlier storms on both variables are the most influential of all the modeling decisions we considered. The original study excluded the two outlier storms with the highest numbers of deaths (Katrina and Audrey) and made no further exclusions. Critics called for excluding either more storms (Christensen and Christensen 2014; Maley 2014) or fewer storms (Simonsohn et al. 2020; Muñoz and Young 2018a). Others suggested "winsorizing" the variables by recoding all values above the ninetieth percentile to the ninetieth percentile (Malter 2014) or for using log damages instead of nominal damages

TABLE 3.2 *Multiverse options and influence analysis for the effect of female hurricane names on deaths*

		Average Interaction coef.	Pct. diff. from mean	
	Overall mean (10,240 models)	0.15	355%	
	Preferred estimate	0.71		
Outliers (damages)	O.1 Drop no outliers[1]	0.17	8%	
	O.2 Drop four extreme outliers[2]	0.16	4%	
	O.3 Winsorize to 90th percentile[3]	0.24	56%	
	O.4 Log damages[2]	0.05	-68%	
Outliers (total deaths)	D.1 Drop Katrina and Audrey[1]	0.19	22%	
	D.2 Drop Katrina only[2]	0.16	6%	
	D.3 Exclude all hurricanes with 100+ deaths[3,4]	0.11	-29%	
	D.4 Winsorize deaths to 90th percentile[5]	0.09	-42%	
	D.5 No exclusions or changes to data[2]	0.22	44%	
Year selection	YS.1 Years 1950–2012 (N = 94 models)[1]	0.21	38%	
	YS.2 Years 1979–2012 (N = 55 models)[1,3,5]	0.10	-38%	
Control for minimum pressure	P.1 Minimum pressure, interact with female[1]	0.22	39%	
	P.2 Min. pressure, interact with female & damages[5]	0.15	-1%	
	P.3 Minimum pressure, no interactions[5]	0.14	-7%	
	P.4 No control for minimum pressure[6]	0.11	-32%	
Model	M.1 Negative binomial[1]	0.21	36%	
	M.2 OLS predicting log(deaths+1)[3]	0.10	-36%	
Gender variable	F.1 Female scale (11-point scale, standardized)[1]	0.17	12%	
	F.2 Female dummy (standardized)[1]	0.14	-12%	

Notes: [1]Jung et al. (2014a), [2]Simonsohn et al. (2020), [3]Christensen and Christensen (2014), [4]Maley (2014), [5]Malter (2014), [6]Muñoz and Young (2018a). The analysis also includes four unreported factors that had little influence on the results: controls for year and US population, population-adjusted death counts, and robust (vs. nonrobust) standard errors.

41

(Simonsohn et al. 2020). The results in Table 3.2 show that the average effect size varies wildly depending on which of these options are used for which variable.

The results are also highly sensitive to the years that are included in the sample. Multiple critics pointed out that hurricane names are inherently confounded with time period: during 1950–1979, all hurricanes were given female names; only after 1979 did they begin to alternate between male and female names. When the analysis is limited to years when storms could have different-gender names (after 1979), the average effect size is much smaller, dropping from 0.20 to 0.11. This means that much of the evidence for a gender effect comes from storms that happened during a time when storms were always given female names.

The story is the same with the next two sets of modeling options: The result is highly sensitive to the way in which the control for minimum air pressure is included (or not included) in the model and also to the use of negative binomial regression rather than OLS log-linear models. Such model specifications seem individually reasonable but hard to uniquely justify.[3] The problem is that there are so many other ways to specify the model that are also reasonable and defensible, and most of those other ways lead to insignificant effects. It is striking that the authors seemingly made just about every modeling decision in a way that produces the largest estimate. The original result depended on a very specific constellation of modeling decisions, and changing nearly any of them undermines the conclusion. This is a potent example of how multiverse analysis can help uncover a nonrobust result and thus contribute to cumulative science.

---

[3] Other modeling decisions have little influence on the result: measuring the gender variable as a dummy variable rather than a continuous index, whether or not population growth is accounted for, controlling for year, or using robust standard errors. Analysts may disagree on which of these modeling decisions are best, but in the end they don't matter much to the result.

4

The Multiverse Algorithm

For nearly one hundred years, applied statistics has been focused on the problem of sampling error (e.g., Fisher 1925). The problem goes something like this: All samples are wrong. No sample exactly matches the true population, and some samples will be highly misleading. Any empirical finding could turn out to be an artefact of random sampling. With this uncertainty in the data, how can we draw credible, confident conclusions? Developing tools to understand sampling error was a paradigm change for empirical science (Bellhouse 1988).

Historically, the only method used to obtain credible data was a census. Censuses are an ancient practice, conducted by many historical civilizations and are discussed in the Bible (appropriately, in Numbers 1:4 of the Old Testament). The concept of sampling, in contrast, is very new. "Before the end of the [nineteenth] century sampling had been rarely employed, and even then ... [studies] never gave an account of how they took the samples ... and did not discuss the accuracy of their result" (Seng 1951: 214). The term *random* at this time still had the connotation of haphazardness – hence a random sample would be a haphazard pile of respondents with no scientific foundation. Sample research essentially did not exist before the turn of the twentieth century, and as a result, early social science was simply not very empirical (Seng 1951).

The conceptual bridge that allowed the jump from census to sample came from probability theory. Probability made it possible to describe a population without everyone needing to be included in the data, so long as "every person or thing has the same chance of inclusion in the investigation" (quoted in Bellhouse 1988: 5). Equal probability sampling does not ensure representativeness of any given sample but rather ensures representativeness *in repeated sampling*. This mathematical intuition was applied in a breakthrough publication by Guinness brew master and statistician William Gosset. Writing anonymously under the pen name "Student," Gosset demonstrated the behavior of a statistic in repeated sampling from a known population and constructed a metric now known as the "Student t" statistic (Student 1908). Gosset took a real dataset of the heights of 3,000 individuals, wrote their measurements on 3,000 pieces of cardboard, shuffled the cards, and then took 750 small samples from this dataset – one of the first bootstraps in the history of science. Of the samples obtained using this procedure, many were unrepresentative, giving individually biased estimates, but together the samples formed a normal distribution of estimates centered around the true mean. The standard deviation of this sampling distribution is today called the standard error of the estimate – the expected margin of error in sampling. Gosset constructed the Student's t-statistic as the ratio of an estimate and its standard error, asking how large an estimate is relative to the usual margin of sampling error.

Ronald Fisher (1925: 42), following in this line of work, developed a threshold for "significance," in which the rate of false positives (p) would be no higher than 5 percent: "the value for which $p = 0.05$, or 1 in 20, is $t = 1.96$ or nearly 2." At this t-statistic threshold of roughly 2, a false positive would "not occur more than once in twenty trials" (Fisher 1926: 504). Fisher advocated that one should "ignore entirely all results that fail to reach this level" (504). (Many years later, Leamer [1985: 308] made the same argument about discounting results that fail to meet model robustness: "A fragile inference is not worth taking seriously.") This Gosset–Fisher method for identifying results that are *robust to sampling error* was a tremendous step forward for empirical science. Statistical significance empowered researchers to use sampling to learn about the world, so long as they acknowledged the margin of error that sampling involves. In the early decades of the twentieth century, sampling became a new paradigm that transformed the social sciences: Scholars embraced both the promise of sampling and the constraints on inference imposed by statistical significance.

Yet, today, there is something profoundly odd about the orthodoxy of statistical significance. Significance gives a "strikingly partial ... account of the existence of error" (Ziliak and McCloskey 2008: 8). Early scholars like Gosset, who developed the t-test, were very clear that they were addressing only one source of uncertainty in estimation. And in the following hundred years, the complexity and variety of statistical modeling assumptions and possibilities have grown dramatically. As the statistician George Box famously said, "all models are wrong" (Box 1976: 792). Statistical testing comes with not just sampling error but also modeling error. The "approximate nature of the model must always be borne in mind" (Box and Draper 1987: 424). There is a fundamental equivalence between uncertainty about the sample and uncertainty about the model. Models, like samples, should not be seen as giving exact or definitive results but rather seen as always coming with a margin of error – some likely but unknown error in specification.

The development of sampling, in the history of science, was held back by ingrained beliefs about the unique validity of the whole-population census. Scholars needed an understanding of sampling error and its guardrails to accept sample data as legitimate evidence. In contrast, researchers have scarcely felt a legitimacy constraint in the elaboration of more complex models. The dramatic expansion of modeling that grew slowly at first after Fisher (1925) and then exponentially with modern computing power has never been held in check by a similar understanding of modeling error. One hundred years ago, scholars and their audiences knew there was "something wrong" with using a sample rather than a census of data and sought to understand and overcome the problem of sampling error. Today, we still struggle to recognize that there is "something wrong" when we sample from the possible model specifications. Most research today samples from the available methods without seriously acknowledging model error or the modeling distribution of possible estimates.

Statistical significance, at the conventional 5 percent level advocated by Fisher (1925), is a threshold of expected robustness in repeated sampling. If a $\hat{\beta}$ estimate is significant, it means that under a null hypothesis that the true β is zero, an estimate as large as $\hat{\beta}$ would occur only in one out of twenty samples. By the same logic, significance means that we expect, in repeated sampling, that $\hat{\beta}$ estimates will rarely be zero (though we acknowledge a 5 percent chance of being wrong in that inference). When an estimate is *not* statistically significant, we are saying that we would *not* expect the results to hold up in repeated sampling. Significance is a special case of robustness – reliability in repeated sampling.

Significance is only one dimension of robustness; results can break or go wrong for other reasons beyond sampling. Robustness means being strong in constitution and unlikely to fail. A finding is robust when it is "detected by numerous, diverse means" (Schupbach 2018: 276). Robust results are those that are hard to overturn. If a result is likely to break in repeated sampling, then it is not considered robust. By the same token, if a result is likely to break with a different but still plausible model, it too can hardly be considered robust.

CONFIDENCE INTERVALS ARE MISLEADING

Scholarly research always presents an estimate along with a measure of uncertainty – a standard error that makes a confidence interval around the estimate. The confidence interval places the estimate at the center and allows ±2 standard errors as a possible range of outcomes. The *intuitive implication* is that other studies will get estimates within that range ninety-five times out of a hundred. In practice, confidence intervals of the form "estimate ±2 standard errors" are a very poor guide to what future studies will find. The central problem is that confidence intervals do not incorporate model uncertainty: They assume that future studies by different scholars will make exactly the same modeling choices – an assumption which is almost never true. To understand the shortcoming of confidence intervals, we draw on two key sources of powerful evidence: meta-analysis research and "many-analyst" studies.

Meta-analyses take a research question in the literature, combine together all published (and ideally, all unpublished) estimates, and then study the variation in results across studies. In areas of intensive research, where there are multiple studies on the same question, the estimates across studies tend to vary greatly – by much more than their standard errors would suggest. This is known as "excess variation": differences in results across studies that cannot be accounted for by sampling uncertainty. Excess variation is "the most common finding among the hundreds of meta-analyses conducted on economics subjects ... The observed variation [across studies] is always much greater than what one should expect from random sampling error alone" (Stanley and Doucouliagos 2012: 80). Excess variation occurs when the standard deviation of the estimates across different studies is larger than the standard errors of those studies.

In meta-analysis, the sampling error is known as within-study variance and is simply calculated as the square root of the average standard errors in the studies. Between-study variance is the observed heterogeneity in estimates across studies, attributed to any number of substantive or methodological differences between the studies. Total variance is the sum of these two factors. When all studies generate the same results, total variance is equal to the within-study variance, and sampling is evidently the only source of error or heterogeneity in the literature (Veroniki et al. 2016).

To illustrate, there have been many studies on how political party affiliation (Democrat vs. Republican) influences judges' decision-making. Pinello (1999) collected sixty-six comparable estimates of the effect of party affiliation. The average standard error from the studies was 0.034, but the standard deviation across estimates was 0.275 – more than eight times as large.

Table 4.1 reports comparable results from this and five other meta-analyses in social science; this is not a comprehensive survey, but in our view these are high-quality cases that well illustrate meta-analysis at work. We report the average standard error (column 1) and the standard deviation (column 2) and a total standard error that incorporates both sources of variability (column 3). In all six studies, the standard deviation of estimates across studies is always larger than the sampling standard errors reported by individual studies. As a result, the total standard error is between 2.2 and 8.1 times as large as the sampling standard error (average = 4.2) (column 4); this means that sampling standard errors are a poor guide to what the next study will find.

As an additional metric, we report the proportions of total variance due to sampling and modeling (columns 5 and 6); the second proportion is commonly reported in meta-analysis, where it is known as the I^2 index: the proportion of variability due to between-study heterogeneity (Huedo-Medina et al. 2006: 194). An I^2 index value of 50 percent is considered moderate and 75 percent is considered high. For judicial ideology, the proportion of variance due to between-study features is 98 percent. This is higher than most of the other meta-analyses, but not by a lot. Across the six studies, sampling error accounts for between 2 percent and 15 percent of the total variance (average = 11 percent).

Model specification is only one element of the cross-study heterogeneity, however. Estimates could also differ across studies because of true heterogeneity in sample populations due to time or geography, how the data were collected (e.g., interviewer effects), and more. Meta-analysis findings help motivate the concern about wide variations in results, but they provide a limited understanding of the influence of model specification per se. For a better understanding, we turn to many-analysts studies.

A "many-analysts" study crowdsources analytic judgment using just one dataset. Diverse scholars work with the same question and data, and each develops their own view of the best possible analysis – it is like a multiverse analysis built on volunteer analytical judgment. The principal investigators of a many-analysts study provide the main data to address the question and then invite outside analysts to participate. Examples of many-analysts studies to date have analytic teams ranged from having 8 to 160 members. Each team analyzes the data and reports back their best empirical solution to the question (one or more specifications and the statistical code that produces it). The unique value of many-analysts studies is that the dataset is held constant, so if there are differences in estimates across teams, it can only be explained by model specification. If experienced statisticians tend to gravitate toward the same ("best") model specification, these teams would produce roughly the same results. In fact, the diversity of results is consistently striking.

Table 4.1 shows results from six many-analysts studies across five different projects. In each case, we ask how much of the variance across estimates is due to sampling variation (column 1) versus model variation (column 2). In a study of immigration and policy support (Breznau et al. 2022), 73 teams submitted a total of 1,253 estimates. Many participants used specifications that overlapped with others' specifications, but no two model specifications were fully identical. The average standard error from those estimates was 0.017, but the standard deviation of the coefficients was 0.074 – many times greater.

As with the meta-analyses, sampling variance is never an important part of why estimates vary. Among the six many-analysts studies, an average of 85 percent of estimate variation is due to modeling choices, and only 15 percent is due to sampling. As with the meta-analyses, the modeling error is much greater than sampling error in every single case we examined.

Schweinsberg et al. (2021) have argued that many-analysts projects may even tend to *underestimate* the degree of methodological divergence one should expect to see in real-world applications. For instance, in some studies the participants discuss their methodologies with one another before the project is complete. It is also common for the organizers of a project to decide in advance how key variables should be conceptualized. In the study by Silberzahn et al. (2018) of skin tone bias in professional soccer, all participants used red card decisions as their outcome measure. If the researchers had independently undertaken studies on the same general topic ("Are football referees biased?"), they might have come up with any number of other reasonable outcomes – yellow cards, stoppage time, offside calls – and the variation in results would likely have been even greater than the study reported. In their own many-analysts study, Schweinsberg et al. (2021) left it up to the participating research teams to

TABLE 4.1 *Estimates of model variance and sampling variance in meta-analysis and many-analysts studies*

	(1)	(2)	(3)	(4)	(5)	(6)
	Sampling SE[1]	Modeling SE	Total SE[2]	Ratio: total SE over sampling SE	Proportion of variance from	
					Sampling	Modeling
Meta-analysis of published estimates						
Minimum wages[3]	0.160	1.096	1.108	6.9	2%	98%
Returns to education[4]	0.015	0.036	0.039	2.6	15%	85%
Judicial ideology[5]	0.034	0.275	0.277	8.1	2%	98%
Ethnic discrimination in housing[6]	0.056	−0.148	0.158	2.8	13%	87%
Racial discrimination in hiring[7]	0.187	0.363	0.408	2.2	21%	79%
Motherhood penalty[8]	0.038	0.089	0.097	2.5	15%	85%
Average				4.2	11%	89%
Many-analysts studies						
Compulsory education[9]	0.004	0.015	0.016	4.1	6%	94%
Health insurance[9]	0.019	0.059	0.062	3.2	10%	90%
Skin-tone bias in soccer[10]	0.176	0.256	0.311	1.8	32%	68%
Immigration and policy support[11]	0.017	0.074	0.076	4.5	5%	95%
Competition and moral behavior[12]	0.108	0.226	0.250	2.3	19%	81%
Elasticity of consumption (4 datasets)[13]	0.018	0.112	0.113	6.7	4%	96%
Average				3.8	15%	85%

Notes: [1]SE = standard error; [2]Total SE = $\sqrt{(\text{Sampling SE})^2 + (\text{Modeling SE})^2}$; [3]Doucouliagos and Stanley (2009); [4]Ashenfelter, Harmon, and Oosterbeek (1999); [5]Pinello (1999); [6]Auspurg, Schneck, and Hinz (2019); [7]Quillian et al. (2017); [8]Leonard and Stanley (2020); [9]Huntington-Klein et al. (2021); [10]Silberzahn et al. (2018); [11]Breznau et al. (2022); [12]Huber et al. (2023); [13]Magnus and Morgan (1997) (estimates here averaged across four datasets).

conceptualize the key variables in the analysis, and they found that methods diverged so much that it was not even possible to form a standardized metric of effect size. The authors instead constructed a standardized p-value and reported that the results were "greatly diverging" (238).

What is the greater source of estimate instability and variation in results: repeated sampling or repeated modeling? If there were ten samples of data and ten plausible model specifications, what would be larger: the sampling distribution or the modeling distribution? There is no definitive answer; no doubt there are cases where the sampling distribution is larger than the modeling distribution. But the evidence here suggests pretty clearly that most of the time repeated modeling can be expected to change an estimate more than repeated sampling.

This implies three corollaries:

(1) Standard errors and p-values patently fail to provide reasonable bounds of confidence around statistical estimates.
(2) The published literature contains many "statistically significant" conclusions that are not robust and would be readily overturned by plausible alternative models.
(3) A significance test can be seen only as an initial starting point; surviving a rigorous and critical multiverse analysis is a true measure of a strong result. In short, statistical findings should be evaluated as much by their robustness as their "significance."

Multiverse analysis seeks to simulate the modeling process of many different researchers bringing different prior beliefs to the analysis of a single dataset. To accomplish this, we essentially bootstrap the model, just as one might bootstrap the data.

BUILDING THE MULTIVERSE ALGORITHM

The sampling distribution shows how an estimate varies in repeated sampling, addressing uncertainty about how representative the sample of data is. The modeling distribution shows how the estimate varies in repeated modeling, addressing uncertainty about how correct the model is. Taken together, they address the two fundamental sources of uncertainty: how an estimate might change if we took a new sample and how it might change if we used a different model. Each form of uncertainty produces its own conceptual distribution of possible estimates. Now we combine model uncertainty and sampling uncertainty into an overall framework for estimate instability.

THE SAMPLING DISTRIBUTION

Consider the basic form of a regression model that uses controls to improve inference:

$$y_i = \beta_1 x_{1i} + \sum_{p=1}^{P} \delta_p C_{i,p} + \varepsilon_i \qquad (4.1)$$

The outcome is y_i and the treatment variable (or variable of interest) is x_1, and the treatment effect is defined as β_1 – this is our coefficient of interest. C_p represents a set of P control variables. For an unbiased estimate of β_1, the challenge is to select a set of control variables such that the conditional mean of the error term is zero, that is $E\left[\varepsilon_i \mid x_i, C_{ip}\right] = 0$.

After collecting a sample of data, we compute an estimate b of the unknown parameter β. This single estimate of b is not definitive but is based partly on random chance, since it derives from a random sample. Suppose there are K possible samples that could have been drawn $\{S_1, ..., S_K\}$, and each of these samples yields a unique regression coefficient $\{b_1, ..., b_K\}$. In repeated sampling, we would draw all these K samples, using Eq. (4.1) with each sample to compute all the K estimates, to make up the *sampling distribution*. This sampling distribution defines what is possible when a researcher draws one sample and computes one estimate. For clarity, the mean of the estimates is denoted as $\bar{b}$, and the standard deviation is $\sigma_s = \sqrt{\dfrac{1}{K}\sum_{k=1}^{K}\left(b_k - \bar{b}\right)^2}$. This sampling standard error, σ_S, indicates how much an estimate would be expected to change if we were to draw a new sample. The sampling distribution has a non-zero variance because each individual sample S_K has a random amount of bias or nonrepresentativeness; some samples will be highly representative of the general population, while others will be poorly representative, and nothing in the sample itself indicates how representative it is. Actual repeated sampling is rarely conducted but is the conceptual foundation of statistical significance testing. Parametric formulas and/or bootstrapping can be used to estimate σ_s, and they are used to decide if an estimate b is statistically significant.

THE MODELING DISTRIBUTION

In classical statistics, the true model that generated the data is assumed to be known, and indeed it is assumed to be the only specification ever applied to the data. This is a simplifying assumption invoked to make the study of sampling distributions more tractable. One must assume that the model is true in order to ensure that the true value of the parameter β_1 (i.e., "the truth") lies at the mean of the sampling distribution. The moment we allow modeling error to enter the equation, then the mean of the sampling distribution may be highly biased. If model error is substantial, then the sampling distribution may greatly underestimate the range and probability of possible results, making statistical significance a poor guide for inference.

In practice, researchers rarely know what the true model is and are limited to working with models that are simply plausible or preferred on some reasonable grounds. Many different versions of Eq. (4.1) could be seen as reasonable. When we admit uncertainty about one or more aspects of model specification, then the sampling distribution alone does not convey the distribution of possible estimates. In other words, there will now be more than K legitimate estimates.

The model space is defined as $\{M_1, \ldots, M_J\}$ possible models, which when applied to a single dataset yields a modeling distribution of J estimates $\{b_1, \ldots, b_J\}$. The average of these estimates is denoted as $\bar{b}$, and the standard deviation of the estimates across the model space is $\sigma_M = \sqrt{\frac{1}{J}\sum_{j=1}^{J}(b_j - \bar{b})^2}$. We refer to σ_M as the *modeling standard error*. This shows how much the estimate is expected to change if we draw a new randomly selected model (from the defined list of J models).

Suppose the model space is defined simply as a set of two plausible control variables, x_2 and x_3, each of which might belong in the true model or might not (and credible arguments could be made either way). With this uncertainty, Eq. (4.1) can be represented in the following set of four possible models:

$$y_i = \beta_1 X_{1i} + \varepsilon_i \quad (4.2)$$

$$y_i = \beta_1 X_{1i} + \delta_1 X_{2i} + \varepsilon_i' \quad (4.3)$$

$$y_i = \beta_1 X_{1i} + \delta_1 X_{3i} + \varepsilon_i'' \quad (4.4)$$

$$y_i = \beta_1 X_{1i} + \delta_1 X_{2i} + \delta_2 X_{3i} + \varepsilon_i''' \quad (4.5)$$

The four equations represent different reasonable ways of specifying the model given the uncertainty about which controls should be included, and they give four plausible estimates of β_1. This is a simple illustration of the all-combinations algorithm, which is the computational backbone of multiverse analysis. For any set of uncertain controls, we generate all possible combinations of those controls. With P plausible controls, there are 2^p unique combinations of those variables. With two cases of uncertainty (regarding two plausible controls), as in the example, there are $2^2 = 4$ unique models. As the number of plausible controls increases, the model space increases exponentially: With twelve possible controls, there are $2^{12} = 4{,}096$ unique models, and with twenty possible controls, there are more than a million unique models.

This modeling distribution is analogous – and complementary – to the conventional sampling distribution of classical statistics. To fully measure the overall uncertainty in our estimates, conceptually we take each possible sample $\{S_1, \ldots, S_K\}$, and for each sample estimate all plausible models $\{M_1, \ldots, M_J\}$, yielding $K \times J$ estimates b_{kj}. Then we take the mean of these estimates $(\bar{\bar{b}})$ and compute the total standard error as

$$\sigma_T = \sqrt{\frac{1}{KJ}\sum_{k=1}^{K}\sum_{J=1}^{J}\left(b_{kj} - \bar{\bar{b}}\right)^2} \qquad (4.6)$$

Equivalently, the sampling and modeling standard errors can be calculated separately and combined using the general formula for compound standard errors: the square root of the sum of the variances. Using the formulas for σ_s and σ_m given earlier, the total standard error is $\sigma_T = \sqrt{\sigma_s^2 + \sigma_m^2}$.

This expression for σ_T encompasses all the sources of estimate instability and includes all reasons why different researchers might arrive at different results: They could use different samples, or different models, or both. The goal of the combined modeling and sampling standard error (σ_T) is to provide a more compelling gauge of what repeated research is likely to find – especially when repeated research involves different authors who may invoke different assumptions. Rather than basing conclusions solely on sampling uncertainty, this incorporates model uncertainty as well.

The analogy between sampling and modeling standard errors is imperfect. Under the usual ordinary least squares or maximum likelihood assumptions, sampling standard errors are better understood than modeling standard errors.[1] Our approach to the modeling distribution is more similar to estimating the sampling distribution for nonlinear models when there is no analytical solution for the standard errors (Efron 1981; Efron and Tibshirani 1993). For example, when estimating the

---

[1] For example, under classical assumptions, the sampling standard error σ_S derives from a normal distribution of parameter estimates in repeated sampling. However, the underlying distribution that the modeling standard error σ_M derives from is unknown.

median (or the conditional median in a least absolute deviation model) there is no formula for the standard errors; all one can do to gauge sampling uncertainty is to bootstrap the median. A second key difference from the classical sampling distribution is that we do not assume that true parameter β_1 is represented by the mean of the modeling distribution. This makes the interpretation of model robustness more difficult than that of sample robustness.

Combining an author's preferred estimate $b_{preferred}$ with the total standard error gives what we term the robustness ratio $:= \frac{b_{preferred}}{\sigma_T}$.[2] This ratio is constructed to be analogous to the t-statistic, but it is worth noting again that the underlying statistical properties of the ratio are not known and will depend on the specified model space. Based on arguments from Raftery (1995) we recommend a critical value of 2 to guide interpretation (i.e., a robustness ratio of 2 or greater suggests robustness), but this is a coarse interpretation and can be misleading in cases where the preferred estimate is found in the tails of the modeling distribution. To augment this, we use graphs of the distribution of estimates across models (i.e., the modeling distribution) for a visual inspection, which is often very informative.

Two simple "vote count" measures can also help make sense of the modeling distribution: The *sign stability* is the percentage of estimates that have the same sign, which can range from 50 percent (half the models have opposite signs) to 100 percent. The *significance rate* is the percentage of models that report a statistically significant coefficient. How many models "vote" for a positive versus negative relationship, and how many of those are significant? Adapting Raftery's (1995: 146) rule of thumb for multimodel inference, we suggest that a significance rate of 50 percent sets a lower bound for "weak" robustness (i.e., at least 50 percent of the plausible models have a significant result). Likewise, when 95 percent of the plausible models have significant estimates, this indicates "'strong" robustness.

Model robustness works on the same intuition as significance testing: Does a result consistently hold up in repeated modeling? Statistical significance and model robustness are both asking questions about estimate stability. The only difference is that significance speaks only to estimate stability in repeated sampling, not stability in repeated modeling.

---

[2] The robustness ratio could also be calculated for the mean estimate, rather than the preferred. We always recommend using the preferred estimate. In the MULTIVRS command in Stata, the mean estimate is used if no preferred estimate is specified.

We argue that sampling and modeling, a priori, have equal standing in the adjudication of the credibility of research results. There is little basis for elevating sample robustness above model robustness. Research results may depend on both the sample and the model, and either or both could be wrong. Model error is no less important than sample error.

The problem with current practice in statistical significance is that scholars treat significance tests as if they account for the potential errors in estimation, when in fact significance greatly underestimates potential estimation error. Indeed, every significance test invokes the assumption that the model specification is correct and is by definition not evaluating possible errors in model specification. We do not criticize significance testing per se (though see Benjamin et al. 2018); science was greatly enhanced by the developing of sampling theory and its tool kit of significance testing, confidence intervals, and standard errors. Rather, we need a parallel set of tools to understand and evaluate model uncertainty and robustness. This is the purpose of multiverse analysis: to extend significance testing into the broader sorts of errors and uncertainties that are involved in the process of statistical modeling.

In the next chapter, we demonstrate the control variable multiverse using real-world data.

NECESSARY CONTROLS AND ESTIMAND-CONSISTENT ROBUSTNESS TESTING

The simple all-combinations algorithm generates a list of what models are *possible*. Multiverse analysis is informed by theory and restricted to the subset of models that are *plausible*. These two sets may be the same, but they can also be different. In mature research lines, there may be widely accepted *necessary* controls that are well established in evidence and practice. In these areas, excluding an important control does not count as an informative robustness test; instead, excluding that control simply shows lack of familiarity with existing knowledge.

Sometimes, control variables are necessary to define the target estimand – the quantity one is trying to estimate (Lundberg, Johnson, and Stewart 2021; see also Auspurg and Brüderl 2021). Consider the question of gender wage discrimination: The US Equal Pay Act demands "equal pay for equal work." The "equal work" clause creates a very specific estimand for legal evidence of discrimination. Under the law, full-time and part-time jobs are not equal work; workers with different skills, education, and abilities are not performing equal work; and so on. Pay differences per se are not unlawful; it is *conditional* wage differences that matter under the law. It remains legally contested how exactly to define equal work, but it is clear that any wage regression needs to control at least for hours of work (part-time versus full-time), education, and labor force experience. Essentially, the Equal Pay Act specifies a set of *necessary* controls for wage discrimination models. Models that exclude these controls do not count as evidence: While such models are testing "equal pay" across genders, they are not appropriately conditioning on "equal work."

When an estimand is defined a priori by a set of controls, the multiverse model set must always include those controls. In these cases, there are necessary controls that have to be in every model to achieve estimand-consistent robustness testing. Models that exclude those controls are, at a minimum, testing a different theory and at worst simply wrong. Plausible models need to yield estimates of the target estimand, not estimates of some other quantity, which in many cases will require always including certain controls. This need for estimand consistency helps flush out what we mean by the term "plausible model."

In general, the more exact the research question and theory, the fewer the subjective "degrees of freedom" researchers have in answering it. When theory brings strong and specific guidance on testing, there is simply less need for multiverse analysis. Indeed, as Bruce Western (1996) emphasized, an important source of model uncertainty is that sociological theory is often vague. Weber's theory of the protestant ethic in the development of capitalism only vaguely translates into a regression model, and it gives very little guidance as to the specification that most convincingly tests his theory (Weber 1904). It is mostly up to applied researchers to figure out the details of the hypothesis testing. The same is true for scholars testing Durkheim's concept of anomie (Durkheim 1933), Marx's view of religion as the opiate of the masses (Marx and Engels 1844), or Goffman's concepts of frontstage and backstage dramaturgy in everyday life (Goffman 1959). When theories can be tested in almost any way a researcher likes, there are many analytical degrees of freedom and wide robustness testing is most appropriate.

The Equal Pay Act, in contrast, does *not* have a "vague theory" of what constitutes discrimination – the law is exact and leaves researchers with little leeway in how they can contribute legally credible evidence.

Another example of necessary controls comes from the research on interstate migration. Do rich people tend to leave high-tax states? Do young people move away from states that ban abortion? For this kind of regression, the outcome variable is migration flows between states, and the focal variable is differences in tax rates or abortion laws. The baseline gravity model of migration is well established in the literature: Migration flows are a function of the population sizes of the origin and the destination, as well as the distance between them (Zipf 1946; Santos Silva and Tenreyro 2006). Thus, two large cities close together will have large migration flows between them, while two small cities far apart will have small flows between them. These are the basic and well-established laws of gravity for migration. These core elements of the model should always be included, and no migration scholar would find it reassuring to see a robustness analysis that excluded them.

When a control variable is well established in the existing literature for well-defined reasons – so that readers and scholars alike know that the control is substantively justified, it need not be subject to robustness testing. Indeed, excluding a well-known and well-justified control, in mature research areas, is more a sign of weak knowledge than of carefulness.

Estimand consistency is an important principle of multiverse analysis but is not a generic excuse to avoid transparency. If dropping a control variable changes the estimand in ways that violate theory or established practice, researchers must be capable of explaining that to readers. Authors need theory – and external evidence – to explain why a control is definitional to their estimand. In our view, any "necessary control" requires a clear causal diagram or definitional justification supported by prior research. Scholars exploring new terrains and empirical territory – as many sociologists are – can rarely invoke the substantive, a priori knowledge needed to justify necessary controls. Necessary controls and the concern about estimand consistency are features of mature research lines where many substantive facts are already known.

Ed Leamer (1983) referred to necessary controls as "dogmatic assumptions," voicing skepticism about how well justified control variables are in most applications. We share this concern and expect high standards for invoking necessary controls. But we also emphasize that multiverse methods and software are flexible, allowing analysts to incorporate many conditions and restrictions to ensure the model space is strongly grounded in sociological and statistical theory. It is computationally easy to introduce theoretically informed constraints on the model space by specifying necessary controls, grouped variables that enter the multiverse jointly or alternately, and the like.[3] We refer readers to the MULTIVRS help file in Stata for many examples and illustrations.

Sometimes, research papers do not justify their model at all but simply describe basic features of the model – for example, "I used a model with Z set of control variables." Authors may well have private reasons for favoring that specification, but without explaining those reasons, any other specification could have been presented in exactly the same way. Other times, researchers do give positive justifications for modeling decisions, saying why these are sensible controls. These justifications, however, only claim that the specification belongs in the model space, not that it is the best specification. Many different models could be justified with positive arguments. Indeed, making arguments is what academics are trained to do. We once heard a colleague say, "If a sociologist cannot come up with ten different arguments in favor of their hypothesis, they do not belong in academia." Stating the reasons why one favors a model is important, because those reasons could be empirically testable in the future. But prudent readers should assume that a large class of plausible models could be justified in a similar way. To exclusively justify one single specification is to show not that it has good properties but rather that it is better than all possible alternatives. Multiverse analysis is ruled out only in the limiting case when an author asserts that a single model specification is absolutely superior for inference to all other specifications (i.e., that it is the true model). We have never seen a research paper that claimed to be using the one true model, and therefore we have never seen a case when multiverse analysis would not be helpful in elucidating alternative estimates and showing the influence of different assumptions.

Researchers can either justify a control variable using a causal diagram of the model, explaining why the control is essential, or use multiverse analysis to show how much the variable matters to the results. Justify it, or multiverse it. Doing neither lacks credibility and gives a free pass to dubious results.

---

[3] Using the MULTIVRS command in Stata, it is very simple to specify variables that must always be in the model. Required controls are bracketed with the focal variable. Consider the following command: multivrs reg wage (gender hours education) region age marital_status. Wage is the outcome variable, gender is the focal variable, and hours and education are the required controls included in every model. In contrast, region, age, and marital status are uncertain controls that may or may not belong in the model.

5

Empirical Multiverses

This chapter shows examples of modeling distributions using empirical applications on the topics of discrimination in mortgage lending and the effectiveness of a job training program. We use the Stata package MULTIVRS in presenting all of the examples (Young and Holsteen 2021). Neither Stata nor the MULTIVRS package is required to do multiverse analysis – the basic process is simply to run the full set of models and then analyze the regression coefficients and standard errors – but the package makes the process very easy. Replication packages for all of the examples are available online at https://osf.io/45ft2/files/osfstorage.

RACE DISCRIMINATION IN MORTGAGE LENDING

We start with an example based on an influential study of racial discrimination in mortgage lending conducted by the Federal Reserve Bank of Boston (Munnell et al. 1996). The dataset includes information about mortgage applications submitted to select banks in the Boston area in 1990. The outcome variable is whether the application was approved, with approval coded as 100 and rejection as 0 (so that the regression coefficients can be interpreted as percentage point changes). The main variable of interest is a dummy for "black" (vs. "white"), and we consider eight other control variables capturing demographic and financial characteristics of the applicants that may be correlated with both race and loan approval rates.

Two illustrative models are shown in Table 5.1. Model 1 includes only race. The intercept, in this simple model, shows the approval rate for

TABLE 5.1 *Baseline regression models for race effect on mortgage lending*

	Model 1	Model 2
Black	−19.1***	−11.4***
	(1.9)	(1.8)
Denied private mortgage insurance		−71.2***
		(4.2)
Payment–income ratio		−50.0***
		(9.3)
Bad credit history		−25.2***
		(2.3)
Loan-to-value ratio		−11.9**
		(3.4)
Housing expense ratio		5.8
		(10.5)
Self-employed		−5.6**
		(1.8)
Married		4.6***
		(1.3)
Female		3.7*
		(1.6)
Intercept	90.7***	113.8***
R^2	0.042	0.229
N	2,380	2,355

white applicants (90.7 percent), and the regression coefficient of −19.1 means that black applicants have an approval rate about 19 percentage points lower than white applicants. When the full set of controls is added in Model 2, the race effect shrinks to 11 points but remains highly significant. This means that the controls explain part of the race gap – black applicants have a lower approval rate in part because they are more likely to have been denied private insurance, to have higher payment–income ratios, and so on. However, there remains a sizeable residual gap that may be attributable to discrimination.[1]

Multiverse analysis can tell us whether the result hinges on this particular set of controls. Since there are eight potential controls, the multiverse includes $2^8 = 256$ models. Box 5.1 shows the Stata commands to load the dataset and run the multiverse.

---

[1] Munnell et al. (1996) find a smaller (though still significant) race gap when they incorporate additional controls for property and neighborhood characteristics.

> **Box 5.1 Stata commands for multiverse analysis of race effect in mortgage lending**
>
> 1. Install the multiverse program.
>    ```
>    ssc desc multivrs
>    ssc install multivrs
>    ```
> 2. Load the dataset.
>    ```
>    webuse set http://cristobalyoung.com/development/wp-content/uploads/2022/02/
>    webuse mortgage.dta, clear
>    ```
> 3. Scale the outcome variable to 100.
>    ```
>    generate accept_scaled = accept*100
>    ```
> 4. Estimate the full regression model with all ten controls.
>    ```
>    regress accept_scaled black denied_PMI PI_ratio bad_history loan_to_value housing_expense_ratio self_employed married female
>    ```
> 5. Conduct the multiverse analysis and save model results to a file named race_effect.dta.
>    ```
>    multivrs regress accept_scaled black denied_PMI PI_ratio bad_history loan_to_value housing_expense_ratio self_employed married female, saveas(race_effect)
>    ```

This is a simple example of using the MULTIVRS command. All models are estimated with ordinary least squares (OLS); no modeling decisions are incorporated other than different combinations of control variables; and all of the command's suboptions are left at their defaults. The command allows a great deal more flexibility than is shown here. It allows estimation commands other than OLS, and it can include alternative versions of any variable, including the outcome variable and main variable of interest. Variables can be marked as "necessary" if they should be included in every model, and variables can be grouped together so that they come in and out of the model together. Saving the model results with the "saveas" option makes it easy to conduct additional analyses or append together the results of separate runs in more complex cases. The "saveas" option also generates a do file providing every regression command run in that

TABLE 5.2 *Model robustness of race effect on mortgage lending*

Linear regression			
Variable of interest	black		
Outcome variable	acceptance	Number of observations	2,355
Possible control terms	8	Mean R-squared	0.14
Number of models	256	Multicollinearity	0.09
Multiverse statistics		**Vote count**	
Preferred estimate	−11.43	Sign stability	100%
Mean estimate	−14.44	Significance rate	100%
Sampling standard error	1.81		
Modeling standard error	2.07	Positive	0%
Total standard error	2.75	Positive and significant	0%
		Negative	100%
Robustness ratio	4.20	Negative and significant	100%

```
. multivrs regress accept_scaled black denied_PMI PI_ratio bad_history loan_to_value
> housing_expense_ratio self_employed married female, saveas(race_effect)
Note: sample size varies across model specifications.
Listwise deletion: 25 out of 2380 observations will not be used.

Calculating 256   models...
Estimated time is 4 seconds (.1 minutes)
```

FIGURE 5.1 Output from Stata MULTIVRS command

multiverse, which is helpful for seeing what the analysis has exactly done (new users should always review this file).

Figure 5.1 shows some of the Stata output from running the multiverse command in step 5. The output reports that sample size varies across model specifications, which is an indication that the controls have different amounts of missing data. As a default, the MULTIVRS command forces all models to have the same sample size by excluding observations with missing values on any variable Here, there are twenty-five observations with missing values that are excluded from all models. The command also gives an expected run time for how long it will take to estimate the multiverse. For this example, run time is trivial (four seconds), but as the model space grows larger, run time can become substantial.

Table 5.2 shows the results. The average estimate of the race effect across all models is –14.4. This value simply represents the average coefficient and is not necessarily a theoretically defensible estimate. The average sampling standard error is 1.8, and the modeling standard error (the standard deviation of these 256 estimates) is 2.1. This suggests that

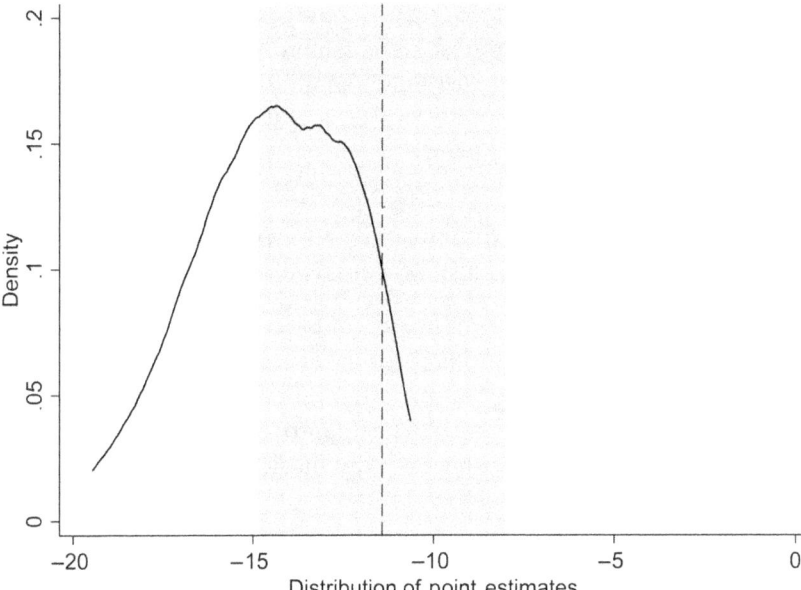

FIGURE 5.2 Modeling distribution of race effect on mortgage lending
Note: The "preferred estimate" of an 11-point race effect, as reported in Table 5.1, is indicated by a vertical line, and the shaded area indicates the confidence interval on that estimate.

uncertainty about the estimate derives about equally from the data and from the model. The total standard error (sampling and modeling combined) is 2.8. The robustness ratio – the preferred estimate divided by the total standard error – is 4.2. By the standard of a t-test, this would be considered a strongly robust result.

The vote count provides additional metrics of robustness. The estimated race effect is negative and significant with every possible combination of controls; both the sign stability and the significance rate are 100 percent. With this list of possible controls, it is not possible to find an opposite-signed estimate, or even one that is nonsignificant.

Figure 5.2 shows a density graph of the modeling distribution. The vertical line marks the preferred estimate from Model 2 in Table 5.1, and the shaded area shows the confidence interval on that estimate. The density curve shows that estimates as large as 20 points are possible in the model space, with the highest concentration around the mean estimate (−14). It is also clear that the preferred estimate is at the smaller end of the modeling distribution, but none of the estimates approach zero.

In our informal testing across many datasets, this kind of outcome – where empirical results are robust – is common. Skeptics of quantitative research may be humbled to see how many different models can support the same basic conclusion. However, in any given research setting, robustness must be demonstrated rather than assumed.

GENDER AND MORTGAGE LENDING: A CASE OF WEAK ROBUSTNESS

Next, we use the same data but change our focus to gender. Table 5.1 reported a rather surprising estimate for the effect of gender. The dummy variable for female had a positive and significant coefficient (+3.7), meaning that women were more likely to be approved for a mortgage than men. How reliable is this estimate – how much does it depend on the choice of controls in the model?

As in the race analysis, the model space includes 256 models – all possible combinations of the eight control variables. However, the two multiverses are not identical, since in the case of racial discrimination, gender was a potential control variable that was only sometimes included in the model specifications. Now, race will take that role in the multiverse for gender effects.

Table 5.3 shows the results. The mean estimate from all models is 2.29. The average sampling standard error is 1.61, which indicates that the mean estimate is not statistically significant. The modeling standard error is 1.60 – the estimates vary across models about as much as would be expected from drawing new samples. The total standard error, incorporating both sampling and modeling variance, is 2.27; combined with the preferred estimate of 3.7, the robustness ratio is 1.63, which is below the rule-of-thumb threshold for robustness.

The vote count leads to the same conclusion. Across the 256 possible combinations of controls, the effect of gender is positive in most (88 percent), but only 25 percent of the estimates are positive and statistically significant. Twelve percent of the estimates are opposite-signed (though none of the negative estimates are significant).

Figure 5.3 shows the distribution of estimates of the gender effect across the 256 models, with a vertical line showing the "preferred estimate" of 3.7 percent from Table 5.1. The modeling distribution is decidedly nonnormal: It is multi-modal, with clusters of estimates around 0, 2.3, and 4.5 percent. We have found that multi-modal distributions are relatively common. The number of modes, or "humps" in the modeling

TABLE 5.3 *Model robustness of gender effect on mortgage lending*

Linear regression			
Variable of interest	female		
Outcome variable	acceptance	Number of observations	2,355
Possible control terms	8	Mean R-squared	0.13
Number of models	256	Multicollinearity	0.19
Multiverse statistics		**Vote count**	
Preferred estimate	3.70		
Mean estimate	2.29	Sign stability	88%
Sampling standard error	1.61	Significance rate	25%
Modeling standard error	1.60		
Total standard error	2.27	Positive	88%
		Positive and significant	25%
Robustness Ratio:	1.63	Negative	12%
		Negative and significant	0%

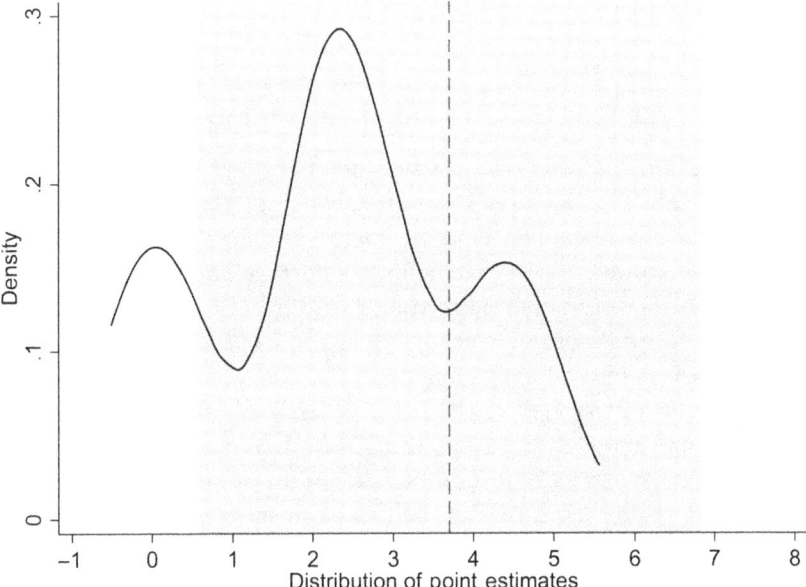

FIGURE 5.3 Modeling distribution of gender effect on mortgage lending
Note: Density graph of estimates of the gender effect from 256 models. See Table 5.3 for more information about the distribution. The "preferred estimate" from Table 5.1 (3.7 percent higher acceptance rate for women) is indicated by the vertical line; the shaded area shows the confidence interval.

distribution, reflects the number of controls (or other modeling decisions) that strongly influence the results. The number of influential controls is the number of modes minus one; in this case with three modes the multiverse has two influential controls, though we do not yet know which controls they are.

It is clear that when we relax the assumption that any one of these control variables must be in the model – allowing us to consider all possible combinations of the controls – there is much uncertainty about the effect of gender on mortgage acceptance. It is hard to draw substantive conclusions from the evidence without knowing more about the modeling distribution. Why do these estimates vary so much? Which controls are responsible for the "humps" in the modeling distribution? What combinations of control variables are critical to finding a positive and significant result? These questions will be answered through influence analysis, which will be discussed in depth in Chapter 6. (Note that influence is an essential part of multiverse analysis and is a standard part of the output from the MULTIVRS command.)

EFFECTS OF JOB TRAINING IN CROSS-SECTIONAL AND EXPERIMENTAL DATA

The next example draws on a classic study by Robert LaLonde (1986). The basic research question LaLonde tackled is this: Do unemployed workers benefit from participating in job training programs? What made his study notable is that he answered that question in two different ways. First, he used data from a field experiment, the National Supported Work Program, which involved random assignment of unemployed workers into a job training program. Next, he set aside the control group from the field experiment, generated a comparison group from national surveys, and conducted a standard econometric analysis with controls to generate a causal estimate of the program's impact. The major distinction then is that the field experiment attempted to control for bias through randomization, while the cross-sectional analysis used a conditioning-on-observables strategy that depended more directly on model specification to address concerns about selection bias. LaLonde found that the nonexperimental methods did a poor job of replicating the experimental result. He concluded: "This study shows that many of the econometric procedures ... would not have yielded accurate or precise estimates of the impact of the National Supported Work Program" (LaLonde 1986: 617).

TABLE 5.4 *Model robustness of the effect of job training programs, field experiment versus cross-sectional analysis*

	(1) Field experiment	(2) Cross-sectional analysis
Number of models	128	128
Mean estimate	1.67	−.81
Sampling standard error	.64	.60
Modeling standard error	.07	2.63
Total standard error	.64	2.70
Robustness ratio	2.61	−.30
Sign stability (%)	100	63
Positive (%)	100	63
Positive and significant (%)	100	16
Negative (%)	0	38
Negative and significant (%)	0	25

We revisit LaLonde's study as the basis for a multiverse analysis.[2] We apply the same basic model to two different datasets. The first is the experimental data from LaLonde's own study ($N = 445$). The second dataset is drawn from a cross-sectional sample of workers from the Current Population Survey (CPS; $N = 16{,}177$). Both datasets contained the same set of treatment and control variables, allowing models to be identically specified in both datasets. We treat the following control variables as plausible model ingredients: past wages and unemployment status, age, race, marital status, and education. Taking all possible combinations of these variables yields 128 unique model specifications, each of which is applied identically to both the experimental and observational datasets.

Table 5.4 reports the results of the two multiverses. Column 1 shows the results with the experimental data, and Column 2 shows the results with the observational data. With the experimental data, the mean estimate is 1.67 (meaning that job training increases wages), and there is remarkably little variation in the results across model specifications. The sign stability is 100 percent. All models have a positive and significant effect. The modeling standard error is only a fraction (12 percent) of the sampling standard error. In other words, with random assignment to job training, model specification

---

[2] We use data made available in Dehejia and Wahba (1999), and we follow the baseline model specification from Athey and Imbens (2015).

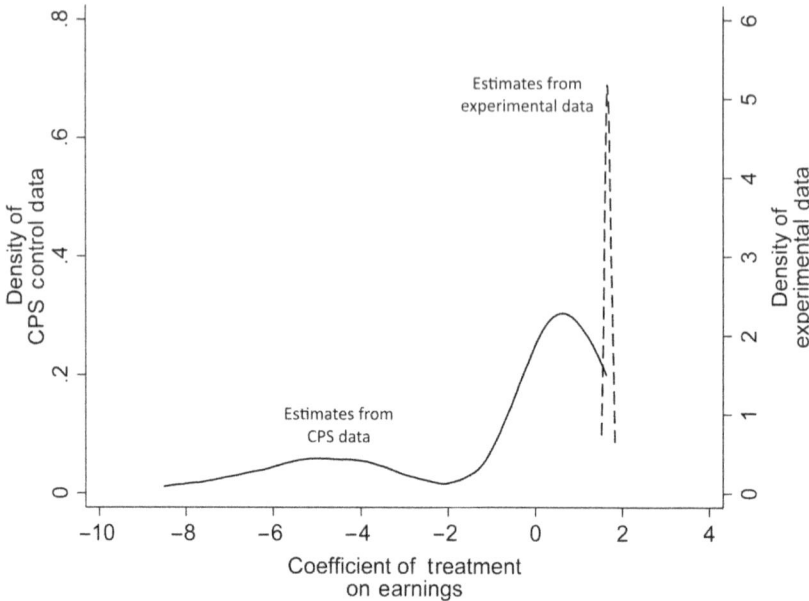

FIGURE 5.4 Modeling distribution of job training program effect
Note: Kernel density graph of estimates from 256 models in each distribution.

has essentially no influence on the results. The modeling distribution is essentially a single spike in estimates, with almost no meaningful variation. The conclusions are given by the data, not by the choice of statistical model.

In the nonexperimental data, the mean estimate is in the opposite direction (-.81, which would mean that job training reduces earnings). Only 16 percent of the models support the general conclusion of the experimental analysis (a positive and significant effect), and more of the models arrive at the opposite conclusion (25 percent show a negative and significant effect). Overall, the modeling standard error (2.63) is more than four times as large as the sampling standard error (.60). This cross-sectional analysis is very far from giving robust results.

Figure 5.4 illustrates how stark the difference is between the two analyses. The analysis using the field experiment data shows almost exactly the same results regardless of which controls are in the model. The cross-sectional analysis, in contrast, allows for a tremendous range of possible estimates, both positive and negative. Across these models, a researcher could easily conclude that the training program significantly raises income, lowers income, or has no impact at all, depending on the preferred model specification.

If we regard the experimental results as the "true" effect of the job training program, then only a handful of possible models from the observational data report the correct results. It is possible that those few models are, in fact, the best models. To understand what control variables are crucial to getting the "correct" results, we will turn to influence analysis in the next chapter.

CONCLUSION

This chapter demonstrated the first step in conducting a multiverse analysis: producing and understanding a modeling distribution. In two of the empirical examples presented, we found the effects to be highly robust (the race effect in mortgage lending and the job training effect from the experimental data). In these examples, the results held regardless of how the model was specified, with any combination of model ingredients yielding the same basic result. In these cases, there is no dispute about whether the data support the basic conclusion of the research. Future studies can find ways to build upon and extend the multiverse, by considering additional modeling options – different controls, different functional forms, different datasets – but the question of whether the result holds with these data and this set of model ingredients is settled.

In the other two examples we showed, the results were not robust (the gender effect in mortgage lending and the job training effect in the cross-sectional data). In these cases, the modeling distributions were wide, and only a minority of models produced a significant effect. This nonrobustness can mean two different things. On the one hand, it might reflect that the conclusion depends on a "knife edge" specification, as in the hurricane names example presented in Chapter 3, and fails to credibly support the hypothesis. On the other hand, it could be that the conclusion depends on only one or two model ingredients – such as the inclusion of a specific control variable – and if those assumptions can be defended as the most sensible assumptions, then the hypothesis result may still be supported. When a result is nonrobust, the second step in multiverse analysis – influence analysis, or the examination of what matters and what does not – will play an especially critical role. This is what we turn to now.

6

Influence Analysis and Scope Conditions

Do research results depend on minor and idiosyncratic aspects of model specification? Is there critical dependence on "convenient modeling assumptions that few would be willing to defend" (King and Zeng 2006: 131)? These questions are not about robustness *writ large*. Rather, the question is about seemingly arbitrary details of a model – of which there could be many – that might affect the conclusions.

When critically evaluating a research paper, scholars often look *outside* the reported model, thinking of new control variables that might moderate or overturn the results. This omitted variable perspective is valuable: It is important to consider what might be missing from a model. It is equally important, however, to probe *inside* the model: to "unpack" a model specification and identify which model ingredients are most influential in the results. This shows which model assumptions matter most – and thus deserve more careful inspection – and which model assumptions have little or no impact on the results. Do certain results depend on including specific control variables? Do different model inputs yield different conclusions?

Multiverse analysis is all about being transparent about the sensitivity of an estimate to choice of control variables and other modeling decisions. In Chapters 3 and 4, we described the first step in achieving that transparency: reporting the full modeling distribution of plausible estimates. It should be made clear how much an estimate would be expected to change not only upon repeated *sampling* but also upon repeated *modeling*.

Robustness testing inherently involves explanatory reasoning (Schupbach 2018). Multiverse analysis, in order to work, needs to say what questionable parts of an analysis are being tested. The source of all robustness testing is doubt – when one or many details of a specification have good alternatives and the correct decision is not known with certainty or scientific consensus. Multiverse analysis addresses specific doubts about a model. The conclusion is never *infinite* robustness but rather robustness to specific factors of concern. This specificity, and limited bounds, means that multiverse analysis is explanatory. Every multiverse provides descriptive explanation of why, or why not, a result is stable in repeated modeling. In this chapter, we will revisit previous analyses and show the value-added of unpacking the modeling distribution.

When a result is not fully robust, the influence analysis provides methodological explanations for the failure of robustness. These explanations can be considered methodological scope conditions – they explain why a hypothesis can be supported in some cases but not in others. Sometimes the influence analysis reveals that many arbitrary assumptions affect the results, suggesting that no credible conclusion is available. Other times conclusions may hinge on one or two important methodological decisions that need to be carefully justified. In exposing these critical assumptions, influence analysis can guide further deliberation about which assumptions are most credible and defensible.

In some studies, influence analysis can even come to take center stage (Engzell and Mood 2023). A textbook case of multiverse analysis, as we have presented it so far, goes something like this: The researcher has estimated a model designed to test a particular hypothesis, and this model gives a single "preferred" estimate of the coefficient of interest. This estimate has been subjected to a multiverse analysis, and the full range of plausible estimates has been presented to the reader so that the finding can be judged to be robust or not. In this textbook case, influence analysis is useful in informing the final judgment – it allows the reader to assess the quality of the modeling distribution and, in cases where models point to different conclusions, to assess whether the models supporting the preferred estimate are based on the more sensible modeling options. But as Engzell and Mood (2023) demonstrated in a recent study on intergenerational income mobility published in the *American Sociological Review*, sometimes the most interesting part is the variation in the estimates. They use registry data from Sweden with a multiverse of 80,000 model specifications to probe the question "Is social mobility declining?" Depending on the specification, one could report that mobility is increasing, flat over time, or declining: The conclusion depends on the model. A key scope condition they identify is that models focusing on daughters rather than sons show robust evidence of declining mobility. Exploring this further, they show that daughters born to high-income parents are "inheriting" more and more labor market success over time, catching up with the advantages that sons have long enjoyed.[1] This influence analysis yields a striking, and unsettling, inference – that rising gender equality leads to less social mobility and more inheritance of advantage.

Nonrobust results motivate a search for explanations, which can turn out to be the most substantively interesting part of the research. In these cases of mixed or weak robustness, multiverse analysis is arguably most informative and constructive, giving deeper insight into what is going on. This is where influence analysis shines, showing methodological scope conditions for a finding (e.g., declining mobility in Sweden is true for women but not men). In contrast, when a result is fully robust, there are no scope conditions to discuss. Influence analysis in this case simply documents what modeling inputs were tested. And when results are very weak, with only one in a hundred models supporting a conclusion, it does not matter very much which modeling inputs make a null result somewhat stronger or somewhat weaker. It is in split cases, where 50 percent of models favor a hypothesis while the other 50 percent favor the null, that multiverse methods and model influence offer the most potentially interesting results.

In every case, however, influence analysis serves an important role in documenting "robustness to what." Influence results show readers what inputs have gone into the modeling distribution and allow readers to judge the credibility of that modeling distribution for themselves. Knowing exactly *what* a finding is robust to provides a clear platform from which future research can build. Engzell and Mood (2023), for example, used multiverse as a method and process of working through all the methodological decisions one confronts (or neglects by taking for granted) when studying social mobility. In this way, regardless of results, multiverse influence is a process of documenting and explaining what approaches were used and how they mattered.

THE LOGIC OF INFLUENCE ANALYSIS

The logic of influence analysis is straightforward: We want to show the impact of each modeling decision on the coefficient of interest. This logic

---

[1] "over time ... women's earnings become a better proxy for their underlying human capital" (Engzell and Mood 2023: 19–20).

Influence Analysis and Scope Conditions

is the same considering all sorts of modeling decisions, but we will start with a discussion of the influence effects of control variables.

Controls are included in a regression equation for a fundamentally different reason than the treatment/focal variable. For the treatment variable, our question is, "Does X affect Y?" When it comes to controls, we are instead asking, "Does Z affect the X – Y relationship?" This question is not directly tested in regression tables, and as a result, readers typically do not learn the answer.

Consider two simple nested models:

$$Y_i = \alpha + \beta X_i + \varepsilon_i \tag{6.1}$$

$$Y_i = \alpha + \beta^* X_i + \delta Z_i + \varepsilon_i^* \tag{6.2}$$

We are interested in how the treatment variable X_i affects the outcome variable Y_i, so β is the coefficient of interest. In the second equation, Z_i is a control variable, and its relationship to the outcome Y_i is given by δ.[2]

In conventional regression tables, it is standard to report the δ estimates. This is a null hypothesis test for the effect of the control variable on the outcome: Is the coefficient significantly different from zero? However, if Z_i is truly a control variable, then this coefficient is not directly interesting. The significance test reported is not the empirical question that controls are there to answer. We want to know the change in β that occurs when Z is added to the model – the difference $\left(\Delta\beta = \beta^* - \beta\right)$. We define $\Delta\beta$ as the influence of including Z_i in the model, or simply the *model influence* of Z_i. This is a comparison of coefficients across models.

The influence of Z_i on the coefficient of interest β is only partly due to the relationship between Z_i and Y_i (i.e., the reported estimate of δ). It is also a function of the correlation between Z_i and X_i, as well as the joint relation of Z_i and X_i with the unknown error term ε_i (Clarke 2005, 2009; Pearl 2011). Thus, the control variables that have the greatest influence on β may not necessarily have a strong or statistically significant relationship with Y_i and may look relatively "unimportant" in the main regression.[3] Similarly, control variables that are highly significant in the main regression may have little or no influence on the estimate of interest.

Suppose that a bivariate regression showed the effect of capital punishment on violent crime (testing the deterrence hypothesis) to be –15

---

[2] Equation (6.2) keeps the notation very simple, but one can think of the δZ_i term in matrix form as $Z_k \delta_k'$, where Z_k is a $k \times 1$ vector of control variables and δ_k' is a $1 \times k$ vector of coefficients.

[3] In other words, δ may be small as long as it is not strictly zero.

percent, so that violent crime is substantially lower when laws permit state executions. However, after adding a set of controls for social demographics, education levels, economic opportunity, safety net generosity, policing levels, and the incarceration rate, the effect of capital punishment falls to zero (no deterrence effect). The question that might naturally arise is, which of the control variables "explain away" the deterrence effect? Adding all of them at once only shows their δ coefficients (how they affect the outcome), not their $\Delta\beta$ effects (how they influence the deterrence coefficient). And since the controls reflect widely varying alternative explanations for violent crime, it is unsatisfying to know simply that together they wipe out the capital punishment effect. It is like a black box of controls that jointly do something important for reasons that no one can directly observe.

A tempting solution to this kind of ambiguity is to add the control variables one at a time, incrementally building from zero controls up to the full model. This allows readers to see how the coefficient of interest changes as each new control is added. Unfortunately, this method does not work. The problem is that there is usually some degree of shared variance, or multicollinearity, among the controls. As a result, the results will often depend on the order in which the controls are added. Consider two control variables, Z and Q, that do an equally good job of accounting for the (X, Y) relationship. In practice, the first control added (Z) gets the first chance to influence or explain away β. The second control added (Q) can only try to improve on Z's alternative explanation. But since Q is only equally good as Z and offers no *additional* explanatory power, it would be deemed noninfluential. However, if the "add one at a time" method had started with Q rather than Z, the conclusion would be the reversed: Q is influential and Z offers nothing more. When there is more than one control, adding them one at a time gives misleading results. We need a method that does not arbitrarily depend on the order in which the controls were considered.

To estimate influence effects more accurately, multiverse analysis borrows from meta-regression analysis. In a meta-regression analysis, comparable estimates are compiled from across studies and become the outcome variable to be explained. Any feature of the sample or the research design can be treated as an explanatory variable. The meta-regression asks, "How did the authors get their result?" Variables could be things like "used panel data," "omitted controls for education," "used European data," or even an author identification variable (in cases where the same researchers published multiple studies on the topic). One meta-analysis coded whether an author engaged in methodological self-criticism (Dolling et al. 2009). Doucouliagos and Paldam (2013) coded a variable called "influence": whether the article acknowledged feedback from another author that was included in the meta-analysis, testing a possible "groupthink" bias (which was positive).

One meta-analytic study of the motherhood penalty coded some 1,895 published estimates (from forty-nine different studies) for whether the estimating equation included each of thirteen different control variables (Leonard and Stanley 2020). Other variables included the year the study was published, the years of data included in the analysis, which countries were included, how motherhood was defined (a dummy versus the number of children), how wages were defined (hourly versus annual), whether the estimate came from ordinary least squares (OLS) or some other model, whether the study was published in sociology (versus economics), and more. They found that studies using fixed effects panel models show a 1.6 percentage point larger motherhood penalty than other studies, and studies that controlled for work experience found a penalty about 1.5 percentage points smaller. Controlling for part-time work or occupation did not affect the size of the motherhood penalty much either way, and other things being equal, estimates published in sociology tended to show larger penalties than those published in economics. In short, a meta-regression documents features of a study that affect the estimate.

Influence analysis also draws on an established technique for identifying outlier observations: the Cook's D approach (Cook 1977; Andersen 2008). In a Cook's D analysis, influence scores for each data point are calculated by excluding observations one at a time and testing how the exclusion of each observation affects the regression estimate. If the exclusion of one specific observation has a "large" effect on the regression coefficient, that observation is considered influential and flagged for further inspection and evaluation. We operationalize a similar strategy to calculate an influence score for each control variable (or other aspect of model specification). However, rather than simply excluding each variable one at a time, we test all combinations of the model ingredients.

Using results from the full 2^P estimated models, we can then formulate an *influence regression* in which the estimated coefficients (for the variable of interest) are the outcome to be explained. The explanatory variables in the influence regression are dummies for whether each modeling ingredient is used in the model. For P possible model ingredients, we create a set of dummy variables $\{D_1 \ldots D_P\}$ to indicate whether each ingredient is used in the model that generated the estimate. OLS regression then reports the marginal effect of using each modeling ingredient. The influence regression is

$$b_j = \alpha + \theta_1 D_{1j} + \theta_2 D_{2j} + \ldots + \theta_P D_{Pj} + \varepsilon_j \qquad (6.3)$$

in which b_j is the regression estimate from the j-th model. The influence coefficient θ_1 shows the expected change in the coefficient of interest (b_j) if the model ingredient corresponding to D_1 is used in the j-th model. Each coefficient estimates the conditional mean $\Delta\beta$ effect for each model ingredient. We offer no explicit definition of a "large" influence; as an intuitive guide, we report the percentage change in the coefficient of interest associated with including each control variable.

INFLUENCE ANALYSIS: RACE AND GENDER
EFFECTS IN MORTGAGE LENDING

To demonstrate the basic process of conducting and interpreting an influence analysis, we revisit the mortgage lending examples from Chapter 5.[4] A baseline model predicting mortgage approval rates, with a full set of control variables, showed two significant effects that we subjected to multiverse testing: a race effect and a gender effect.

Our baseline estimate of the race effect suggested that banks are significantly more likely to give loans to white applicants than to black applicants. The effect was based on a specific directional hypothesis that was well grounded in theory and previous research. The modeling distribution showed that result to be fully robust: 100 percent of the models had a negative and significant race effect. We don't need an influence analysis to know whether this dataset supports the conclusion that there is a race effect: It clearly does. The preferred estimate was at the smaller end of the modeling distribution, though. Most models (94 percent) showed a bigger race effect. To judge whether the preferred estimate is the better estimate, we have to identify which controls yield smaller estimates and determine whether those controls are the most sensible. Do the smaller estimates come from especially compelling model specifications?

In contrast, the gender effect was exploratory. The study was not designed to test for a gender effect; it was merely an interesting result that appeared in the model. We had no hypothesis about the role of gender in mortgage lending, and the effect went in a surprising direction, suggesting that banks

---

[4] Replication packages for all examples are available online at https://osf.io/45ft2/files/osfstorage.

TABLE 6.1 *Influence statistics for race effect on mortgage lending*

	Average race coefficient (ß)	Effect of inclusion (Δß)	Δß as a percent of mean estimate
All models	−14.4		
Bad credit history			
Not included	−16.0		
Included	−12.9	3.2	−22%
Denied insurance			
Not included	−15.4		
Included	−13.5	1.9	−13%
Loan-to-value ratio			
Not included	−15.1		
Included	−13.8	1.3	−9%
Payment–income ratio			
Not included	−14.9		
Included	−14.0	1.0	−7%
Married			
Not included	−14.6		
Included	−14.3	0.3	−2%
Housing expense ratio			
Not included	−14.5		
Included	−14.4	0.2	−1%
Self-employed			
Not included	−14.3		
Included	−14.6	−0.2	2%
Female			
Not included	−14.2		
Included	−14.7	−0.5	4%

Note: Estimates based on 256 models.

are more likely to approve loans for female applicants than for men. The modeling distribution for the gender effect was wide, with only 25 percent of models having a positive and significant effect. These facts – that the gender effect wasn't hypothesized and that it wasn't robust – do not mean that the gender effect isn't real. It just means that the finding deserves special scrutiny. In order to make a judgment about whether there is a gender effect, it is necessary to look closely at the influence analysis to determine which controls are driving the effect and to assess the quality of those controls.

Table 6.1 shows the influence results for the race effect. For all 256 models in the multiverse, the average effect is about −14.4 points, which

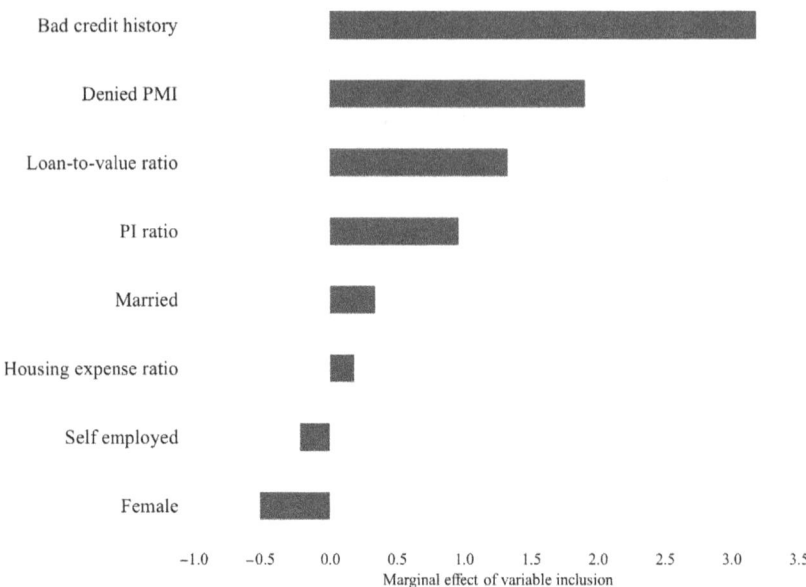

FIGURE 6.1 Influence effects for race effect on mortgage lending

would suggest that the approval rate for black applicants is about 14.4 percentage points lower than the rate for white applicants. Then the table shows the influence effects of each potential control variable: first the average effect in models that don't control for that variable, then the average effect in models that do control for it, and finally the difference, which is what we refer to as the influence effect of the variable. To ease interpretation, the table also shows delta ß as a percentage of the mean estimate. Figure 6.1 shows a graph of the influence effects. Since the race effect is negative, the positive bars make the effect "smaller" and negative bars make it "larger."

The most influential controls are bad credit history, having been denied private mortgage insurance, and loan-to-value ratio. Controlling for any of these variables makes the estimate of the race effect smaller by more than a percentage point. Other controls have little influence on the result: Controlling for any of marriage, housing expense ratio, or self-employment changes the average effect size by only a trivial amount. It makes little difference to the estimate of the race effect whether these variables are included in the model or not.

Table 6.2 shows the influence results for the gender effect. Here, the full multiverse has an average effect size of about 2.3, which would mean

TABLE 6.2 *Influence statistics for gender effect on mortgage lending*

	Average gender coefficient (ß)	Effect of inclusion (Δß)	Δß as a percent of mean estimate
All models	2.29		
Married			
Not included	1.06		
Included	3.53	2.47	108%
Black			
Not included	1.34		
Included	3.25	1.91	83%
Housing expense ratio			
Not included	2.19		
Included	2.39	0.19	8%
Denied private insurance			
Not included	2.30		
Included	2.28	−0.03	−1%
Payment–income ratio			
Not included	2.38		
Included	2.20	−0.18	−8%
Bad credit history			
Not included	2.41		
Included	2.18	−0.23	−10%
Loan-to-value ratio			
Not included	2.41		
Included	2.17	−0.25	−11%
Self-employed			
Not included	2.44		
Included	2.14	−0.30	−13%

Note: Estimates based on 256 models.

that the approval rate for women is 2.3 percentage points higher than the rate for men. The control with the largest influence on the gender effect is marital status (a dummy for "married"). Models that don't control for marital status have an average gender effect of only 1.1, and models that do control for marital status have an average effect of 3.5 – controlling for marriage more than triples the average estimate. The other control that stands out as influential is race. Controlling for race (with the dummy variable "black") increases the gender effect from 1.3 to 3.3, more than doubling the estimate. The other controls have less model influence.

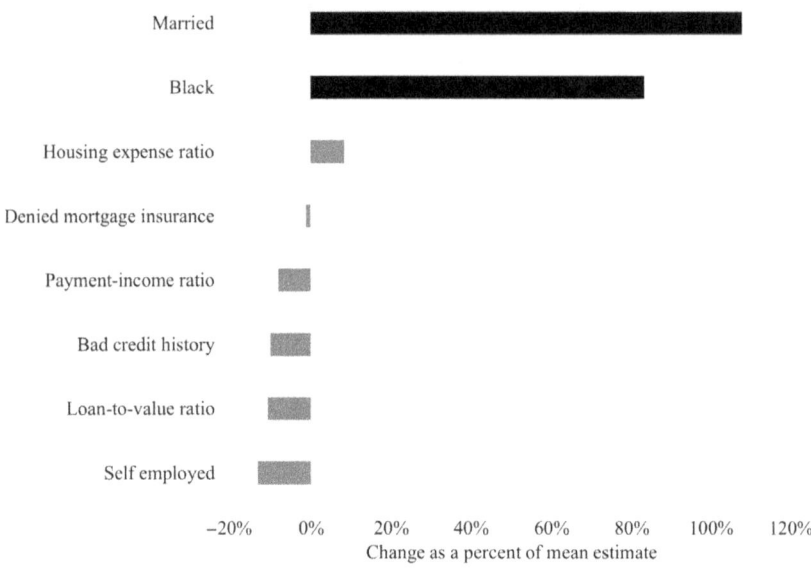

FIGURE 6.2 Influence effects for gender effect on mortgage lending

Figure 6.2 shows a bar graph of the influence effects, with the bars showing the influence effects as a percentage of the mean estimate. Positive values mean that a control makes the gender effect larger; negative values mean that a control makes the effect smaller. In this graph, the outsize influence of the marriage and race controls is clear.

Note that the variables with the most model influence are not necessarily the variables that are most important in predicting mortgage approval rates. In the influence analysis for the race effect, the most influential variables were roughly the same as those that are most important in predicting approval rates. (See regression output from the previous chapter, Table 5.1.) But for the gender effect, this isn't the case. For instance, the variable that is most significant in the baseline regression model is having been denied private mortgage insurance by a third-party insurer. When an applicant has been denied private insurance, banks rarely approve the loan – it reduces the acceptance probability by roughly 70 percent. However, this variable is also the least influential control – it is largely irrelevant to the analysis of how gender affects mortgage lending. Similarly, a bad credit history has a striking effect on lending decisions, reducing the approval rate by 25 percent. Yet credit history has very little model influence, with no real bearing on conclusions about

TABLE 6.3 *Model influence regressions for race and gender effects on mortgage lending*

	Race effect	Gender effect
Bad credit history	3.18	−0.23
Denied mortgage insurance	1.91	−0.03
Loan-to-value ratio	1.32	−0.25
Payment–income ratio	0.96	−0.18
Female	−0.52	
Married	0.34	2.47
Self-employed	−0.22	−0.30
Housing expense ratio	0.18	0.19
Black		1.91
Constant	−18.02	0.50
R^2	0.99	0.98

Note: Each model based on 256 estimates.

the gender effect. The underlying reason for the low influence of these two variables is that they have essentially zero correlation with gender. They are tremendously important in predicting mortgage acceptance but are irrelevant to the gender effect.[5] Moreover, the variables that are critically influential in assessing the gender effect (race and marital status) have modest coefficients in the main regression and do not stand out as key determinants of mortgage approval. Influential variables may be nonsignificant, and significant variables may well be noninfluential. This highlights the critical difference between the significance of a control variable and its model influence. Conventional regression tables focus on the former and give little insight into the latter.

Table 6.3 shows the same basic results as in Tables 6.1 and 6.2 but now in the form of influence regressions. In these models, the sample size is equal to the number of models in each multiverse ($N = 256$), the outcome variable is the size of the race/gender effect, and the predictor variables are a set of dummies indicating whether each control is in the model. For example, in a model with no controls, the expected race effect is −18. If a control for bad credit history is added, the expected estimate shrinks by 3 points, to −15. Controlling for having been denied private mortgage insurance shrinks the estimate by about 2 points. The high R^2

---

[5] This also helps one appreciate that prediction and inference are different goals and use different methods of analysis.

for the model (0.99) suggests that the influence effects are roughly linear; they are about the same regardless of which other variables are in the model, such that controlling for both bad credit history and having been denied private insurance shrinks the expected race effect by the sum of their individual effects, or about 5 points.

The gender regression can be interpreted the same way. The model without controls has an expected effect of only 0.5. Controlling for marriage increases the expected effect by 2.5; controlling for race increases it by about 2 points; and controlling for both of those variables increases the expected effect by about 4.4 points.

For another look into the modeling distribution, we graph effect sizes by the number of controls in a model, as suggested by Brodeur, Cook, and Heyes (2020). Figure 6.3 shows the average size of the race and gender effects by the number of controls. Each dot in the graphs represents the effect size estimated from a single model, and the black lines show the average effect size at each number of controls. For the race effect, the model with no controls has a very big race effect of about 19 points. There are eight models that include one control variable, and the average effect of those models is −17.5. As the number of controls in the model increases, the average effect size continues to get smaller. This is generally how we think control variables work: The raw correlation captures the effects of other (confounding) variables. By stripping out the effects of these other variables, adding controls usually makes the coefficient of interest smaller but more credible.

The second panel shows how the gender effect varies by the number of controls. Here the model with no controls has a gender effect of essentially zero, and the effect size gets larger as more controls are added to the model. We can say that the gender effect is "suppressed" in the raw data; controls are invoked to reveal a relationship that does not appear in the raw data.

This type of suppression effect is common in published papers. Lenz and Sahn (2021) replicated forty-nine observational studies published in the *American Journal of Political Science* between 2013 and 2015. They found that at least 30 percent of those studies depended on suppression effects to achieve statistical significance. In other words, the bivariate relationship between the main treatment variable and the outcome was null, and it became significant only when controls were introduced. Moreover, none of the articles that relied on suppression effects actually disclosed this – none of them reported the bivariate relationship. There were crucial control variables generating the authors' conclusions without this being disclosed to readers. As Lenz and Sahn note, this does not

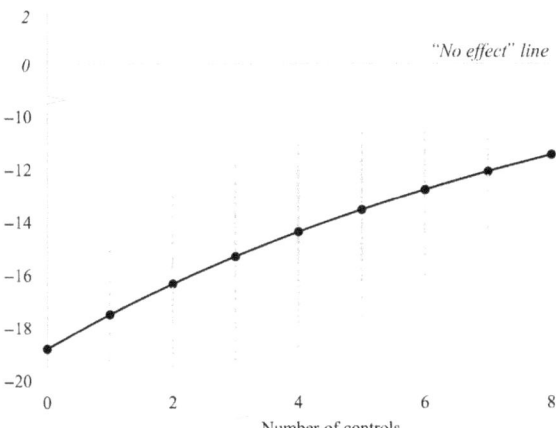
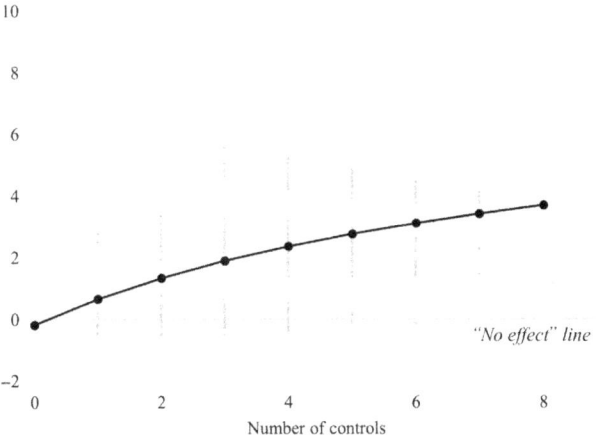

FIGURE 6.3 Average size of race and gender effects on mortgage lending, by number of control variables
Notes: Each gray dot represents a single model. The black line shows the average effect size for each number of controls. The "no effect" line shows where zero is located on each graph, as the graphs have different y axes.

necessarily mean that all of those results are false positives, but it does mean that those studies were avoiding scrutiny and failed to justify their model specifications. As Crede, Gelman, and Nickerson (2016: 2) argue, "suppression effects are considered statistical artifacts unless there is a strong theoretical explanation for their occurrence." Thus, the general rule of thumb when dealing with a suppression effect is that it should be made transparent; the reader should know that the bivariate relationship is the opposite of the "preferred" estimate.

This brings the influence analysis of the race effect to a logical conclusion. We found the race effect from the original model to be highly robust, and there is nothing in the influence analysis to cast much doubt on that conclusion. Furthermore, it would seem that the reported "preferred" estimate of the race effect is probably one of the more defensible estimates, even though it is one of the smaller estimates. The controls that drive that estimate – bad credit history, having been denied private mortgage insurance, loan-to-value ratio – are all things that are correlated both with race and with approval rates, and they can all be, in our view, comfortably justified as confounders in the relationship between race and loan approval (see Chapter 7 on criteria for good and bad controls). Future research might build on the finding by identifying further omitted controls, by examining patterns in other times or places, and by considering modeling options other than the selection of controls.

On the other hand, our influence analysis of the gender effect requires digging further. We have determined that two control variables are critical for getting a positive and significant gender effect: marital status and race. In essence, there are two distinct modeling distributions. In one set of models, the controls for race and marital status are always included. In this distribution, the average gender effect is 4.4, and the significance rate is 100 percent – complete robustness. The second distribution is defined by models that include only one of these two variables or neither of them (i.e., race but not marriage, or marriage but not race, or neither). This second distribution has an average effect size of 1.6, and only one estimate (out of 192) is significant. In this distribution, there is virtually no evidence of a gender effect. In order to draw conclusions from these data, it is necessary to make a substantive judgment about whether those two controls should be treated as strictly necessary.

When we look more closely at how race and marital status influence the gender effect, it becomes clear why these controls are so critical: There *is* a gender effect but only among single black applicants (Table 6.4). Banks treat unmarried black men as especially high credit risks; unmarried black women have an approval rate that is almost 13 points higher, and the result is reasonably robust (59 percent) despite the small cell sizes for this test. In contrast, there is no significant gender effect among white applicants, whether single or married, and there is no significant gender effect among black applicants who are married.

TABLE 6.4 *Mortgage approval rates by gender, race, and marital status*

	Single black applicants	Married black applicants	Single white applicants	Married white applicants
Approval rate: women (N)	76.5% (102)	68.2% (22)	91.2% (284)	96.5% (86)
Approval rate: men (N)	63.8% (69)	73.6% (140)	86.1% (469)	91.9% (1,188)
Gender effect	12.7	−5.4	5.1	4.6
Effect significant with controls?	Yes	No	No	No
Multiverse significance rate	59%	0%	6%	0%

Ultimately, a close inspection of the nonrobust gender effect brings us vividly back to race. What is robust about the gender effect is its contingency on race: that black men face greater barriers with banks than black women. Indeed, recent research emphasizes how the burden of black racial discrimination falls most heavily on the men (Chetty et al. 2020; Reeves, Nzau, and Smith 2020).

Further inspection of Table 6.4 reveals deeper problems with a gender analysis that includes married couples. Mortgage applications are made at the household level. If a single person applies for a mortgage, the data on gender is easy to interpret. When a married couple applies for a mortgage, it is unclear what it means that the applicant is male or female (especially in the 1990s when these data were collected). Presumably, the married couples represented both genders, but more than 90 percent of the time, married couples are coded as male applicants. These are administrative data created by banks processing applications, not social scientists ensuring that variables match theoretical understandings. Most of the married people in this dataset probably represent couples where the couple's "gender" is the gender of the primary breadwinner. The small number of married applicants coded as women are likely some combination of couples where the woman is the primary breadwinner, women separated from their husbands and trying to purchase homes on their own, data entry errors, and who knows what else. For an analysis of gender, our conclusion is that the analysis should be limited to single applicants. This is a case where the influence analysis flags a variable for close inspection, which in turn leads to significant concerns about variable construction – a topic we will address in detail in future chapters.

Our best inference from this evidence is that there *is* a credible effect of gender on mortgage lending, but not in the simple way we initially imagined. The only reasonably robust finding (with 59 percent significance) is of a *less negative* evaluation of single black women than single black men. This seems mostly a story of the gendered stigma of race, rather than a narrative of banks being unwilling to lend to women more broadly. No less important, influence analysis highlighted the critical importance of marriage as a control variable; closer inspection reveals obvious problems in how the "gender" of married couples is coded. The analysis told us where to look for deeper insight, and following those leads was highly informative (cf. Young and Holsteen 2017).

INFLUENCE ANALYSIS OF JOB TRAINING PROGRAM EFFECTIVENESS

In Chapter 5, we also showed a multiverse analysis of the effect of a job training program on participants' future earnings. The treatment group of unemployed men who participated in the program were compared to two different control groups. The first was from a randomized, controlled experiment in which the treatment and control groups were created through random assignment. The second is a nationally representative sample of men from the Current Population Survey (CPS). The purpose of using this second dataset was to assess how well a standard regression analysis using nonexperimental data was able to replicate the experimental result.

We showed the modeling distributions of the estimated program effects using each of the datasets in Chapter 5. In the experimental data, the program had an effect size of 1.7 (which would mean that the program increased men's earnings by $1,700, in 1982 dollars). This estimate was significant, and it was highly robust to choice of controls. Every estimate in the control variable multiverse fell in the narrow range between 1.5 and 1.85, and all estimates were significant. The results with the CPS control group were far more complicated. Using that dataset, a model with all controls had an effect size of $1,100 but was insignificant. The multiverse analysis showed the estimate to be drawn from a very wide modeling distribution: Estimates ranged from –$8,500 (meaning the program made participants much worse off) to +$1,600 (comparable to the result from the experimental data). Only 16 percent of models supported the general conclusion of the experimental analysis, while many models pointed to the opposite conclusion (25 percent show a negative and significant effect).

At first glance, this might sound like evidence that the CPS dataset failed to produce the "correct" result. This isn't necessarily the case, however. The relative robustness of the experimental result is to be expected – experimental data will tend to produce narrower modeling distributions in a control variable multiverse, because controls aren't needed to make the treatment and control groups comparable. The opposite is true of the CPS dataset. The CPS sample is nationally representative of all men aged 55 or under, and no analyst would argue that comparing the participants of the job training program to *all men under 55* would be a reasonable way to assess the program's impact. A strong set of controls is necessary for a fair comparison; models with too few controls would surely give a badly distorted estimate. This means that the wider modeling distribution, with some extremely off-base estimates, is unsurprising and not, in and of itself, a reason to reject the nonexperimental results. It might well be the case that the 16 percent of models with a positive, significant effects are the models that contain the most sensible combinations of controls; it might well be that a reasonable analyst would be likely to choose one of the models that come closest to the experimental estimate. A careful examination of the influence analysis thus becomes critical for drawing any substantive conclusions about the CPS dataset – either about the program's effect or how well it replicates the experimental finding.

Figure 6.4 shows the results of the influence analysis for both datasets. The top graph shows the influence effects in the experimental dataset, and the bottom graph shows the influence effects in the CPS dataset. The bars show how much the inclusion of each control changes the average effect size (i.e., the average estimate in models that include that control minus the average estimate in models that exclude it). Positive numbers mean that a control increases the effect size; negative numbers mean it decreases it.

For the experimental data, the influence analysis simply reiterates that none of the controls has much influence on the result and that any combination of controls gives about the same estimate of the program's effect.

For the nonexperimental dataset, the controls are far more important. In fact, the least influential control (age) changes the estimate by more than the most influential control in the experimental analysis (high school

88 Part II: The Computational Multiverse

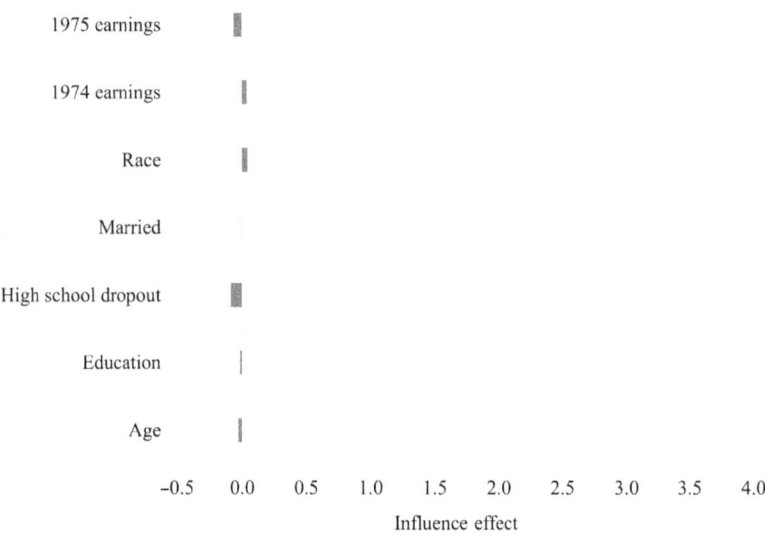

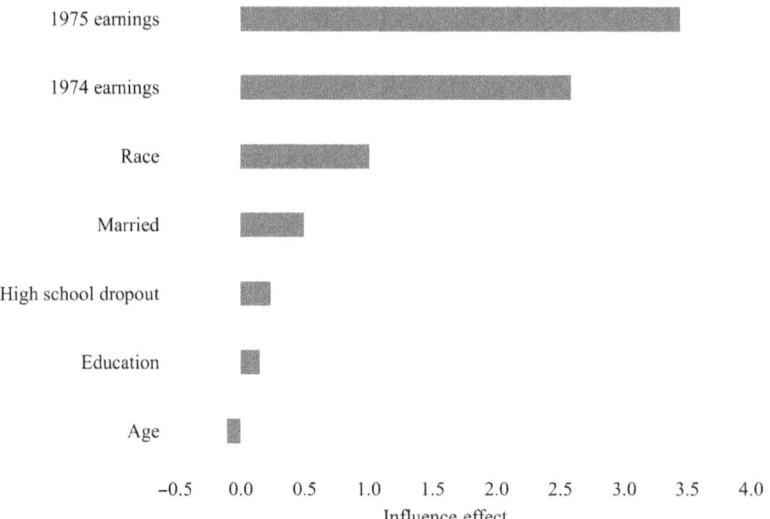

FIGURE 6.4 Influence effects, experimental data versus cross-sectional data

TABLE 6.5 *Model influence regressions for effect of job training programs, CPS dataset*

	Model 1	Model 2
1975 income	3.4	6.0
1974 income	2.6	5.1
1975 income × 1974 income		−5.1
Race	1.0	1.0
Married	0.5	0.5
High school dropout	0.2	0.2
Years of education	0.2	0.2
Age	−0.1	−0.1
Constant	−4.7	−6.0
N (number of models)	128	128
R^2	0.72	0.95

dropout status). The most influential control is 1975 earnings: Models that control for this variable have an average effect size that is more than three points ($3,000) larger than models that don't. Controlling for 1974 earnings has nearly the same influence, and controlling for race increases the average effect size by about a point. Overall, six of the seven controls make the program effect seem larger; only controlling for age makes the average effect size smaller.

Table 6.5 shows influence regressions for the CPS dataset, in which each of the 128 models is an observation, the outcome variable is the estimated program effect size, and the predictors are a set of dummy variables for whether or not each control is included in the model. The constant term reflects the expected program effect in a model with no controls (−5), and the regression coefficients show the expected change in the effect size from including each control in the model. Model 1 suggests that controlling for 1975 earnings increases the estimated effect by 3.4, controlling for 1974 earnings increases it by 2.6, and so on. This model reproduces the influence effects shown in Figure 6.4.

Notice, however, that the R^2 of Model 1 is only 0.72. Properly specified influence regressions tend to have values of R^2 around 0.9 or higher. Those high values indicated that the influence effects are linear – that is, the influence effect of any one variable is about the same regardless of which other variables are in the model. If R^2 is much lower than 0.9, it usually means that there is at least one important interaction between the influence effects that is not accounted for. In this example, the key

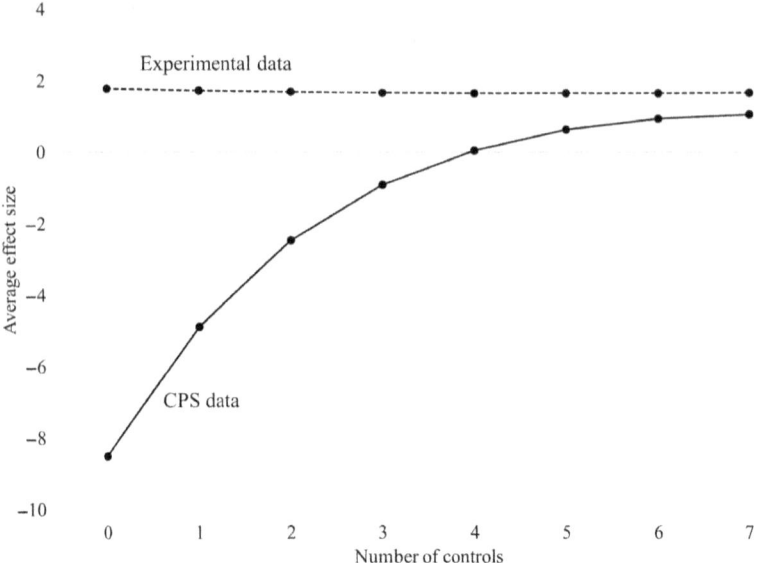

FIGURE 6.5 Average size of job training program effect, by number of control variables

interaction is between the two earnings variables. Model 2 adds the missing interaction term, and the R^2 jumps to 0.95.

The two earnings variables measure the same underlying concept: prior earnings. We can see clearly in Figure 6.4 that prior earnings is the most influential control, and it isn't surprising that when program participants are compared to nonparticipants with the same low level of earnings before the program began, the program's effect appears larger. But there is a strong interaction between the two earnings variables: Adding either of them to the model alone changes the effect size a lot; adding the second changes the effect size only a little bit more. This is clear from model 2. Adding 1975 income to a model with no income control increases the expected effect size by 6.0; adding 1974 income to a model with no income control increases the effect size by 5.1. The interaction term reflects how much those influence effects change *if the other earnings variable is already included*. If 1974 earnings is added to a model that already includes 1975 earnings, it increases the expected effect size by essentially zero, since the magnitude of the interaction term is about the same as the magnitude of the main effect.

Figure 6.5 shows the average effect size by the number of controls. In the experimental data, the number of controls is irrelevant. The average estimate is about 1.7 regardless of how many controls are in the model. In contrast, the CPS models are highly sensitive to the number of controls. In the model with no controls, the program participants appear to be substantially harmed by the program, seeing earnings fall by $8,000. As the number of controls increases, the average effect size moved toward zero and becomes positive in models with four or more controls. If we assume that the experimental results give the true effect of the program, then adding controls strongly improves inference and gets to results that are close to the truth. If this were how control variables always performed in regression, scholars would be much more positive about OLS as a tool for credible causal inference (Heckman and Navarro-Lozano 2004).

To make a final judgment about the results of the nonexperimental data, we can also look more closely at the characteristics of the models that do have a significant effect. There are twenty-one models with a positive and significant effect, and all of them include two controls: 1975 earnings and race. Most of the other controls appear in just over half of the significant models (compared to *exactly* half of the full set of models). Among the models that control for both of these variables, 100 percent find a positive result and 66 percent are significant.

Given that the model with all controls does not have a significant result, it is hard to argue that an analyst looking at the CPS results alone would conclude that the job training program had a significant effect on earnings. However, if the analyst looked not just at the full, preferred, model but at a multiverse of plausible models, they would see that many combinations of the controls do produce a significant result. The most likely outcome is that an analyst looking at this dataset without having knowledge of the experimental result would make no strong conclusions either way and would call for further research to settle the matter.

Another goal of the study was to assess whether the nonexperimental dataset could reproduce the result of the experiment. Given that goal, another standard by which we might evaluate the CPS results is this: Do the most defensible models produce estimates that fall within the confidence interval of the experimental estimate? The experimental estimate was positive, significant, and highly robust, but it also had quite a large confidence interval, ranging from 0.4 to 2.9. While we can say with confidence that the job training program led to a significant increase in participants' earnings, the experimental result does leave quite a bit of uncertainty about the *size* of the program's effect. It turns out that about half of the models in the CPS multiverse fall within that confidence interval, including 80 percent of models with at least five controls and 100 percent of models that control for both race and 1975 earnings. By this standard, the nonexperimental analysis performs reasonably well.

ROBUSTNESS TO UNKNOWN FACTORS: SENSITIVITY ANALYSIS

Another approach to robustness is known as "sensitivity analysis," meaning sensitivity to possible *unobserved* variables. This approach is an extension of the omitted variable bias formula. The goal of sensitivity analysis is to characterize whether an estimate would be robust to plausible (but unknown) omitted variables. First, we will discuss the main features of this framework and then consider how it could augment a multiverse influence analysis.

A t-test presents an effect size divided by its standard error: Is the estimate larger than the noise expected from random sampling? The sensitivity test, in contrast, presents an effect size divided by plausible effects of omitted variables: Is the estimate larger than the (hypothesized) omitted variable bias? Sensitivity analysis does not tell us whether there is an omitted variable problem but only what effect it would have if it existed.

Using the omitted variable bias formula, one can calculate the features of an omitted variable (i.e., its partial correlations with X and Y) that would render the effect zero (or, alternatively, not statistically significant). While it is simplest to think of this as a single unobserved covariate, the same applies to a linear combination of many unobserved covariates. Written in terms of correlations, consider $r_{x \cdot y}$ to be the observed correlation between x and y, while $\hat{r}_{x \cdot y}$ is what we *would* observe if an unobserved confounding variable, cv, were added to the model (Frank 2000; VanderWeele 2011). The formula is

$$\hat{r}_{x \cdot y} = r_{x \cdot y} - \left(r_{x \cdot cv} \cdot r_{y \cdot cv}\right) \tag{6.4}$$

The omitted variable bias term is given by the product of the correlation between x and cv ($r_{x \cdot cv}$), and the correlation between y and cv ($r_{y \cdot cv}$). What motivates sensitivity analysis is realizing that if both $r_{x \cdot cv}$ and $r_{y \cdot cv}$ are equal to $\sqrt{r_{x \cdot y}}$, then including cv in the model will shrink the correlation to zero.

There are some simple rules of thumb for understanding what magnitude of correlation is needed with the omitted variables to shrink $r_{x \cdot y}$ to zero. The short answer is that generally both the correlations in the product $\left(r_{x \cdot cv} \cdot r_{y \cdot cv}\right)$ need to be larger than $r_{x \cdot y}$ to overturn the correlation and render $\hat{r}_{x \cdot y}$ zero. If $r_{x \cdot y} = 0.5$, and so are both the correlations with the confounding variable, then the bias term will be 0.25 and therefore $\hat{r}_{x \cdot y} = 0.25$. When two small correlations are multiplied together, they become very small. In general, correlations with the omitted variable need to be substantially strong than $r_{x \cdot y}$ itself to eliminate the correlation. One can also discuss how much other controls in the model are correlated with x and y to give a sense of what it takes to null the result.

When an effect size is small, it is easy to imagine omitted variables that would explain away the result. The larger is $r_{x \cdot y}$, the harder it will be to find omitted variables that can overturn the result. These types of observations lead authors to comment on the plausibility of omitted variables existing that could overturn one's conclusions. Almost inevitably, users of this method conclude that it would be unlikely that any remaining omitted variable cv could have large enough correlations with x and y to null the results. In essence, authors often use sensitivity analysis to claim their results are too big to fail.

Some notes of caution are very important here. First, this is a purely hypothetical exercise. This "sensitivity analysis" is *not* a robustness test and does not establish any new empirical facts. It is a postestimation calculation of how large a set of correlations would be needed for some unknown omitted variable to overturn a result. If one actually had the confounding variable, they would include it in their multiverse and see how it actually affects the results. Sensitivity analysis is only used to *hypothesize about unknowns*.

Second, describing the correlation levels needed to overturn a result can be of little value if readers do not have good intuition about the distribution of such correlations in the universe of relevant data. Moreover, in Eq. (6.4) any cv can stand for multiple unobserved variables – a vector of confounders that jointly have a stronger correlation with x and y than any one variable alone. Statements that cv needs to have large correlations to matter are often weakly informative in practice. In a way, sensitivity analysis is just reminding readers about the role that confounders play in regression.

A case study on how this kind of sensitivity analysis goes wrong is offered by Mazumder (2018) and the critical replication by Biggs, Barrie, and Andrews (2020). The original study examined how local civil rights protests had long-term and liberalizing influence on racial attitudes in America. Whites living near the sites of prominent civil rights protests in the 1960s have more liberal views on race, even when measured decades later. Mazumder invoked sensitivity analysis to claim there was unlikely to be any omitted variables that could overturn the results. Biggs et al. promptly responded with a replication documenting readily available omitted variables that overturned the results.

Mazumder (2018: 932) claimed to have included "an exhaustive set of ... confounders" and used sensitivity analysis to assert that remaining omitted variables would need to have implausibly large effects. He wrote, "Such an unmeasured variable would have to explain more than twice the amount of variance ... than observed predictors such as urbanization, median income, and percent black ... It is difficult to think of an unobserved confounder that has such a large effect" (Mazumder 2018: 929–930).

On this basis, the author stated, "using a series of formal sensitivity analyses, I demonstrate that the correlations presented can be interpreted as a causal relationship" (932). Another interpretation of the sensitivity results given is: "my results are insensitive to the inclusion of additional potential explanations" (928). These are remarkable causal claims given that all sensitivity analysis does is state what magnitude of correlations could overturn the results.

A team of leading scholars on social movements replicated these results with three main conclusions (Biggs et al. 2020). First, the list of confounders was not exhaustive; the dataset included variables for college education (which is intimately connected to civil rights protests) that were omitted from the original analysis. Second, once college education variables are included, local civil rights protests no longer have a significant effect on racial attitudes. Third, the college education variables overturn the results in exactly the way the sensitivity analysis predicted: They explain two to three times as much variance as the original controls. In short, calculations from the sensitivity analysis were correct; the problem was in claiming that omitted variables with those features were unlikely to exist. As Biggs et al. (2020: 1) conclude, "tests for sensitivity can induce complacency about the risk of confounding."

Sensitivity analysis does not show robustness to anything. Any observational result can be overturned by a hypothetical omitted variable. Regression results are always provisional, and nothing can be considered robust to unknown problems in estimation and identification. There is something about the method of sensitivity analysis that seems to encourage overstepping the bounds of careful inference. Used judiciously and with careful interpretation – Sharkey and Elwert (2011) provide a good example – sensitivity analysis can aid interpretation and help think through the likely effect of omitted variables. When used carelessly, it is simply a way of waving off concerns about omitted variables whose effects are unknown.

SENSITIVITY TO MULTIVERSE INFLUENCE

From this discussion, we settle on the idea of *sensitivity* to mean the *potential model influence* of unknown and/or unobserved variables. If a variable is observed in the multiverse, it has an influence score (the $\Delta\beta$ showing how it changes the results when included in the model). When a variable is unobserved, its $\Delta\beta$ is unknown, so instead of observed influence we speak of (potential) sensitivity. The distinction between influence and sensitivity, in other words, is whether or not the variable was actually included in the multiverse. This language is perhaps not ideal, but it clarifies and links together the terms that are used in these two different literatures.[6]

With this in mind, we highlight how multiverse analysis can help inform discussions of sensitivity to unknowns. First, consistent with sensitivity calculations, we think main effect sizes should always be compared to the observed model influence estimates. A preferred result can be compared to the $\Delta\beta$ value (as in our Tables 6.1 and 6.2) to give a sense of how large the influence is and, equivalently, how close a control variable comes to making a result become null. This is simple to do, since everything one needs is already available in the standard MULTIVRS output. The preferred estimate for the effect of race on mortgage lending was 10 percent; the single largest influence effect was 3.2 percent – so it would take three variables with that level of influence in order to overturn the result. Does that sound likely to be observed in practice? Alternatively, let's consider the range between the largest and smallest estimates in our control variable multiverse: 10 percent to 20 percent – a gap of 10 points. From this view, it is clearly possible that different combinations of controls can shift the result by 10 points, which is what it would take to get a zero coefficient. So, if there exist another set of controls "like these" out there, one should expect to observe models with null results. If scholars want insight into how their coefficient of interest might change if new variables were added, the multiverse influence analysis is the best immediate source of that information.

At the same time, we reiterate that researchers should be very cautious in claiming robustness to hypothetical omitted variables. Multiverse

---

[6] In our view, "influence" is something caused by an added variable, while the term "sensitivity" sounds like an x–y relationship's susceptibility to influence. Linguistically, these two things would seem to be symmetric and empirically analogous. In practice, these terms have evolved to signify discussions of the effect of observed versus unobserved variables.

analysis shows robustness to specific model ingredients, in any combination. It does not show robustness to anything that is *not* tested in the multiverse. It is always tempting to infer that because a result is robust to ten control variables it is probably robust to five more controls. But that involves inferring from the known to the unknown and involves untested assumptions about the features of unknown controls. Sensitivity analysis shows the problem of pushing robustness claims beyond what is specifically tested – of generalizing from an *observed* robustness test to imagining the results of an *unobserved* robustness test. It is a caution that users of multiverse methods should well remember. Multiverse analysis is a way to think about, organize, and reveal analytical alternatives in a way that is as provisional and open-ended as science itself: It embraces new observations, variables, and analytical insights as they become available. No amount of robustness testing renders a conclusion definitive, or robust to unknown model features, as the multiverse always allows more branches of analysis that could yield new results.

CONCLUSION

Influence analysis is an essential component of multiverse methods. When a result is not robust, it can make clear why different methodological choices lead to different conclusions. Not all nonrobust results are "wrong," and influence analysis provides the additional details needed to help draw sound conclusions. Sometimes the influence analysis will show a result to be dependent on a mish-mash of assorted modeling assumptions that are hard to defend, which casts doubt on the robustness of the finding. Other times, it may show a result to be dependent on specific assumptions that *can* be defended – in these cases, it is incumbent on the author to be transparent about what assumptions are required to get the result. Whether a finding is robust or not, influence analysis can make clear the *methodological scope conditions* under which a finding is robust and guide further deliberation and research.

Overall, our empirical testing shows three basic patterns of model robustness:

1. A statistical result holds no matter how the model is specified; any combination of the model ingredients yields the same basic result (see race and mortgage lending).
2. A conclusion depends only on one or two model ingredients – such as a specific control variable – which in turn suggests informative

follow-up analyses to better understand why the control variable is so important (see gender and mortgage lending).
3. A conclusion depends on a "knife edge" specification, supported in only one in a hundred plausible models (see hurricane names).

Without conducting a multiverse analysis, it is impossible to say whether a single regression represents a robust finding or whether the modeling assumptions are entirely shaping the results in ways that would be hard to justify or explain.

In the next chapter, we revisit the assumptions behind the use of control variables and review multiple reasons why control variables need explicit justification and should be treated as suspect when authors do not provide clear theory explaining why the control belongs in the model.

7

Good and Bad Controls

Statistical models with long lists of control variables are a routine part of data analysis in the social sciences. Anyone scrolling through the pages of a typical research journal in a field like sociology, political science, or economics will notice long tables of control-heavy models. The use of controls is attractive to analysts because they help us examine causal relationships and make causal claims even when data from randomized controlled experiments are not available – and in the social sciences, such data are often not available (Heckman 2005). Control variables are also a component of models designed for specific forms of causal inference, such as instrumental variables, difference-in-difference models, fixed effects panel models, and regression discontinuity analysis.

The dangers of not controlling for potential confounding factors are well known. When causal claims are based on observational data, there is always concern that the claims might be biased due to omitted variables; it is for good reason that data analysts (and their reviewers) are trained to consider carefully which variables left out of a model might be generating a spurious result. This fear of reporting a spurious relationship is perhaps responsible for the widespread view that control variables are inherently good. The unspoken attitude often seems to be "the more controls, the better," and rarely is the inclusion of every control in a model defended or theorized. Instead, each additional variable is assumed to improve the like-with-like comparison between people who have received some treatment and those who have not; every control is seen as reducing the ever-present threat of a spurious result (or, at the very least, it is seen as doing no harm).

There should be much more skepticism about the proliferation and careless use of control variables (Clarke 2005, 2009; York 2018; Wysocki,

Lawson, and Rhemtulla 2022). There are myriad ways in which the overuse of controls can harm an analysis. Adding variables to a model can have unpredictable consequences, and a poorly selected control can easily introduce bias rather than eliminate it. Telling the difference between "good controls" and "bad controls" is hard, requiring careful judgment and scrutiny.

Long lists of controls are especially dangerous when analysts look at many different models before selecting one or a small number of "preferred" models to report. The decision of which controls to include in a model gives analysts leeway to fish for a good-looking result, even when they are not actively trying to do so. Even a seemingly benign practice such as dropping insignificant variables can cause problems, leading to significance inflation and an increased number of false positives (Freedman 1983).

TYPES OF GOOD AND BAD CONTROLS

Bad controls can wreak havoc in statistical models and bias estimates of causal effects. We will show stylized examples of some of the more common types of controls: confounders (the good controls) and then mediators, colliders, and proxies (some of the more common types of bad controls). There are more complicated versions of all of these. It is also possible for a variable to fall into one or more of the categories – for instance, a control can be both a confounder and a mediator. The goal is to show the many ways that controls can do harm and to motivate the usefulness of the control variable multiverse (Cinelli, Forney, and Pearl 2022).

When researchers disagree about what control variables belong in a model, these are the issues they are concerned about. A multiverse analysis might include the wrong set of controls; this section discusses why it would be wrong. These criteria are the reasons why controls do or do not belong in an inferential regression analysis.

COMMON CAUSE CONFOUNDERS: THE GOOD CONTROLS

The ideal control variable is a common cause confounder (or just "confounder"). Most data analysts are well familiar with the role of confounders and how to deal with them, but we review the mechanics as a reference point for how "bad" controls go wrong.

A confounder is shown in the causal diagram in Figure 7.1. In this analysis, we are interested in the relationship between X and Y, and

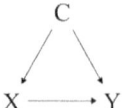

FIGURE 7.1 Causal diagram of a confounder (C)

there is a third variable C that causes them both. If we looked at X and Y alone, we would find them to be correlated, even if there were no true relationship, because of the causal connections they each have to C. By controlling for C, or by holding C constant, the true relationship between X and Y can be revealed. In other words, the uncontrolled estimate of X on Y is biased, and adding C as a control eliminates the bias. In a causal diagram, the direction of the arrows is absolutely central. What makes C a good control is that the causal arrows point away from, not toward, C.

An easy example of a common cause confounder is the relationship between shoe size and reading skills among elementary-age children. Shoe size and readings skills are correlated but not because one causes the other. Older children have larger feet, and they also have more developed brains. Age is a confounder, and without control, we get misleading estimates of the true relationship between shoe size and reading ability (which is null).

CAUSAL HELPERS: MEDIATORS AS BAD CONTROLS

Sometimes control variables increase bias in the estimate of a causal effect because they *mediate* – or help cause – the relationship between the two variables. For instance, if we wanted to know the effect of earning a college degree on income, we wouldn't want to include occupation as a control because it mediates the relationship between them. In other words, one way earning a college degree affects income is that the diploma provides access to higher-income occupations.

Figure 7.2 shows a causal diagram of a mediator, where X causes Y, but it causes Y in part through a third variable C. X may have a direct effect on Y, but it also has a mediated effect on Y, which passes through C; the total effect of X on Y includes both the direct and the mediated effect. If we control for C, then part of the pathway through which X causes Y is eliminated, and bias is introduced into the causal estimate. Controlling for C strips out the fact that college is critical for accessing the occupation.

Good and Bad Controls

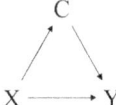

FIGURE 7.2 Causal diagram of a mediator (C)

The direction of the arrows in Figure 7.2 is central. Because C has an arrow pointing to it, we can say the control is endogenous: C is determined by other variables in the equation, so it should be a left-hand side variable. By treating C as a right-hand side control variable, the regression is misspecified because it does not account for the fact that C is caused by X; instead C is treated as a causal factor that is independent of X but may have an accidental correlation with X. If X is the puppet master, giving C its marching orders, then X is the only true causal factor in the model and C should not be included.

The problem of controlling for a mediator can be illustrated with a vivid example: gender discrimination in high-tech industries. The basic model for this is $Wage_i = \alpha + \beta Female_i + \ldots + \varepsilon_i$, where β gives the difference in wages between men and women who work for high-tech companies. The analytic goal is to include control variables that help formulate a "fair comparison" between men and women who are otherwise similar.

Google (2017) reported on the results of such an analysis among their employees, concluding that "there is no gender pay gap at Google." However, this finding, which Google described as "extremely scientific," used promotions and subjective performance evaluations as control variables. Yet these controls seem like classic mediators: Evaluations and promotions are at the discretion of the company; if there is bias, they would be central to how men and woman can be sorted into different wage levels. By controlling for these factors, the Google report controlled away the pathways by which gender discrimination may well occur (Niedig 2017). In terms of Figure 7.2, variable C represents potentially biased performance evaluations and promotion practices, which are caused by gender (X) and result in higher wages (Y). After controlling for C, the partial effect of X on Y shows the *remaining* wage discrimination after factoring out biased promotions. In essence, Google is saying, *if you control for potential bias, there is no discrimination*.

It is often unclear whether a particular control represents a confounder (a good control) or a mediator (a bad control). Note that the only difference between Figures 7.1 (showing a confounder) and 7.2 (showing a mediator) is the direction of the arrow between X and the confounder/mediator C. As a confounder, X causes C ($X \to C$), while as a mediator, C causes X ($C \to X$). In both cases, X and C will be correlated in the data, and often there is no immediate way to know for sure which way the causal arrow goes. Further complicating the issue is that C could be *both* a confounder and a mediator.

For instance, Google could argue that performance reviews are largely unbiased, promotions based on fair criteria, and that these variables provide an accurate reflection of job performance. If that is true, then performance reviews and promotions are confounders (good controls) rather than mediators (bad controls) and thus belong in the model as fair explanations of wage differences between male and female employees. But to include these controls without careful justification is to close off a large portion of the debate over discrimination. Indeed, in 2022, Google settled a $118 million class action lawsuit over gender pay discrimination (Grant 2022). The suit was brought by 15,000 female employees, who specifically alleged that the company discriminates first "by assigning and keeping women in job ladders and levels with lower compensation ceilings and advancement opportunities than those to which men with similar skills, experience, and duties are assigned and kept" and second "by promoting fewer women and promoting women more slowly than it has promoted similarly-qualified men" (Niedig 2017). These are exactly the conditions which would invalidate conditioning on promotions in an analysis of gender discrimination.

Interestingly, Apple also produces pay equity statistics that control for job level and performance evaluations and similarly claims to have achieved gender pay equity. It refuses to release the raw gender pay gap in the company and argues that without these control variables the pay gap is not "a meaningful metric for Apple" (Apple 2023). This insistence on looking only at the controlled wage difference seems like a sure indicator that the uncontrolled wage gap is less favorable to the company.

Ultimately, a basic wage regression analysis will not be able to settle the debate over whether evaluations and promotions are biased – and whether these variables are confounders (as the companies assert) or mediators (as the class action suit alleged). What the wage regression can do is show *how much* of the raw wage difference operates through evaluations and promotions. To show this, one first reports the wage regression *excluding* evaluations and promotions and then reports the regression that includes them and observes how large the difference is. (This kind of influence analysis is the focus of Chapter 6.) If the difference is large, this means that this pathway accounts for a lot of potential discrimination, and more research is needed to understand the fairness of the promotions process itself.

It may seem unsatisfying to leave the question of discrimination in tech unsettled. But important progress has been made: We have converted an unquestioned and potentially very biasing modeling assumption into a new question for important follow-up research. A key part of methodological rigor is revealing problematic assumptions even if there is no quick statistical fix for the problem. And the process of transforming analytical *assumptions* into research *questions* is in many ways the essence of scientific progress. Requiring that every important assumption be justified with compelling evidence is what makes science a "knowledge machine" and fuels its relentless push for understanding.

COLLIDERS AS BAD CONTROLS

Another way that a control variable can serve as a "bad control" that biases the estimate of a causal relationship is when the control is a collider. Figure 7.3 shows a causal diagram of a collider. We want to know if X causes Y, but both X and Y cause a third variable C. The language of a collider variable comes from this type of diagram, where the causal forces of X and Y "collide" at C. The crucial distinction of a collider is that Y causes C (Y → C), or stated differently, that C is endogenous to Y. In this case, controlling for C, or holding it constant, can distort the relationship between them (Cinelli et al. 2022; Wysocki et al. 2022).

A good example of a collider comes from Rohrer's (2018) work on the science of science. What is the relationship between methodological rigor and innovativeness in scientific research? Suppose that we gather a sample of published papers that differ by their innovativeness and methodological rigor and find a negative correlation: Innovative papers tend to be less rigorous, and rigorous papers tend to be less innovative. (In conversations, we find that academics frequently believe that this negative correlation is true.) However, suppose we worry that published papers are not representative of all scientific research, and so we collect a new sample of *unpublished* papers, repeat the same analysis, and

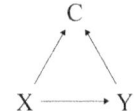

FIGURE 7.3 Causal diagram of a collider (C)

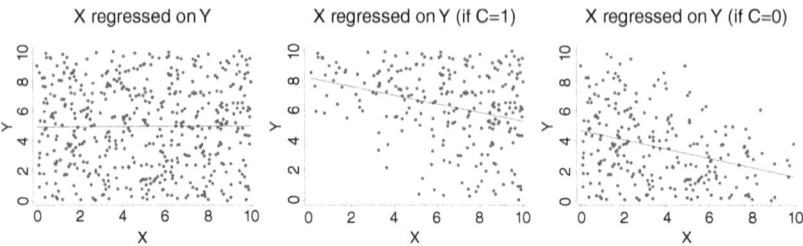

FIGURE 7.4 Simulation of a collider (C)

again find a negative correlation. A careless analyst might conclude that innovativeness must indeed be negatively correlated with methodological rigor, since the pattern is apparent among both unpublished and published papers. The more sophisticated researcher will realize that publication status may be serving as a collider, because either innovativeness or methodological rigor would make a paper more likely to be published – in other words, they are both causes of publication. In Figure 7.3, imagine that X is rigor, Y is innovativeness, and the collider variable C is the publication status. With all papers combined, there is no relationship. When we split the cases into published (C = 1) and unpublished papers (C = 0), an inverse relationship appears among both groups. The same result occurs if the samples are combined and a dummy for publication status is included in the model (to "take into account" publication).

A simulation of how a collider works is shown in Figure 7.4.[1] The variables X and Y are each randomly selected from a uniform distribution from 0 to 10, and there is no relationship between them. This is clear in the first panel, where the regression line is nearly flat. In the next two panels, the cases are split by a collider variable C. To calculate C, we took the sum of X, Y, and a random noise variable and then coded scores above the median as C = 1 and those below the median as C = 0. This means that cases with higher values of either X or Y are more likely to be coded as C = 1, cases with high values of *both* X and Y are nearly all coded as C = 1, and cases with low values of both X and Y are nearly all coded as C = 0. Splitting the sample on the collider creates a negative association at both levels of C, as the bottom left quadrant is missing at C = 1 and the top right quadrant is missing at C = 0. The

---

[1] A replication package for this simulation is available online at https://osf.io/45ft2/files/osfstorage.

TABLE 7.1 *Simulation of a collider: regression models predicting Y*

	(1) All cases (no control for C)	(2) C = 1	(3) C = 0	(4) All cases (control for C)
X	0.01	−0.29***	−0.31***	−0.30***
	(0.04)	(0.06)	(0.06)	(0.04)
Collider (C)				3.62***
				(0.25)
N	500	250	250	500
R^2	0.00	0.09	0.10	0.31

Note: ***$p < 0.001$, **$p < 0.01$, *$p < 0.05$. Constant is included in all models.

regression results in Table 7.1 show that there is no true effect of X on Y (Column 1), but the effects at each level of C are negative and statistically significant (Columns 2 and 3), and the effect of X on Y controlling for C is also negative and significant.

Collider bias has multiple moving parts and can be tricky to follow. Next, we consider another applied example to try to anchor the concept. How does personal happiness change as people grow older? One prominent study concluded that happiness is "U-shaped" over the life course with lowest happiness at middle age (Blanchflower and Oswald 2008). In a critical response, Glenn (2009) argued that the results are driven by the authors' use of a bad control variable (marriage) and showed that the results are reversed when the control is excluded.[2] The model estimated by Blanchflower and Oswald (2008) is the following:

$$\text{Happiness}_i = \alpha + \beta_1 \text{age}_i + \beta_2 \text{age}_i^2 + \beta_3 \text{Married}_i + \varepsilon_i \quad (7.1)$$

Including marital status as a control is tempting because it is correlated with age (highest in middle age), and it is reasonable to think that marriage has a causal effect on happiness. The problem is that there is also reverse causation between marriage and happiness. People with happy dispositions are more desirable marriage partners; their happiness attracts marriage proposals, and they are selected out of singlehood and into marriage faster and younger than unhappy individuals. If this reverse

---

[2] Glenn critiqued multiple controls in Blanchflower and Oswald's study, but we focus here on marital status as an example of a collider.

FIGURE 7.5 Diagram of marriage as a collider

causation pattern is strong, then controlling for marriage induces collider bias in the estimated effect of age on happiness. The alternate explanation for these correlations is as follows: (1) Happiness is not affected by age, but (2) each year the happiest single people get married, and (3) the rate of people getting married is U-shaped with age. Figure 7.5 shows a diagram where both age and happiness point to marriage; they "collide" at marriage. The young and the happy get married first. A regression of happiness on age by itself would show no age effect, but after controlling for marriage, the regression would show happiness declining with age. As people grow older, the happiest singles switch their status to married; the remaining pool of singles are increasingly unhappy due to the selection effect of marriage. The problem here is (1) reverse causation in marriage (happiness causes marriage), which in turn is (2) also caused by age because marriage rates are correlated with age.

Figure 7.6 graphs the relationship (in simplified and exaggerated form, to demonstrate the role of the collider more clearly). In this graph, the solid gray dots are married people, and the unfilled dots are unmarried people. At age twenty-five, only the happiest 20 percent of people are married. By age thirty, the happiest 30 percent are married, and so on. As a greater percentage of the population gets married, and those people tend to be the happiest people, the trendlines in happiness for both married and unmarried people slope downward. Age "causes" marriage to increase; happiness "causes" marriage; and thus controlling for marriage distorts the relationship between age and happiness.

The contribution of Glenn (2009) was to recognize the potential for collider bias in the causal relationships between these variables and then show that conditioning on marriage induces the correlation between age and happiness that is consistent with collider bias. Part of the problem with the original Blanchflower and Oswald (2008) article was that the authors never reported the uncontrolled effects – the effect of age without controlling for marriage. This is an example of using control variables to turn a null finding into a significant result, without informing readers the crucial role the controls are playing; as Lenz (2021) notes, this is a common problem in the social science literature.

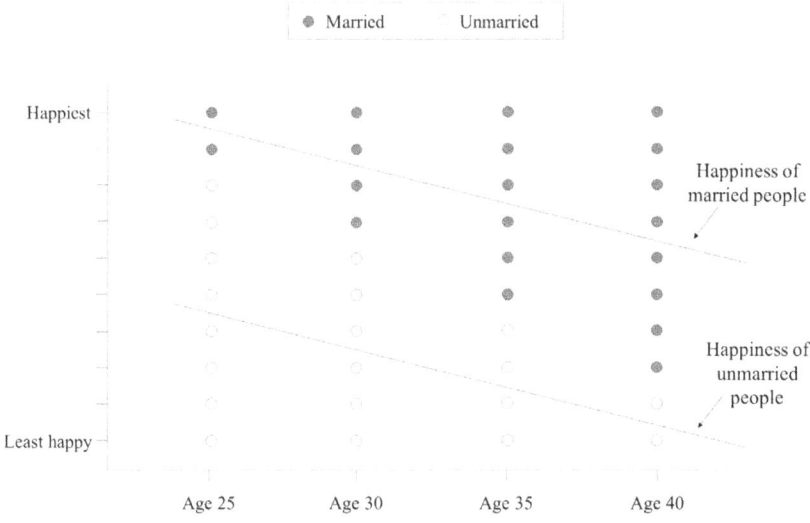

FIGURE 7.6 Marriage as a collider between age and happiness

The final example of a collider variable comes from research on education: How does a student's home environment influence their academic performance? A commonly used measure of environment is the number of books in the home, which many studies find to be the single most important determinant of student performance. However, this variable is likely endogenous to academic performance in two ways (Engzell 2021). First, students who are good at reading tend to accumulate more books: books are partly *the result* of student ability, not the cause. Parents are only one factor in book purchases, and the student's interest and aptitude play a key role as well (and increasingly as they get older). Second, students with little interest in reading tend to underreport the number of books in their home. This endogenous measurement error artificially increases the correlation between books in home and student performance. Engzell (2021) provides interesting evidence of both forms of endogeneity and concludes that endogeneity accounts for a large portion of the observed relationship between books and performance. Now, suppose books in home is used as a control variable, say in a regression of student performance on teacher quality – controlling for home environment to help isolate the true effect of teachers. If great teachers improve student performance, then they also presumably stimulate student demand for books and increase student awareness of the books available to them. The control variable books in home is on the causal pathway between teacher quality (X) and student performance (Y), being at least partly caused by both. This is the definition of a collider variable: In the causal diagram, both X and Y point to the control. In this case, including books in home diminishes the effect of teacher quality, giving the impression that student performance is more about what happens in the student's home rather than in the classroom. This, in turn, suggests lower returns to investing in high-quality education.

PROXIES AS BAD CONTROLS

Consider a case where a control variable C is caused by X but has no effect on Y (as shown in the causal diagram in Figure 7.7). This situation by itself is unproblematic: C should have a zero coefficient in the regression on Y and should not affect the estimated relationship between X and Y. This control variable is simply not needed for unbiased estimation. Suppose, however, the likely case that X is measured with error, so that our model includes not X but X'. In this case, both X' and C are proxies for the same underlying variable, and the true effect of X on Y is distributed across the coefficients of X' and C. In this case, some of the effect of X will be erroneously attributed to C.

Imagine, for instance, that we want to know the impact of earning a college degree on wages, and we control for the number of college t-shirts a person owns. The t-shirts themselves have no effect on wages, but people with college degrees tend to have more college t-shirts. If college graduation is measured perfectly, then controlling for t-shirt ownership will not have much impact on the causal estimate. But suppose we don't have a perfect measure of college graduation and that we must rely on a proxy. This would no doubt result in some people being misclassified, and we would then be predicting wages with two imperfect proxies for having a college degree. The real impact of the degree on wages will be split between the two proxies: The effect of t-shirts will appear larger than it really is, and the effect of a college degree will appear smaller. The greater the error in X' relative to X, the greater this proxy bias will be.

It is common in social research to have multiple measures of the same underlying concept, and there are a number of aspiring methods for

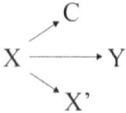

FIGURE 7.7 Causal diagram of a proxy variable (C)

dealing with them. One common situation is to have a variable that is measured at multiple points in time. For instance, in studies of intergenerational income mobility, researchers often have measures of parents' income in multiple years. They want to use all of the data available, since income measured in any particular year is only a messy proxy for more stable, lifetime income. But if all of the income variables are included in the same model, the true effect of parent income will be distributed across multiple income coefficients. They will all be smaller and less significant than would be a true single measure of lifetime income (Lubotsky and Wittenberg 2006). Typically in this situation, the researcher simply takes an average of multiple years of income (Solon 1992; Zimmerman 1992; Mazumder 2001; Chetty et al. 2014).

Another common situation is to have multiple and different variables that are all intended to measure the same underlying concept. For instance, the Demographic and Health Survey is a large cross-national dataset often used to answer social scientific research questions, but it doesn't contain a direct measure of household wealth or income. Instead, it contains a list of twenty-one variables indicating whether a household has different types of assets, such as a television, a refrigerator, and electric lighting. All of the twenty-one variables are imperfect proxies for household financial wellbeing. If they are all put into the same model, the true impact of household wealth will be distributed across the many variables and diluted in magnitude and significance. Better practice would be to use a principal components analysis to create an index of household assets, but that assumes awareness and transparency about the multiple proxies problem (Filmer and Pritchett 2001).

When the researcher is aware of the presence of multiple proxies, there are well-established methods for dealing with them, and they can even reduce bias by allowing better measurement of the underlying concept. The problem arises when researchers add proxies to a model without realizing that they have done so. When controls are carelessly added to a model, it can be easy to inadvertently include a control that is a proxy for the treatment variable of interest. When this happens, the presence of the proxy will bias the estimate of the causal effect.

EVEN GOOD CONTROLS CAN BE BAD

Adding controls to a still-incomplete model is not necessarily helpful. Leaving a confounder out of a model can substantially bias an estimate of a causal effect, and this concern drives the impulse to pad regression models with an abundance of controls. The problem is that the classic case of the confounder applies only under particular conditions: There is only one omitted variable, which is then added to complete the model, so that the final regression is the true model of how the data were generated. In practice, the true model is almost never known. Social phenomena are messy and complex, and analysts are nearly always constrained to choose a subset of control variables from the full array of true confounders. The intuition might be that including ten controls out of twenty is better than including five out of twenty, but this intuition is not grounded in the mathematics of regression analysis. Controlling for some but not all variables can increase bias just as well as reduce it (Clarke 2005, 2009).

This point has been demonstrated by the political scientist Kevin Clarke (2005), who conducted a simulation to show what happens when *some but not all necessary controls* are added to a model. He considered a situation where the true model is the following:

$$y_i = \beta_0 + \beta_1 x_{i1} + \beta_2 x_{i2} + \beta_3 x_{i3} + \varepsilon_i \qquad (7.2)$$

where y is the outcome variable and x_1 is the treatment variable of interest. We want to know if x_1 causes y, so our goal is to obtain an unbiased estimate of the regression coefficient β_1. The variables x_2 and x_3 are confounders; it is necessary to include them in the model to obtain an unbiased estimate of β_1.

Clarke considered two misspecified models:

$$y_i = \beta_0 + \beta_{11} x_{i1} + \varepsilon_{i1} \qquad (7.3)$$
$$y_i = \beta_0 + \beta_{12} x_{i1} + \beta_2 x_{i2} + \varepsilon_{i2} \qquad (7.4)$$

The difference between the two is that Model 7.3 omits both x_2 and x_3, while Model 7.4 omits only x_3. Clarke poses the question: Is Model 7.4 better than Model 7.3, in the sense that it gives a less biased estimate of β_1? Does adding x_2 to the model improve the estimate of β_1 even if there is still another remaining omitted variable? Put more precisely, he wanted to know the conditions under which the error on β_{12} is less than the error on β_{11} (which one might presume it would be).

Clarke ran a mathematical simulation to find the answer. He identified two values of particular importance in calculating the amount of bias on β_{11} and β_{12}: the correlation between x_2 and the omitted variable x_3 (r_{23}) and the coefficient of the omitted variable (β_3). He allowed both of these values to vary, setting r_{23} to vary over its full range (−1 to 1) and β_3 to vary from −5 to 5. To make computation tractable, he then set β_1 and β_2 to 4, all variances to 1, and the correlation of x_1 with each of x_2 and x_3 to 0.5.

With these assumptions, he was able to calculate, for each combination of r_{23} and β_3, the amount of bias on the main coefficient of interest β_1.

The result? "Including [x_2] in the regression is just as likely to increase the bias on [β_1] as it is to decrease it" (Clarke 2005: 345). In half of the models in his simulation, adding x_2 to the model without also adding x_3 decreased the bias on β_1, but in the other half of the models it actually increased the bias. Clarke (2005: 346) concluded: "Unless a researcher knows the remaining omitted variable, and furthermore knows the relationship of that variable with the newly included variable, she cannot know the effect that the newly included variable will have on the bias of a coefficient of interest. The newly included variable may decrease the bias, but it is just as likely to increase the bias."

This is a sharp warning against kitchen sink models that control for "everything in sight." First, controls need to be justified theoretically, explaining why the variable is believed to be a confounder (Clarke 2005; Cinelli et al. 2022; Wysocki et al. 2022). Second, the impact of a control variable on the results and conclusions should be transparently revealed to readers – to show that the influence of a control is consistent with the theory that justified the use of the control.

FREEDMAN'S SCREENING REGRESSION AND THE DANGERS OF ITERATIVE MODEL REFINEMENT

It is common practice for data analysts to consider many different control variables before selecting a final model. These are "screening regressions" in which the coefficients are used to choose the model. This practice creates new potential for harm through the selection of control variables, even when the variables being decided upon are not, in and of themselves, "bad controls." We consider how combinations of controls can be bad because noise in a particular dataset creates the desired correlations between those sets and the causal effect of interest. Iteratively refining a model allows researchers to "fish" for a combination that looks good to them.

A further risk of looking at many combinations of controls before selecting a preferred combination is the natural "significance inflation" that happens when the least-significant variables are dropped from a model. In inferential statistics, false positives are inevitable but assumed to be rare. When we choose a 5 percent level of significance for our tests, we accept that 5 percent of the time our analyses will be wrong. However, this expectation holds true only under very particular circumstances: when a scholar conducts a "classical" statistical test, formulating their hypothesis prior to seeing the data, and then only running a single regression model that they believed before seeing any results. If the researcher formulates a new model after seeing preliminary results, that second test will not be expected to have a 5 percent error rate – it will be higher, and possibly much higher.

Berkeley statistician David Freedman (1983) demonstrated this phenomenon in a classic simulation. Freedman constructed a dataset of "pure noise" (153): He generated a matrix with 100 rows (cases) and 51 columns (variables), and every value in the matrix was randomly selected from a standard normal distribution. He designated the last column the dependent variable, and then he estimated a regression model predicting that variable using the other fifty variables. The noise-on-noise model he estimated had one variable that was, purely by chance, significant at the 5 percent level. Freedman then estimated a second regression model, but this time he included only the fifteen variables that were significant at the 25 percent level in the first round. The result? In the second-round model, five more variables became significant at the 5 percent level, bringing the total to six. In repeated simulation, the second run always produced many more significant effects than the first run.

Freedman's screening regression simulates the process of researchers choosing controls in the absence of clear guidance from prior theory, using a simple heuristic of dropping the least-significant controls. The result is excess false positives – wrong results. Yet this type of model pruning reflects common practices in applied analysis. Researchers often start by casting a wide net of potential variables and then screen out those that appear unimportant. Indeed, we suspect that nearly every applied researcher in American social science today has dropped variables for a lack of statistical significance. On the surface, it seems a benign practice, a straightforward way to present a more parsimonious model. In reality, it is another way that selecting controls without clear theoretical guidance can lead to a "bad" combination of controls.

CONCLUSION

Control variables are a core element of nearly all inferential models using observational data. Even when other identification strategies like panel data, instrumental variables, or regression discontinuity are invoked, these strategies themselves also rely on control variables to improve inference. In any case, control variables require theory to explain the role they are expected to play in a regression model.

How do we know that a control variable is a textbook-style common cause confounder? How do we know it is not, instead, a mediator, or a collider variable, or another proxy for the treatment/focal variable? A confounder, a mediator, and a collider can all have very similar statistical relationships in the data; distinctions between these kinds of variables is generally made on theoretical grounds (Urminsky, Hansen, and Chernozhukov 2016).

These are modeling assumptions that are rarely empirically tested when a control variable is invoked. Justifying a control variable requires assumptions about cause and effect between the controls, the treatment variable, and the outcome variable. Causal claims involving controls are no easier to justify than the causality of the x–y relationship itself. This means that when a regression result depends on a certain control variable, the validity of that result in turn depends on the causal assumptions that invoked the use of the control variable. And for each control variable that a result depends on, there is an additional set of causal assumptions that need to be true in order to believe the result.

These points are not meant to be an existential critique of control variables in social science. There is no assumption-free way of conducting empirical analysis, and our goal is transparency in the assumptions. This chapter walks through the complex criteria needed to demonstrate the validity of a researcher's claim that a control variable is strictly necessary to their analysis.

In our view, three basic principles come out of this chapter. First, readers should always know what control variables, if any, are central to sustaining an empirical conclusion. Studies that do not report, at least in an appendix, model influence statistics for their controls are not being transparent with readers about what assumptions are driving their results. Second, any control variable that is necessary for a conclusion requires clear theoretical justification: a causal diagram showing the assumed relationships between the control, the treatment, and the outcome. Without this explicit justification, all controls should be by default treated as uncertain and subject to multiverse testing. Third, the influence results of a control variable should be consistent with its assumed role in the model. For example, control variables are often invoked as a way to rule out alternative explanations of an x–y association, meaning that the control is expected to *reduce* the magnitude of that association. When a control variable, in contrast, serves to *increase* the magnitude of x–y treatment effect, as in the case of gender and mortgage lending, authors need to be especially careful in explaining why that would occur.

Researchers often invoke long lists of controls with little or no justification of the causal assumptions they are making about those controls. This practice has proliferated under an outdated view that control variables "do no harm." We now know there are many ways in which adding a control variable to a model can increase bias and degrade inference. This means that studies need to be much more clear about the exact role that control variables are playing in their results.

The multiverse allows readers to see for themselves what kind of decisions and assumptions the author has made about the controls and to understand how the results would change if different controls had been used instead. Sometimes, multiverse analysis will reveal that a control doesn't have much impact on the results one way or the other and neither analyst nor reader need waste much time deliberating over it. Other times, a result is highly sensitive to the inclusion of a particular control, and the control variable multiverse will draw attention to those cases. It then becomes incumbent on the author to justify its inclusion (or exclusion) from the model.

In the next chapters, our discussion of robustness and influence will be extended to other aspects of model specification: functional form assumptions and data processing decisions. A full-developed multiverse, in our view, documents and explains what every aspect of a specification is doing in the analysis. Up to this point, we treated the choice of controls as the only modeling decision to be made. Having addressed control variables in depth, we are now ready to tackle modeling aspects that are harder to computationally multiverse but potentially as important as, if not more important than, the choice of controls.

8

Some Alternative Approaches

The previous chapters laid out a vision of multiverse analysis that is, in our view, compelling and comprehensive. Nevertheless, multiverse analysis can be done in different ways. In this chapter, we consider several elements of the multiverse that could be conducted differently. We cover them here to recognize interesting leads and promising approaches that go beyond the main multiverse analysis. We also emphasize the boundaries of the multiverse, showing where multi-model approaches start to serve different purposes – especially model robustness versus model selection.

MODELING DISTRIBUTION VERSUS SPECIFICATION CURVE

In the current literature on model robustness, there is a divergence of sorts in multiverse methods, between thinking about a modeling distribution (Young 2009; Young and Holsteen 2017; Muñoz and Young 2018a) and a specification curve (Simonsohn et al. 2020). This is mostly a difference in language and presentation rather than substance: Both methods seek the same goal of understanding how different models can generate different results using the same basic all-combinations algorithm. Yet there are also differences in presentation that make the output of these two methods look and feel different.

We emphasize the conceptual unity between the classical sampling distribution of estimates and the modeling distribution that comes from bootstrapping the model. For this reason, we use the probability density graphs that are common in statistics to show the properties of a sampling distribution. Density graphs visually convey the distribution of different possible estimates, showing the mean, median, and mode(s) of the results. In contrast, Simonsohn et al. (2020) emphasize the idea of a specification curve and present their distribution of estimates as a *cumulative* graph. Both kinds of graphs (probability density and cumulative) contain the same information, but they are different to read and interpret.

In Figure 8.1, we compare the density and cumulative graphs for modeling distributions we analyzed in earlier chapters. The first step

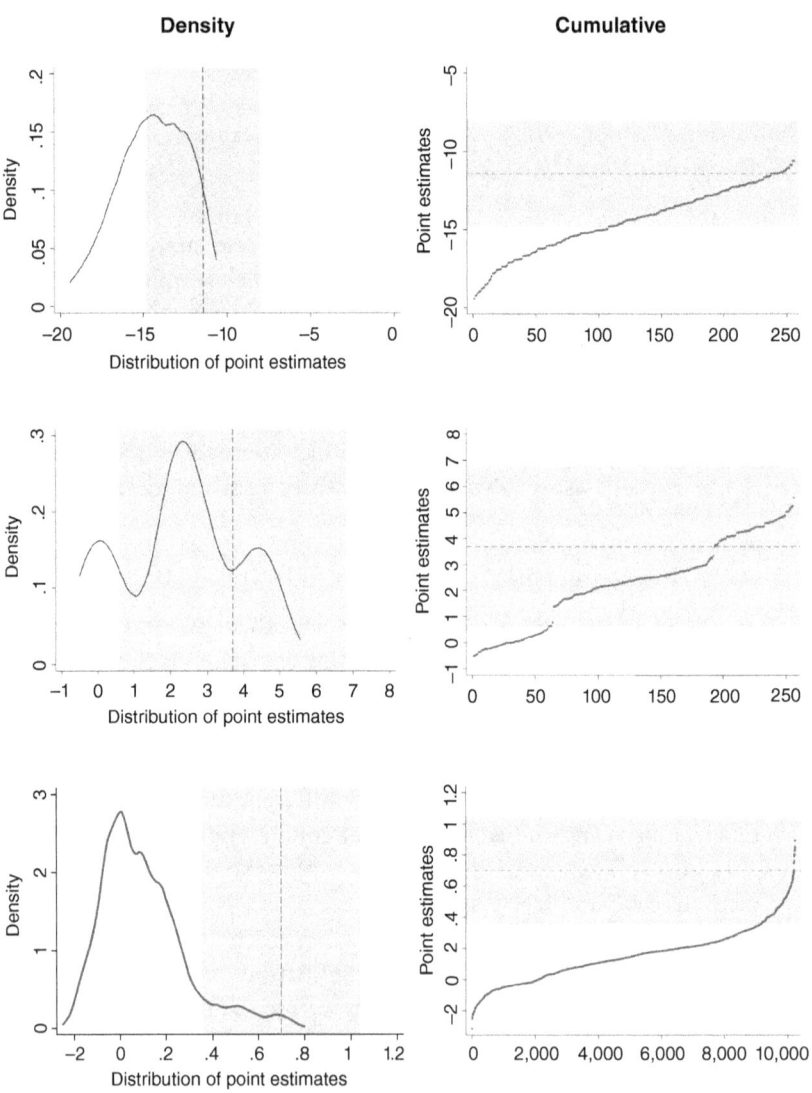

FIGURE 8.1 Density graphs of modeling distributions versus specification curve graphs. (A) Race effect in mortgage lending, (B) gender effect in mortgage lending, and (C) hurricane name effects.

is that compared to a typical sampling distribution graph, the cumulative flips the *x* and *y* axes. This immediately makes distributions hard to compare with commonly known sampling distributions. Moreover, in every case, the cumulative graph flattens the visual distribution, making it harder to see key features of the distribution such as the mean, median, or mode. Finally, in example C, both graphs report that the preferred estimate (dashed line) is an extreme outlier. While both graphs technically say the same thing, the density graph conveys this evidence much more intuitively in our view.

The language of a "specification curve" has been catchy, and we welcome anything that draws attention to robustness analysis. But in our assessment the cumulative graph is relatively uninformative about modeling distributions and comes with a loss of intuition about what we are looking at (something comparable to a sampling distribution). Ultimately, however, the difference is more stylistic than methodological.

ATHEY AND IMBENS: "A MEASURE OF ROBUSTNESS TO SPECIFICATION"

Some researchers may take a dogmatic view and insist that all of their control variables are necessary to the analysis: No controls can be dropped without sharply biasing the results, and thus, there is no control variable multiverse at all – there is only one single permissible specification.

Athey and Imbens (2015) offer a fresh source of modeling variation to gauge robustness without excluding any controls. They propose using the one fixed set of controls but splitting the sample in many different ways based on covariate values. Here is how their approach works. Begin with an outcome variable (y), an explanatory variable of interest (x), and a set of Z_k control variables. The baseline model for k controls is

$$y_i = \beta_0 + \beta_1 x_{i_1} + \sum_{k=1}^{K} \beta_k Z_{i,k} + \epsilon_i \tag{8.1}$$

Suppose a regression model is first applied to a whole sample (yielding an estimate $\widehat{\beta_{1,\,\text{full}}}$), and age is one of the Z_k controls. Next, the dataset is partitioned at the mean of age, and the same regression model is run on each sample separately (yielding two new estimates $\widehat{\beta_{1,\,\text{young}}}$ and $\widehat{\beta_{1,\,\text{old}}}$). A simple test of estimate stability is whether the weighted average of ($\widehat{\beta_{1,\,\text{young}}}$ and $\widehat{\beta_{1,\,\text{old}}}$) is equal to $\widehat{\beta_{1,\,\text{full}}}$. If a model is correctly specified, the estimates should be similar across sample splits. If the baseline model gives a different estimate than the split-sample-recombined estimate, asymptotically it indicates the presence of a specification error.

This sample splitting is conducted for all Z_k controls, and in larger samples there could be multiple splits for each control – rather than at the mean, splitting could be at each quartile or even decile of Z_k (the authors propose a machine learning method to optimize the number of sample splits for each control). This process generates many sample partitions yielding many unique estimates of $\widehat{\beta_1}$. As in multiverse analysis, they use the variance of estimates across sample splits to construct a modeling standard deviation (i.e., an estimated standard error). The mean estimate across sample splits divided by the standard deviation across sample splits gives a measure of model robustness. Their framework treats both the traditional sampling variance and the modeling variance as equally important in evaluating the credibility of the results.

This analysis is similar and complementary to our framework: Nonrobustness occurs when arbitrarily different models are leveraging idiosyncratic aspects of the data and giving different estimates. What is interesting is that the Athey and Imbens approach perturbates the model without changing the set of control variables. It sets aside the question of omitted variable bias: All models in this analysis use the same baseline specification with the full set of controls. It does not show the effect of including or excluding controls, but it explores many nonparametric effects of controls. If splitting the sample gives different estimates, that is the marker of estimate instability. They assert – as we do – that the data contain evidence about the robustness and reliability of a preferred estimate, which can be revealed through additional computation – through robustness analysis.

In their full implementation, Athey and Imbens use machine learning tools to develop many feasible sample splits depending on the sample size and variation in each variable. They never released their code for the analysis, and we have not taken the time to code it ourselves, but it remains a promising approach.

ROBUSTNESS VERSUS SELECTION

Readers of multiverse analysis have sometimes wanted a different product. Some researchers do not actually want to know about estimate instability or the influence of modeling choices on the results. Rather, they want a *model selection tool* that cuts through uncertainty and returns the single best model specification selected by machine learning. Rather than acknowledging and reporting uncertainty around the estimates, they want model uncertainty to be somehow resolved by an algorithm that chooses the single best specification. We sympathize with this desire. It would be a great leap forward if computational power could not only reveal the set of possible estimates but also tell us which estimate is the *true causal effect*.

Multiverse analysis, however, is about robustness rather than selection. Multiverse analysis shows the possible estimates, but it does not select which one is best. This is because there is nothing in the distribution of estimates per se that tells us which is the true effect of x. The criteria for including or excluding a control variable are very complex. The formula for omitted variable bias is correct only when the true model is known, and it is merely suggestive when there are other unmeasured variables – especially if there are "unknown unknowns": remaining omitted variables that no one has even thought of measuring. Endogenous controls are often recognized only in mature research areas with extensive accumulation of scholarship – and even there remain debated and poorly understood, as in the case of controlling for promotions in research on gender wage inequality. Collider variables are even harder to identify but are probably common in social science. If we want a model selection algorithm to tell us the best model for inference, it would have to process these questions at least as well as human experts can.

Model selection algorithms are widely used in data science today, but they are designed for predictive rather than inferential tasks. These algorithms aim to select a set of right-hand-side variables that minimize prediction error in y, with an ultimate goal of out-of-sample predictive accuracy. This is a very different task from inference. Let's consider again a regression model with many potential Z_k controls:

$$y_i = \beta_0 + \beta_1 x_{i1} + \sum_{k=1}^{K} \beta_k Z_{i,k} + \epsilon_i \tag{8.2}$$

Predictive modeling does not make a distinction between x and the Z_k variables – they are all predictors. The aim is to predict $\hat{y}$, not generate an unbiased estimate of a *specific $\hat{\beta}$*. Prediction is not trying to tease out any specific inference question and is happy to mix together any number of causal effects – or incidental correlations with causal effects – into a joint prediction function. How the predictions are actually made is generally a "black box." Even when the predictions are right, predictive models cannot be disaggregated to explain *why* an event happened (Pearl and Mackenzie 2018). The parameter estimates in a predictive model are not estimates of individual causal effects: The goal is that *all* the right-hand-side predictors *together* will be able to predict y.

Consider this difference between prediction and inference: Teachers can often correctly guess which of their students will perform best in the final exam (the y variable). But this does not mean they know the root causal forces that lead to student success (the true coefficients on x variables). What works well for one task – prediction of an outcome – does not work well for the other – disentangling specific causal effects. (We discuss this in greater depth in Chapter 13, "Weighting the Multiverse.")

For inference, what is missing from prediction is the omitted variable bias formula. Predictive models focus entirely on correlations between predictors and the outcome but do not care about correlations between the predictors themselves. Belloni, Chernozhukov, and Hansen (2014) have made first steps toward an algorithm for selecting inferential models, based on the omitted variable bias formula. They recommend its use, however, only for cases of high-dimensional data where there are more control variables than observations (i.e., $K > N$). The Belloni et al. selection algorithm is meant to aid in sifting through hundreds or thousands of potential controls that are too numerous to individually evaluate. It is meant to narrow down a set of controls that merit careful attention.

One day, we may well have a good artificial intelligence (AI) algorithm for inferential model selection, a kind of ChatGPT that tells us what is the best model for a given inference question. But this AI would work in a very unique way. It would not focus on running a lot of regressions. Rather, it would absorb existing scientific knowledge – both theoretical and empirical – about causal associations between all potentially relevant variables and distill that knowledge into a vast causal directed graph that best summarizes knowledge about a focal x–y hypothesis and everything correlated with it.[1] It would summarize both quantitative and qualitative understanding about the relationships between all relevant controls identified from all past scholarly literature. From this, the AI would identify which set of controls best approximates the true causal model, given what variables are unobserved or not measured. This would tell us (1) what would be the perfect model if all variables were observed; (2) which feasible model to use given what is observed and unobserved; and (3) how much bias from omitted variables remains in the best feasible model. This is the goal of cumulative science: understanding how all variables in a system are causally related. But to be clear, the AI in this vision is

---

[1] It would develop weights (probabilities) for the likelihood that each model ingredient belongs in the true model, but based on a summary of arguments and recorded evidence, rather than correlations in any particular dataset.

primarily summarizing existing theory and evidence, rather than conducting multi-model estimation.

It can be hard to accept, but "untestable assumptions are always required for the identification of causal effects" (Lechner 2008: 194). Model selection for inference requires choosing the best assumptions. The data in hand that are used for estimation never tell us which model assumptions are best. Science iteratively works toward better-informed assumptions but is never assumption-free. Model selection is always uncertain and always requires multiverse analysis to acknowledge that the assumptions could be wrong and different credible estimates are possible.

CONCLUSION

There is room for disagreement about the best way of doing a multiverse analysis and how exactly it should be implemented. However, the fundamental principle is greater transparency about how analytical choices affect the results.

Multiverse analysis is ultimately about reducing the asymmetry of information between author and reader. The goal is to relax assumptions about how the model "must" be exactly specified and relinquish some of the author's control over which estimates readers are allowed to see. If a result depends on a very specific constellation of controls or other modeling decisions, this should be made clear to the reader, and it is incumbent on the author to make the case that the specific model specification is the one that is the most theoretically sound – in full view of what other estimates are possible.

PART III

EXPANDING THE MULTIVERSE

9

Functional Form Robustness

Coauthored with Sheridan A. Stewart[*]

Social scientists face a dual problem of model uncertainty and methodological abundance. There are many ways to conduct an analysis. When the "true" model is unknown, authors have wide scope to cherry-pick or "p-hack" to find estimates that best support their prior views or publication goals. This leaves it unclear how much conclusions come from the data and how much they come from an author's modeling assumptions, which is a feature of the "crisis of credibility" in science. Multiverse analysis embraces this challenge by estimating and reporting results across hundreds or thousands of plausible model specifications. Existing multiverse work has often focused on the choice of control variables as model features most tractable for combinatoric methods, with scant attention to functional forms issues. We extend the multiverse approach to new dimensions, demonstrate its application, and test the ground truth validity of the approach.

Model specification involves at least two core elements: choosing which controls to include and choosing a functional form that relates the left- and right-hand sides of the equation. From this set, many different modeling combinations are plausible, creating a garden of forking paths that offers multiplying chances to find statistically significant results (Borges 1941; Gelman and Loken 2014). Choosing which model to report in a paper is "difficult, fraught with ethical and

---

[*] This chapter is based on a working paper previously circulated as "Functional Form Robustness: Advancements in Multiverse Analysis" (Young and Stewart 2021).

methodological dilemmas, and not covered in any serious way in classical statistical texts" (Ho et al. 2007: 232; Winship and Western 2016). There is wide concern today that many statistically significant results published in scientific literatures are not robust and fail to replicate (Camerer et al. 2018; Christensen, Freese, and Miguel 2019; Engzell, Mood, and Jonsson 2020). This is in part because of asymmetric information between authors and readers: Authors can run nearly endless alternative models to learn about possible results, but readers typically only see a handful of estimates curated for publication (Young 2009). In an age of vast and growing computational power, we need better ways of transparently revealing the range of estimates that the data can support.

This study is part of an agenda to build comprehensive multiverse analysis encompassing all the major analytical decisions that feed into an empirical estimate (Leamer 1983; Steegen et al. 2016; Young and Holsteen 2017; Muñoz and Young 2018a; Brodeur et al. 2020). The central goal is to improve the transparency of research. Multiverse analysis emphasizes that there are multiple universes of plausible, alternative modeling assumptions. One author may strongly defend the assumptions behind their estimates, but that same author might invoke different modeling assumptions under different circumstances – for example, if their role was to be a critic rather than the author. Multiverse analysis allows one to backtrack along the garden of forking paths, showing the sensitivity of each modeling assumption to reasonable alternative specifications. It uses computational power to estimate hundreds or thousands of theoretically reasonable models, estimating all unique combinations of plausible model ingredients. The result is a modeling distribution of estimates, similar to a bootstrap sampling distribution – a bootstrap of the model assumptions. This can show how each model ingredient affects the coefficient of interest.

We build on existing methods for the multiverse of control variables, expanding to include functional form decisions. Often, there is limited consensus on what functional form researchers should use: logit, probit, the linear model, or something else? In matching models, researchers face a choice among many approaches to matching, such as propensity score and coarsened exact matching (King and Nielsen 2019; Ripollone et al. 2020). All of these offer different ways of estimating an effect while conditioning on observables, each of which may leverage idiosyncratic aspects of the data in different ways. Given the data, how much do results differ across functional forms and possible estimation commands?

Empirically, we demonstrate the functional form multiverse in two sociological applications: the effect of job loss on subjective wellbeing and the role of education on voting in the 2016 presidential election. We show that different functional form assumptions can generate different and less stable modeling distributions than others. Some functional forms (such as matching and inverse probability weighting [IPW]) appear much more sensitive to modeling assumptions than others (the linear model and logit).

Next, we test the ground truth of computational multiverse analysis by reexamining data from a large many-analysts study (Silberzahn et al. 2018). We compare the computational multiverse to a pool of estimates generated by many analysts in a crowdsourcing study. Does the multiverse algorithm reproduce the work of many human analysts? How does the consistency and reliability of computational multiverse methods compare to the work of well-informed human researchers?

METHODOLOGICAL ABUNDANCE

The variety, novelty, and abundance of statistical techniques available in social science is remarkable. The *Handbook of Econometrics*, for example, runs across seventy-seven chapters and more than 5,000 pages (Heckman and Leamer 2007). New methods continually aim to improve estimation but also come with unknown sources of error and bias; they expand the garden of forking paths, render the literature harder to evaluate, and increase researcher degrees of freedom in the reporting of results (Glaeser 2008; Muñoz and Young 2018a).

Different analysts studying a topic scarcely ever use the same model specifications. The problem is not simply that some scholars are doing bad analysis: Divergent results are common even among equivalent levels of competence and methodological quality. The "many analysts, one dataset" project, for example, recruited twenty-nine teams of social scientists to probe discrimination by skin tone in professional soccer (Silberzahn et al. 2018; cf. Magnus and Morgan 1997). The result was wide-ranging empirical strategies, diverse results, and a roughly 70–30 split on the empirical conclusion across analysts. The range of findings was not readily explainable: Neither the researchers' level of experience and training nor their personal confidence in their own analysis nor peer ratings of methodological quality explained why some estimates were larger or smaller, significant or nonsignificant. Different researchers studying a dataset do not consistently produce the same result.

The problem of the multiverse is not that many methods exist but rather that the selection of their use is not transparent. Authors can selectively choose a preferred result from among many plausible estimates. Scientists are susceptible to biases and conflicts of interest in a world of "publish or perish." Researchers often test theories against a generic zero-effect null that they do not believe and are willing to change their modeling assumptions when the estimates seem "wrong." Scholars suffer from the problem of motivated reasoning and can convince themselves that favorable model assumptions are clearly superior. Objectively incorrect beliefs can be sincerely held; such views are wrong but "feel right" to the authors and were generated through a process of painstaking, though motivated, reasoning: The authors "convinced themselves."

Multiverse analysis is one way of addressing problems of transparency and asymmetric information in science and is especially well-suited to observational research. Next, we discuss the construction of a multiverse analysis, starting from control variables and advancing to functional form.

THE MULTIVERSE OF CONTROLS

Generating a model specification involves two central elements: choosing the controls to include and the functional form that relates the left- and right-hand sides of the equation. We assume there is a true model that generated the data: a correct set of controls and a correct functional form. Research is evaluated and debated based on how well applied work approximates these elements of the (unknown) true model. However, all models are approximations and should not be treated as definitively correct; there are always errors in modeling.

The set of possible control variables in an analysis can be represented as

$$y = f(x, Z, Q) \tag{9.1}$$

where y is the outcome, x is the variable of interest, Z is a vector of control variables deemed essential to the analysis, and Q is a vector of n plausible controls $[q_1, q_2, \ldots, q_n]$, each of which may or may not be included in the model. The goal is to estimate the effect of x on y (a parameter β). The vector Z allows authors to impose strict assumptions (as "known facts") about necessary controls to ensure the model space is credible. Z represents established beliefs about good control variables; in contrast, Q represents model uncertainty: For these variables, prior theory does not inform which elements belong in the model, leaving different analysts to make their own debatable judgments.

The purpose of multiverse analysis is to understand how much the results change when including any element of Q in the analysis. It is important to note that in Eq. (9.1), f is a fixed functional form assumed to be correct. As the number of Q model ingredients increases, the model space grows exponentially: With n plausible control variables, there are 2^n unique combinations of those variables. With two cases of uncertainty (regarding two plausible controls) in the aforementioned example, there are $2^2 = 4$ unique models. With ten possible controls, there are $2^{10} = 1{,}024$ unique models, and with twenty possible controls there are over one million.

THE MULTIVERSE OF FUNCTIONAL FORMS

The well-known omitted variable bias formula gives guidance to what is expected when a control variable is omitted from a regression. However, there is no analogous formula for "wrong functional form bias," though scholars are often just as concerned about functional form as about choice of controls and debates around functional form are common in the literature. What happens when using an incorrect functional form? Does that bias estimates in a similar way as a wrong (or omitted) control variable?

The existing literature has struggled with the tractability of functional form robustness because different functional forms often yield estimates on different and incompatible scales. Our contribution is to incorporate functional form into a multiverse algorithm while maintaining directly comparable coefficients.

To anchor thinking about many possible functional forms, consider the generalized linear model, which provides an umbrella concept that treats the link function as a variable (McCullagh and Nelder 1989). This specifies a family of models that can link the left- and right-hand sides of an equation. The link could be the linear probability model (LPM), logit, probit, ordered logit or probit, multinomial logit, Poisson, negative binomial, and more. This is an analogy, as we extend this to consider algorithmic "functional forms" such as matching, as well as hybrid approaches like IPW. From a statistical programming perspective, link functions can be thought of as estimation commands.

In more formal terms, the choice of functional form generalizes Eq. (9.1) as

$$Y = f_m(x, Z, Q) \qquad (9.2)$$

where the function f is now a variable with subscript m, indicating a vector of models $[f_1, f_2, \ldots, f_M]$. For example, the link function f is LPM if $m = 1$, logit if $m = 2$, propensity score matching (PSM) if $m = 3$, and so on. Our goal is to allow a range of possibilities – each paired to different assumptions about which functional form would provide the least-biased estimate of β. For any link function that changes the scale of the β coefficients, the resulting estimates are converted into comparable units – either transforming odds ratios into average marginal effects or transforming marginal effects into implied odds ratios. With n uncertain control variables and m plausible link functions and algorithms, there are $2^n \times m = J$ unique models.

Retrieving the estimated effect of x from each model provides a modeling distribution that is analogous to the sampling distribution. From a multiverse perspective, estimates of the modeling error are exactly analogous to those of the sampling error. Indeed, sampling and modeling are simply two sources of estimate instability. The mean of the modeling distribution is $\overline{\hat{\beta}_1} = \frac{1}{J}\sum_{j=1}^{J} \hat{\beta}_{1j}$, and the modeling variance is $V = \frac{1}{J}\sum_{j=1}^{J}\left(\hat{\beta}_{1j} - \overline{\hat{\beta}_1}\right)^2$. The square root of V is the modeling standard error.[1] This is computed the same way as sampling standard errors in a bootstrap process and can be thought of as a standard error that comes from bootstrapping the model, rather than the sample (Efron and Tibshirani 1993). As with sampling standard errors, large observed modeling standard errors cast doubt on the reliability of a point estimate. To the extent that the specified multiverse captures rival views of how best to conduct an analysis, the modeling distribution shows the range of estimates that would be found in a skeptical replication or an "adversarial collaboration" with other researchers (Bateman et al. 2005).

Alternative functional forms can affect the modeling distribution in two different ways, changing either the mean or the variance. Statisticians traditionally evaluate estimators by focusing on the mean and the variance of their *sampling* distributions – behavior in repeated sampling. We are interested in the mean and the variance of the *modeling* distributions – behavior in repeated modeling. Different functional forms could shift the mean of the distribution, analogous to omitted variable bias.[2]

---

[1] Recall that the term standard error simply means "estimated standard deviation" – in other words, the standard deviation of the sampling distribution.

[2] For this analogy, imagine that an incorrect functional form has an omitted feature that biases the effect estimate, and correcting the functional form removes that bias.

This systematic influence would call for greater deliberation about which is the best functional form assumption; even if that is hard to definitively resolve, more and better evidence can always be brought to bear (Battey, Cox, and Jackson 2019). Different functional forms could also change the *variance* of the modeling distribution – having wider or narrower modeling distributions. In this case, the influence of functional form is seen more in the tails of the distribution: One functional form gives more extreme estimates – both larger *and* smaller – than another form. The greater the variance of estimates generated by a functional form, the more the degrees of freedom it gives for researchers to select a preferred estimate. Other things being equal, variance is a negative property – meaning less reliability – and researchers should favor functional forms that produce the smallest variance in estimates (Coker, Rudin, and King 2020).

Next, we briefly discuss the types of functional forms empirically tested in this study.

MATCHING VERSUS REGRESSION

Matching is a common method for effect estimation when the treatment variable is binary. Matching aims for balance in covariates between "treatment" and "control" groups. The goal is to match each treatment case with at least one control case that has (very) similar observable characteristics. Early studies often viewed matching as a method that directly provides causal estimates (reviewed in Arceneaux, Gerber, and Green 2010). It is now recognized that matching relies on the same unconfoundedness assumption as ordinary least squares (OLS): It offers no solution to problems of endogeneity or omitted variable bias (Morgan and Harding 2006; Imbens 2015; King and Nielsen 2019). Still, matching is often invoked for properties that may offer superior estimation over OLS. It is nonparametric, or at least semiparametric. It does not impose the strict linearity assumption of OLS, and it offers ways to restrict the analysis to the basis of common support and exclude or down-weight observations that are poorly matched – thus potentially improving the covariate balance between comparison groups. A downside of matching, however, is the abundance of proposals of how to implement it in practice. The *idea* of matching has been much more popular than any single approach of how to match (Morgan and Harding 2006; Stuart 2010). This leaves considerable discretion in choosing a preferred matching method.

Matching is a two-stage process. First, one estimates the probability that a unit is in the treatment group, based on the observed covariate z and selected elements of Q_n. In PSM, the propensity score is

$$\pi_i = \Pr(X_i = 1 \mid z, Q_n) \tag{9.3}$$

π_i is often estimated using predictions from a logit model. In the second stage, the estimated propensity score $\widehat{\pi}_i$ is used to analyze the outcome equation, which could be simply the mean difference

$$E[Y \mid x, z, Q_n] = E(Y \mid x = 1, \widehat{\pi}_i) - E(Y \mid x = 0, \widehat{\pi}_i) \tag{9.4}$$

In coarsened exact matching (CEM), rather than using the first-stage regression of Eq. (9.3), an algorithm temporarily coarsens the continuous z and Q_n variables into bins that allow treated cases to be matched to similar control cases (Iacus, King, and Porro 2012). Cases with the same values for all coarsened variables are grouped together into a stratum (e.g., high, medium, and low). The goal is to coarsen z and Q_n just enough to match treated ($x = 1$) and control ($x = 0$) observations into comparable strata. The CEM estimate comes from aggregating all comparisons of treated and control cases within each stratum. There is an active debate over the properties of these two matching approaches. Some argue that "propensity scores should not be used for matching" (King and Nielsen 2019: 435), while others report that CEM often leads to "high bias and low precision" relative to PSM (Ripollone et al. 2020: 613).

Matching methods illustrate the problem of novelty in statistical methods. While new techniques can improve estimation or causal inference, they also come with unique uncertainties and poorly understood biases. New techniques often generate considerable enthusiasm but merit large doses of skepticism because of the researcher degrees of freedom that novelty brings (Glaeser 2008).[3] Some scholars argue that matching reduces model dependence in empirical results – in other words, matching offers more reliable and robust effect estimates than regression (Ho et al. 2007; King and Nielsen 2019). Others caution that matching can produce biased or even nonsensical results in applied settings (Arceneaux et al. 2010). This well captures a wide

---

[3] In a review of 100 political science articles published since 2009 using the method, the most common articulated case for matching was to address endogeneity – something that methodologists agree matching does not accomplish any better than OLS regression (Miller 2020).

range of views about matching: The method might improve the quality and consistency of estimation over OLS, might worsen them, or might not make much difference at all.

INVERSE PROBABILITY WEIGHTING

The propensity score π_i (Eq. (9.3)) not only is used for matching but can also be used as a weight for a regression analysis when there is concern about missing data. When data are missing completely at random, listwise deletion is an unbiased solution (Allison 2002). If one deletes all cases that have any missing information, the subsample will still be representative of the full sample. When data are missing due to unobserved systematic factors, there is no obvious solution for potential bias. However, there are intermediate cases of systematic missingness that can be corrected. Imagine that respondents are more likely to be missing if they are in the treated group versus the control group (or when x is large rather than small). If that difference can be explained by observed variables (such as age, education, and home ownership), then IPW can correct for selection bias in the treatment effect (Wooldridge 2007). In the case of binary treatments, the weight for individuals in the treated group is $w_i = 1/\hat{\pi}_i$ and for those in the control group is $w_i = 1/1-\hat{\pi}_i$. Specifying a simple regression equation with inverse probability weights gives

$$\frac{y_i}{w_i} = \frac{\beta_1 x_i}{w_i} + \frac{2 z_i}{w_i} + \frac{\varepsilon_i}{w_i} \qquad (9.5)$$

Intuitively, IPW gives greater weight to control observations that are more similar in the probability of treatment as the treatment cases. This puts weight on ideal control cases – those most likely to receive the treatment but who were not treated.

LINEAR VERSUS NONLINEAR: LOGIT VERSUS LINEAR PROBABILITY MODEL

Modeling choices are often interconnected with the structure of the data. When an outcome variable is binary, sociologists commonly adopt a logit model. Economists traditionally favored probit in such cases (Angrist and Pischke 2009: 102–107). Either way, research with binary outcomes often uses a nonlinear functional form for a variety of reasons (Long 1997). In contrast to the linear model, logit and probit are written as

$$\text{Logit}: \Pr(Y = 1 \mid x, z) = \left(1 + e^{-(\beta_1 x_i + \beta_2 z_i)}\right)^{-1} \quad (9.6)$$

$$\text{Probit}: \Pr(Y = 1 \mid x, z) = \Phi\left(\beta_1 x_i + \beta_2 z_i\right) \quad (9.7)$$

where Φ is the cumulative standard normal distribution function. These models are similar. Both restrict the predicted probabilities to between 0 and 1 and feature nonlinear effects of x on y. However, there are also serious shortcomings of these nonlinear models, including problems that can prevent convergence and challenges in interpreting results across nested models (King and Zeng 2001; Mood 2010).[4] In light of various problems with nonlinear models for binary outcomes, Breen, Karlson, and Holm (2018) recommend the LPM as the default.

In summary, there are many different functions or algorithms that relate the left- and right-hand sides of a model. This variety of functional forms may be desirable in many ways. A downside, however, is the expanding degrees of freedom it offers researchers, in which a multiplicity of plausible methods may provide many additional chances to find and selectively report a statistically significant result. Each functional form, potentially in combination with each control variable, offers a new opportunity to leverage idiosyncratic observations or give greater weight to chance associations in the data. A researcher might initially estimate a null result and then react to that disappointment by trying out alternative functional forms until a statistically significant result is found. In this way, the choice of functional form can serve as a backstop, rescuing a hypothesis from disconfirming evidence.

SCALE OF COEFFICIENTS

A challenge in functional form robustness is that different functional forms may report estimates on different scales (Williams 2011; Mize, Doan, and Long 2019). The linear model produces estimates on the probability scale as marginal effects. Logit models give estimates as log-odds (alternatively, odds ratios), while probit estimates are reported on the z-score scale. Because changing functional forms simultaneously changes the scale of the coefficients, it is not possible to directly compare logit or probit results to OLS estimates. However,

---

[4] Contributing factors in convergence failure include small sample sizes, "wide" datasets (i.e., a high explanatory variable to observation ratio), flat gradients, multiple local maxima, and collinear explanatory variables (Long 1997).

in postestimation, odds ratios can be converted into average marginal effects, and alternatively marginal effects can be converted into implied odds ratios (Greene 2012: 689–690). The conversion is possible since the odds of an outcome ($Y = 1$) is the probability the outcome occurs divided by the probability that it does not occur. If we think of the probability (P) of an outcome in treated (t) and control (c) groups, then the marginal effect is ME $= P_t - P_c$, while the odds ratio is $OR = \dfrac{P_t / 1 - P_t}{P_c / 1 - P_c}$. The necessary probabilities for either metric can always be calculated regardless of the preferred functional form. Ensuring comparability of estimates is critical to a functional form multiverse analysis. Another possibility for putting coefficients on a common scale is to convert t-statistics into partial correlations, using the formula: $r = t / \sqrt{t^2 + df}$ (Stanley and Doucouliagos 2012). We do not pursue this method here, but note its potential value in comparing across many possible types of models.

Table 9.1 illustrates the problem of different scales across different functional forms. Consider an analysis of voting for Donald Trump in the 2016 presidential election as a function of voters' race (coded as white or nonwhite). The logit coefficient for white is 3.3, meaning that whites have more than triple the odds of voting for Trump compared to nonwhites. The probit coefficient is 0.64, which is hard to interpret but looks very different from 3.3. The next row shows the estimate from the linear model, 0.10, meaning that whites are 10 percentage points more likely to vote for Trump than nonwhites (from an overall sample mean of 46 percent). These are all very different numbers, because they are on different scales. Do these estimates all mean the same thing, or are they giving substantively different results?

In the final rows of Table 9.1, we convert the logit odds ratios and probit coefficients onto the probability scale as average marginal effects.[5] Once these estimates are on the same scale as LPM, we see that

---

[5] The average marginal effect is a postestimation procedure that computes the expected difference in outcome probability due to a unit change in the treatment variable. In this case, the AME is calculated from the logit/probit regression results by predicting the outcome probability for each observation ($\widehat{\text{Vote\_Trump}_i}$), treating all cases as if they were white respondents. Next, the outcome probabilities are predicted as if each respondent were nonwhite. The difference between these two probabilities is the marginal effect *for each case*. Averaging the difference across all cases gives the average marginal effect, which can then be directly compared to the OLS coefficient (Williams 2011, see also Bartus 2005). Note that this procedure linearizes the effect of x on y (Mood 2010).

TABLE 9.1 *Comparison of coefficient magnitudes*

	White (vs. nonwhite)	Democrat
Logit (odds ratio)	3.30	0.01
Probit	0.64	−2.66
LPM	0.10	−0.77
Logit (AME)	0.11	−0.76
Probit (AME)	0.11	−0.76
		−0.76

Notes: Models control for income, gender, age, age squared, and marital status. AME = average marginal effect. Data: American National Election Survey 2016 Time Series. $N = 1{,}701$.

the logit and probit results are much the same as the estimates from the linear model (both 0.11, meaning whites are 11 percentage points more likely to vote for Trump, compared to 10 percentage points in the linear model). When coefficients are placed on the same scale, it can easily turn out that different functional forms produce equivalent results – a fact that is not transparent before converting coefficients to marginal effects. If logit coefficients were routinely converted to marginal effects and compared to LPM (or vice versa), how often would the differences be large enough to matter?

THREE EMPIRICAL APPLICATIONS

We now apply the functional form multiverse analysis in a series of cases. First, we analyze data from the Panel Study of Income Dynamics (PSID) on unemployment and wellbeing. This features a binary treatment (job loss) allowing comparison between matching and regression. Next, we examine American National Election Study data on the effect of a college degree in voting for Donald Trump in 2016; as both the outcome and explanatory variables are binary, we can compare linear regression, logit, and matching. Our third application considers the effect of skin tone on receiving red cards in professional soccer. These data are drawn from a crowdsourcing study in which many analysts considered logit, linear regression, and Poisson as possible functional forms (as well as choosing among a set of possible controls). This invites a correspondence test for the range of results in a computational multiverse analysis, compared to the estimates of many different scholars each contributing one preferred estimate.

Application I: Unemployment and Wellbeing

How does job loss affect an individual's subjective wellbeing? We draw on data from the PSID to address this question. With a binary treatment variable (job loss = 1, no job loss = 0), we compare OLS, IPW, PSM, and CEM estimates of the effect of losing a job in a two-wave panel. We use fixed-effects analysis for examining the transition from working to unemployed (Young 2012: 622, Table 3).[6] A set of ten plausible time-varying controls includes income, part-time work, children in the home, marital status, homeowner status, zero/negative wealth, not having one's desired food, not having enough food, being eligible for unemployment insurance, and receiving food stamps. While each of these controls is plausibly related to changes in wellbeing (and employment status), some of them could be posttreatment or endogenous controls that could potentially bias the results (Elwert and Winship 2014; Montgomery, Nyhan, and Torres 2018). It is properly cautious to allow dropping any one of these controls, as might occur in a skeptical replication. All combinations of these ten controls give a covariate multiverse of $2^{10} = 1,024$ unique specifications. Next, we extend the multiverse to incorporate four different functional forms: OLS, IPW, PSM, and CEM. This broader multiverse yields a modeling distribution of 4,090 point estimates. In our baseline linear regression model, including all ten controls, job loss leads to a 0.4 standard deviation drop in wellbeing (table not shown). As Young (2012) notes, job loss has a larger effect on wellbeing than any other variable.

Panel (a) of Figure 9.1 shows the modeling distributions from OLS, IPW, CEM, and PSM separately, illustrating how the multiverse of controls depends on functional form. The modeling distribution from OLS is highly concentrated – appearing largely as a spike in estimates near the baseline of –0.4: None of the controls meaningfully changes the results. IPW, CEM, and PSM all have similar means but show a much wider range of estimates. Table 9.2 provides more detail: The average estimate by functional form is –0.44 (OLS), –0.46 (IPW), –0.40 (CEM), and –0.39 (PSM), revealing little systematic difference. However, the ranges are far larger using non-OLS functional forms. The modeling standard errors are many times greater using IPW (0.07), CEM (0.08),

---

[6] Specifically, the data are first-differenced so that all functional forms are analyzing the change in wellbeing between waves 2003 and 2005 as a result of transitioning from employed in the 2003 wave to unemployed in the 2005 wave. See Young (2012) for a more complete discussion.

TABLE 9.2 *Functional form robustness of effect of job loss on wellbeing*

	Average estimate	Range	Average sample standard error	Modeling standard error	Significance rate ($p < 0.05$)
OLS	−0.44	[−0.45, −0.42]	0.08	0.01	100.0%
IPW	−0.46	[−0.64, −0.32]	0.12	0.07	100.0%
CEM	−0.40	[−0.52, −0.15]	0.09	0.08	98.5%
PSM	−0.39	[−0.90, −0.12]	0.13	0.09	86.9%
Pooled distribution	−0.42	[−0.90, −0.12]	0.11	0.07	96.4%

Note: Estimates from 4,090 model specifications. Data: PSID (2003–2005 waves). $N = 6,192$.

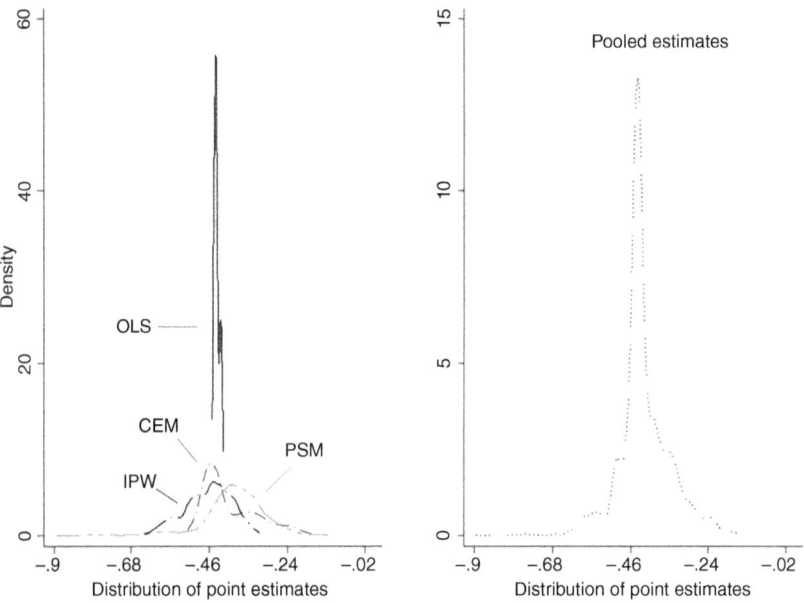

FIGURE 9.1 Modeling distributions: effect of job loss on subjective wellbeing
Note: Estimates from 4,090 model specifications. Data: PSID (2003 and 2005 waves). $N = 6,192$.

or PSM (0.09) than for OLS (0.01). This reflects idiosyncratic differences across functional forms. In particular, PSM permits point estimates that are more than twice as large in magnitude than any OLS estimate, as well as some small and nonsignificant estimates. These nonsystematic differences mean that the results are more open to debate among scholars on relatively loose methodological grounds. It also means that researchers have more (undisclosed) flexibility to choose a preferred estimate.

Nevertheless, as Figure 9.1, panel (b) shows, the core empirical finding of psychological harm from unemployment is not in serious question; rival functional forms produce debate about the magnitude, but not the existence, of painful psychological effects of job loss (Young 2012; Brand 2015). Pooling across all four functional forms, all of the estimates are negative, and 96 percent are statistically significant – strongly robust by the Raftery (1995) standard. In these 4,000+ models, fewer than 1 in 20 report a nonsignificant result. If an author preferred a null result, they could curate a table of models supporting a null conclusion. However, it is clear those null results are fragile specifications that would be very difficult to substantively justify. In contrast, if an author preferred one of the extremely large (long left tail) estimates reported in a few matching models, these would be equally difficult to justify once the multiverse of estimates is known.

More broadly, the findings of Application I show that even if the *average* estimate may be quite similar across functional forms – where there is little *systematic* difference – some functional forms may be much more sensitive to the choice of controls. Figure 9.2 offers one visualization of model influence: how the number of controls in a specification affects the coefficient of interest, by functional form type. OLS estimates are almost entirely insensitive to the number of controls included in a specification. For CEM, the estimates trend slightly closer

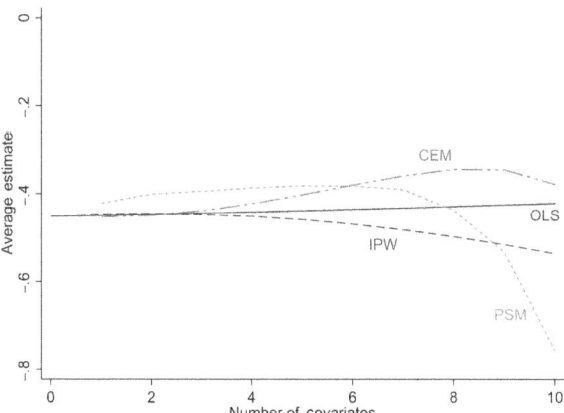

FIGURE 9.2 Effect size of job loss by number of control variables
Note: Based on results from 4,090 model specifications. Data: PSID (2003–2005 waves), $N = 6,192$.

to zero as the number of controls rises, while in IPW they trend slightly *away* from zero. For PSM, the estimated effect of job loss grows dramatically when more than eight controls are included. These three functional forms are adjusting for covariates in different ways, with some surprisingly different impacts.

Consider the effect of controlling for family income. In OLS, this control has no influence on the effect of job loss on wellbeing; in CEM, controlling for income makes the effect of job loss *smaller* (explaining away the effect of job loss); in PSM, controlling for income makes the effect much *larger* (see Appendix, Table A9.1, at the end of this chapter). These patterns seem difficult to explain as anything other than estimation noise. The intersection of functional form and control variables often leverages chance associations in the data in different and unintuitive ways.

Application II: Voting for Trump in the 2016 Election

Who voted for Donald Trump in the 2016 presidential election? Historically, college graduates have tended to vote republican while working-class voters leaned democrat (Pew 2018). Intuition tells us that 2016 did not follow that pattern, reflecting a realignment in party coalitions. We draw on the American National Election Study to analyze the effect of having a college degree on voting for Trump.

This application compares the linear model, logit, and the matching estimators. We consider seven plausible control variables: race, gender, age, square of age, marital status, party affiliation, and income. Taking all possible combinations of these controls gives a modeling space of $2^7 = 128$ unique specifications. This set is estimated with four different functional forms: the linear model, logit, PSM, and CEM.

Figure 9.3 shows the results. The modeling distributions from all four functional forms clearly overlap, but with noteworthy differences. Panel (a) reports the distribution of results from the linear model. Depending on the set of controls used, one can find estimates ranging from a 7 to 16 percentage point lower probability of voting for Trump among college graduates. The distribution is bimodal, indicating that one of the control variables has strong influence on the results. In the Appendix, influence analysis shows this variable is party affiliation (republican vs. democrat): Including this variable shrinks the estimate for education by about 50 percent (Table A9.2). Party affiliation may well be an endogenous control/collider variable, something more like an intermediate outcome than an exogenous factor to be controlled (Morgan 2018). Either way,

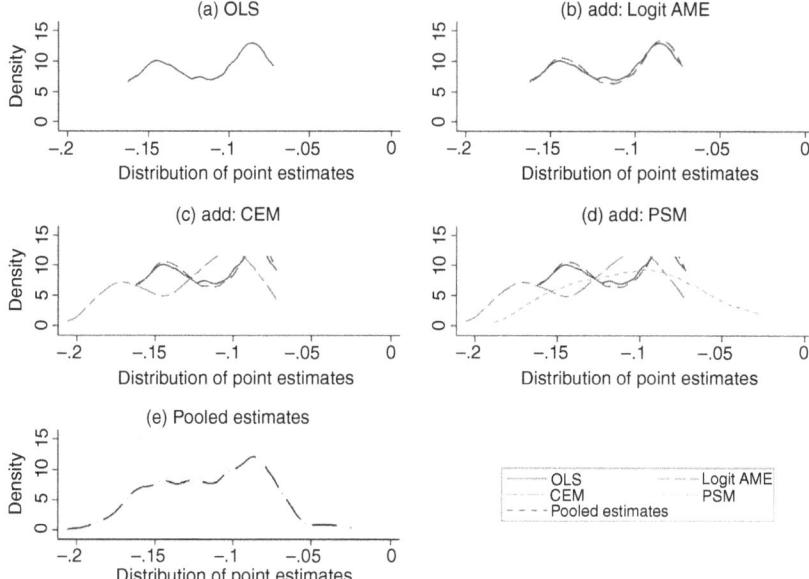

FIGURE 9.3 Modeling distributions: effect of college degree on voting for Donald Trump in 2016
Note: Estimates from 510 model specifications. Data: ANES 2016 Time Series. $N = 1,701$.

informed consumers of this research should be aware that the decision to control for party affiliation clearly influences the results.[7]

In panel (b), we add the modeling distribution from logit, reporting average marginal effects. These two functional forms offer identical modeling distributions: Nothing is at stake in the analytic choice between LPM and logit in this case. In panel (c), we add the distribution from CEM. While this distribution largely overlaps with those of LPM and logit, it is wider, with some estimates being larger in magnitude (longer left tail). In panel (d), we add the modeling distribution from PSM, which further expands the distribution, with some estimates being closer to zero (longer right tail). Finally, panel (e) shows the pooled distribution of the estimates: results from all possible combinations of the seven plausible control variables and the four different functional forms. Matching produces both larger and smaller estimates, depending on what set of

---

[7] Race and income also have some modest influence, while gender, age, and marital status are irrelevant to the results. While gender and age are often important factors in support for Trump, they do not matter as controls for the current analysis (the effect of education in voting for Trump).

TABLE 9.3 *Functional form robustness of effect of college degree on voting for Donald Trump in 2016*

	Average estimate	Range	Average sample standard error	Modeling standard error	Significance rate ($p < 0.05$)
OLS	−0.114	[−0.163, −0.072]	0.019	0.031	100.0%
Logit (AME)	−0.113	[−0.161, −0.073]	0.019	0.030	100.0%
PSM	−0.104	[−0.189, −0.025]	0.024	0.037	91.3%
CEM	−0.126	[−0.206, −0.072]	0.021	0.034	100.0%
Pooled distribution	−0.114	[−0.206, −0.025]	0.021	0.034	97.8%

Note: Estimates from 510 model specifications. Data: ANES 2016 Time Series. $N = 1,701$.

controls is included. This shows idiosyncratic influence of controls on the modeling distribution, regardless of the functional form.

Table 9.3 offers further detail. Logit and the linear model have nearly the same point estimates, sample standard errors, and modeling standard errors. Matching methods produce similar average estimates, but the differences are noticeable. PSM gives the smallest average estimate (−0.104), and for nearly 9 percent of the models the estimate is not statistically significant. CEM gives the largest average estimate (−0.126), and all its estimates are significant. CEM and especially PSM have larger ranges and modeling standard errors than the linear model or logit. These longer tail distributions are worrisome because researchers have greater flexibility in their conclusion. Some PSM models allow a null conclusion, but 98 percent of this multiverse finds that a college degree reduces the chance of voting for Trump, by about 11 percentage points on average. The pooled distribution has twice the range of either the OLS or logit distributions.

Influence analysis continues to show that different functional forms control for covariates in somewhat different ways. For example, in both LPM and logit, controlling for income reduces the effect of education on voting for Trump by 8 percent. However, in PSM, controlling for income reduces the effect size by 25 percent, and in CEM controlling for income has no effect on the estimate of interest (Appendix, Table A9.2). This again illustrates how different functional forms can adjust for controls in different ways.

Figure 9.4 shows that the influence of adding additional controls depends on the functional form. PSM is most sensitive to the number

Functional Form Robustness

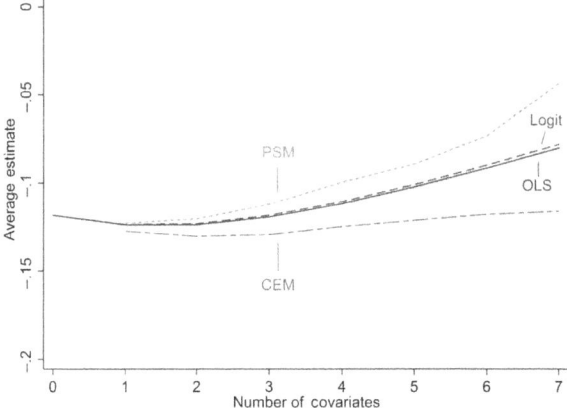

FIGURE 9.4 Effect size by number of control variables, voting data
Note: Based on results from 510 model specifications. Data: ANES 2016 ($N = 1,701$).

of controls (pushing the estimate toward zero), CEM is less sensitive (the number of controls is irrelevant), while the linear model and logit curves – which are virtually indistinguishable from one another – lie between these ranges.

Application III: Evaluating the Ground Truth of Computational Multiverse Analysis

Our final application aims to evaluate the "ground truth" validity of the functional form multiverse method. How accurate are the modeling standard errors that emerge from a computational multiverse analysis? How do we know if the range of estimates is realistic or rather too wide or too narrow? Some scholars voice concern that taking all combinations of plausible controls and functional forms yields a haystack of models that have never been specifically justified, many of which no one would ever estimate, and thus likely produce a lot of wild and unreliable estimates (Lundberg et al. 2021). From this perspective, the computational modeling distribution is too large, gives an artificial view into what models different researchers would actually choose, and sets an unrealistic bar for robustness. On the other hand, an algorithm has no preference or desire for a specific result, does not engage in motivated reasoning, conducts no further data processing, and will not do any "extra work" after seeing the results.

To address these crucial questions of ground truth validity, we reanalyze the work of a many-analysts crowdsourcing project (Silberzahn et al. 2018). The many-analysts study is a kind of multiverse analysis in which each specification was carefully selected by a skilled and knowledgeable research team using their best independent judgment. Drawing on one original dataset, twenty-nine teams of researchers conducted their own analysis and each submitted their preferred estimate. We reanalyze the data using the same core modeling inputs described in the original study and estimate over 3,000 unique specifications. How similar are these two modeling distributions: the set of 29 estimates carefully selected by human researchers and our set of 3,000+ estimates generated computationally from the same dataset?

The empirical case focuses on discrimination in professional soccer: whether players with darker skin tone receive more red card penalties from referees. Red cards are penalties for player misconduct or violence on the field, and referees have wide discretion in assigning them. Are referees more likely to give red cards to dark-skinned players than to light-skinned players? To address this question, Silberzahn et al. (2018) collected data on European leagues. Skin tone is measured on a five-point scale ranging from very light to very dark, coded from player photographs. The outcome variable is at the player–referee dyad level, recording the number of red cards each player received from each referee they played with in their career. There are 146,028 dyads of players and referees in the data. The number of red cards in each dyad ranges from 0 to 2, with a mean of 0.004 – red cards are very rare events at the dyad level. In other words, the outcome is nearly binary but is technically a count variable.

The original research teams nearly all used one of three general functional forms: logistic (52 percent), Poisson (21 percent), and the linear model (21 percent). Following Silberzahn et al. (2018), in all specifications the main effect of skin tone is calculated as an odds ratio – the odds of a very dark skin player receiving a red card over that of a very light skin player.[8] The original authors had chosen from a set of ten possible right-hand-side variables, with teams using between one and eight of those – reflecting a range of preferences for parsimonious versus richly

---

[8] Poisson models report the incident rate ratio (IRR). When the outcome is a rare event (e.g., less than 10 percent) as in this case, the odds ratio and the IRR are on the same scale. For nonrare events, the odds ratio is always larger than the IRR and direct comparisons require a conversion formula. For the linear model, we convert marginal effects to odds ratios using the margins command.

specified models. The controls include player height, weight, and age; the number of goals, ties, victories, and defeats; the number of yellow cards they received from the referee; their position on the team; and their national league (France, Germany, England, or Spain). The number of games played with each referee is treated as a necessary control – serving as an exposure variable. With ten plausible controls there are 1,024 possible specifications for each functional form.

Figure 9.5 presents the functional form plus controls multiverse, compared to the full set of results from the original study. Both distributions are strongly centered around an odds ratio of 1.3 – dark-skinned players have 30 percent higher odds of receiving a red card than light-skinned players. Functional form assumptions have little influence on the average estimate. However, results from many-analysts show a considerably wider range and variance than the multiverse analysis. In particular, the many-analysts study shows a much longer left tail, including opposite-signed effects (odds ratios less than 1).[9] The computational multiverse effects range from 1.23 to 1.64 (i.e., from 23 percent to 64 percent higher odds), and all estimates are statistically significant (Table 9.4). The many-analysts results range from 0.88 to 1.71, and only 69 percent are statistically significant. The modeling standard error in many-analysts (0.170) is more than three times greater than in the computational multiverse analysis (0.048). In other words, human analysts produce a much wider range of results than does the multiverse algorithm.

In discussing their results, Silberzahn et al. (2018) focused on the choice of controls and functional form as representing the modeling differences across analysts and results. However, these core elements do not fully explain the diversity of their results. By comparison, the functional form multiverse is missing the left tail of the many-analysts

---

[9] The original study included two outlier (far right tail) nonsignificant estimates which turned out to have errors in scaling. These two estimates (2.93, 2.88) were more than twice the magnitude of all other estimates, despite being non- or barely significant. On close inspection rerunning the original authors' code, we identified and corrected the scaling errors. Team 21 used tobit, with the outcome as red cards/games played, setting tobit limits to censor the outcome at 0 and 1. This led to a large rescaling of the estimate and its standard error; we corrected this using fractional regression and replicated the same result using OLS (an odds ratio of 1.31). Team 27 interacted skin tone with all other controls but still reported the coefficient on skin tone as a main effect. Since none of the interactions were significant, we simply reran their R code without the interaction terms – which rescaled both the coefficient and its standard error, without affecting the significance level (odds ratio of 1.29). Silberzahn et al. issued an update agreeing with these corrections.

TABLE 9.4 *Functional form robustness of effect of skin tone on receiving red cards*

	Average estimate	Range	Average sample standard error	Modeling standard error	Significance rate ($p < 0.05$)
Logit (odds ratio)	1.30	[1.23,1.38]	0.110	0.035	100.0%
OLS (odds ratio)	1.30	[1.23,1.36]	NA	0.034	100.0%
Poisson (IRR)	1.34	[1.23, 1.64]	0.119	0.059	100.0%
Pooled distribution	1.31	[1.23, 1.64]	NA	0.048	100.0%
"Many analysts"	1.27	[0.88, 1.71]	NA	0.170	69.0%

Note: Estimates from 3,072 model specifications: Three functional forms each with ten possible controls. Data: Silberzahn et al. (2018). N ranges from 350,448 to 373,067, depending on the selection of controls. Sampling standard errors were not computed for OLS odd ratio results and were not directly reported in the "many analysts" study.

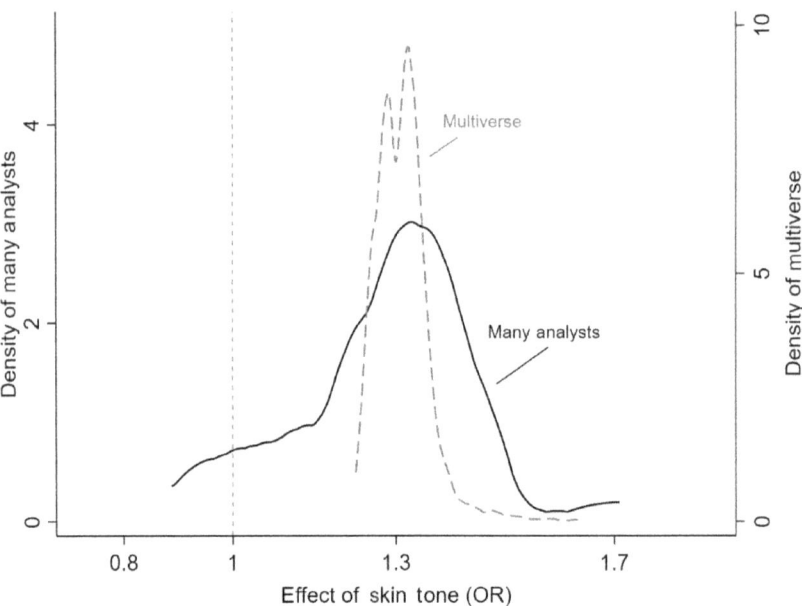

FIGURE 9.5 Multiverse results: effect of skin tone on red cards
Note: Multiverse – odds ratio estimates from 3,072 model specifications. Many analysts – 29 estimates reported in Silberzahn et al. (2018). Two corrections noted in footnote 10. Data: Silberzahn et al. (2018). N ranges from 350,448 to 373,067, depending on the selection of controls.

results – and ultimately appears as a conservative estimator of what results can be found in repeated modeling. This is reassuring for baseline validity of the computational multiverse: No empirical result emerged from the multiverse that was not previously reported by the many-analysts group. At the same time, this suggests that a truly rigorous multiverse needs to go further still and incorporate more inputs into the modeling process – especially data processing decisions like variable coding, treatment of outliers, and the handling of missing data (Steegen et al. 2016).

DISCUSSION

In this chapter we developed a multiverse estimator that models all plausible combinations of specified functional forms and control variables. We then apply this method to a series of empirical cases: the effect of unemployment on subjective wellbeing, the role of education in voting for Trump in 2016, and the effect of skin tone on assigning red cards in professional soccer. Across these cases, we compute over 7,500 unique model specifications. Our interest is not in any single estimate but rather in understanding how functional form uncertainty can change the apparent evidence and possible conclusions. Some functional forms – such as logit and probit – report coefficients on noncomparable scales. Reporting estimates on a common scale (converting either to marginal effects or odds ratios) greatly clarifies what difference there is between LPM, logit, probit, Poisson, and matching estimates. Once the estimates from different models are on comparable scales, we can evaluate the modeling distribution analogously to the sampling distribution. We arrive at two (local) empirical conclusions, one for the mean and one for the variance of the modeling distributions we observe.

To what extent can researchers obtain a new result by choosing a different functional form? First, different functional forms, in our results, have similar central tendencies. Estimating across all plausible combinations of controls, the average (or modal) estimate from functional forms – including linear regression, logit, probit, IPW, Poisson, PSM, and CEM – are very similar. Sometimes a functional form can shift the entire modeling distribution in one direction or another, but we find systematic shifting to be modest. On average, it may not matter much, for example, whether researchers use logit or the linear model as long as effect sizes are reported on a common scale (Breen et al. 2018).

Second, different functional forms can also affect the stability or *variance* of the modeling distribution, such as when an estimator is prone to more long-tailed estimates in repeated modeling. When functional forms have the same central tendency, scholars should favor those with the smallest modeling variance over those that give more dispersed and scattered estimates. This is analogous to the efficiency criteria in repeated sampling and minimizes researcher degrees of freedom in repeated modeling. None of the functional forms considered here improve on linear regression: Alternatives like logit, Poisson, IPW, and matching could at best match the stability of OLS, not improve it. In Application II, CEM had longer *left* tail estimates than LPM or logit, while PSM had longer *right* tail estimates than the others. In Application I using panel data, the long tails from matching models were even more dramatic: PSM, in particular, could yield estimates either twice as large or half as small, as any possible linear regression estimate. Moreover, different functional forms can sometimes adjust for controls in different ways, creating haphazard results for certain combinations of controls and functional forms. This is troubling, given that matching in the past has been advocated as a way to reduce model dependence and improve estimate stability.

Finally, we test the ground truth of computational multiverse analysis, comparing to a many-analysts crowdsourcing study that used the same set of possible controls and functional forms. While some may be skeptical of the all-combinations algorithm as a way to generate plausible models, human analysts in fact produced a wider range of estimates. While the many-analysts and multiverse approaches converged on the same average estimate, many-analysts found many more left tail and nonsignificant results than are available from all combinations of the basic modeling ingredients. If social scientists worry that the multiverse algorithm can produce idiosyncratic or hard-to-explain estimates, they should be even more worried about what their colleagues can do. This also calls for more, rather than less, multiverse expansion, especially into areas of data cleaning and processing.

CONCLUSION

Empirical research is often seen as "data analysis," implying that the data have priority in this process. In reality, authors' choices about how to do the analysis can be just as important as the data. All empirical results are a joint product of both the data and the analytical assumptions. We consistently find that modeling variance is greater than the sampling variance – more uncertainty stems from the choice of model than from random sampling of the data. Traditional uncertainty about the sample data – captured by *t*-statistics, confidence intervals, or sampling standard errors – seems less important than uncertainty due to the multiverse of plausible models.

In the "crisis of science" today, many recognize that current research practices fail to assure an impartial assessment of the evidence. Analysts are not blinded to how their methods support or disfavor a preferred conclusion, but for readers, the modeling process is opaque and difficult to evaluate. Social science needs better practices that reduce the asymmetry of information between analysts and readers and more transparently show what estimates are possible. Edward Leamer (1983: 31) once called this a matter of taking "the con out of econometrics."

Multiverse analysis is not the only pathway to improving transparency in science. In preregistration, all analytical decisions, including the exact statistical specification, are decided prior to collecting the data, with a detailed preanalysis plan placed in a time-stamped public archive (Miguel 2021). Preregistration aims to ensure that researchers are blinded to the empirical results when making analytical choices – they have to choose their methods and model specifications before knowing which method, in their data, most favors their preferred result (Christensen et al. 2019). Yet preregistration was conceived with experimental studies in mind and is difficult to implement for the analysis of observational data. When the data already exist, authors can explore the data prior to registering their analysis – making it unclear what if anything was truly preregistered. Moreover, when researchers are not creating the data themselves, they generally do not know in advance what will be in the data, how they are structured, or how exactly they will be analyzed (Christensen and Miguel 2018). Observational research often "involves myriad judgement calls that may be challenging to anticipate and specify in advance" (Miguel 2021: 206). When authors cannot (or do not) preregister their exact analyses, and thus are unconstrained in searching the model space, multiverse methods can show the range of results available to authors that the data could support. In this sense, multiverse and preregistration are alternative approaches to transparency and suited to different kinds of data. But they are also complementary. Some experimental researchers are forceful advocates for multiverse methods (Simmons et al. 2011; Simonsohn et al. 2020) in addition to preregistration and indeed recommend preregistering not just a single, preferred, specification but a credible multiverse of specifications. Likewise, for researchers using observational data, even when the data already exist, writing a preregistration document can be the most productive and principled way to start thinking through the "thicket of possible models" and identifying the analytical branches of the multiverse that seem most important to explore (Leamer 1985: 308).

In the past, multiverse thinking had been limited by computational constraints. Realizing an entire multiverse – the garden of forking paths of an empirical analysis, where all the reasonable "paths not taken" are brought to light – was computationally infeasible. However, this is becoming a reality as more elements of analysis – such as the functional form – are brought into a multiverse framework. Our methodological approach can be extended in multiple ways. For outcomes measured on a Likert scale, how much do results depend on modeling those as continuous (OLS) or ordinal (ordered logit/probit)? For outcomes measured as percentages or fractions, how much does it influence results to use fractional regression rather than OLS (Wooldridge 2011)? What about models that are less sensitive to outliers than OLS, such as least absolute deviations or quantile regression (Andersen 2008)? Finally, we advocate including data processing – alternative ways of cleaning, coding, and categorizing variables – as a further dimension of the multiverse that may be more important than often recognized (Leahey, Entwisle, and Einaudi 2003; Steegen et al. 2016; Young and Holsteen 2017).

The challenge facing social science is not simply that there are many ways of doing a thoughtful analysis. The problem is transparency: showing whether results are robust and compelling or – as critics sometimes suspect – are instead based on fragile model assumptions that are hard to justify or explain. For many modeling decisions, we lack good evidence on how much our choices even matter, leaving it unclear how much analysts can select the supposedly empirical conclusions they arrive at. Multiverse analysis offers a way forward, showing the other empirical worlds that different analytical assumptions can see. Extending multiverse analysis beyond control variables, into the realm of functional forms, is a key advancement.

FUNCTIONAL FORM APPENDIX:
EXPANDED INFLUENCE RESULTS

Application I: Unemployment and Wellbeing

In Application I, the influence of many control variables is different across functional forms. Even the signs of the influence scores frequently switch depending on the functional form. For example, how does controlling for self-reported food problems ("not having enough food") change the estimated effect of job loss? PSM shows a notable *negative* influence of this control (−0.021), while CEM (0.030) and OLS (0.011) both find a positive influence of the control. A very similar pattern is seen for the variable "children at home." For homeowner status, CEM and PSM agree on the sign of its influence (negative), but in CEM the influence is nearly fifteen times larger than in PSM (−0.044 and −0.003, respectively). Another striking difference across functional form is for income: It has no influence in OLS (−0.001), modest positive influence in CEM (0.017), and a large negative influence in PSM (−0.046). These differences in the influence scores – in how a control variable affects the coefficient of interest – seem very idiosyncratic.

Table A9.1 gives a broader view of these idiosyncratic influence effects. In OLS, the number of controls has no noticeable effect on the job loss coefficient. In CEM, additional controls tend to modestly shrink the estimate toward zero. In PSM, controls generally have no effect unless there are many of them, in which case adding controls greatly increases the estimate (i.e., expands it away from zero). In this troubling case, an author's (extreme) result could depend not on *which* controls are in the model but simply on the discontinuous effect of including *many* controls. The PSM results, in particular, seem haphazard.

TABLE A9.1 *Influence effects for effect of job loss on subjective wellbeing*

	OLS		PSM		CEM	
	Effect	% change	Effect	% change	Effect	% change
Not enough food	0.011	−2.5%	−0.021	5.4%	0.030	−7.5%
Not desired food	0.010	−2.3%	0.008	−2.0%	−0.005	1.4%
Eligible for unemployment	0.004	−0.8%	0.022	−5.7%	0.118	−29.4%
Children at home	0.002	−0.5%	−0.026	6.7%	0.011	−2.7%
Homeowner	0.001	−0.2%	−0.003	0.8%	−0.044	11.0%
Part-time work	0.001	−0.2%	0.036	−9.3%	0.030	−7.4%
Married	0.001	−0.1%	−0.003	0.8%	0.005	−1.3%
Zero/negative wealth	0.001	−0.1%	−0.002	0.4%	0.016	−4.0%
Food stamps	0.000	0%	−0.002	0.6%	0.006	−1.6%
Log income	0.000	0%	−0.046	11.7%	0.017	−4.2%
Average estimate	−0.439		−0.391		−0.401	
N	1,024		1,023		1,023	
R^2	0.916		0.147		0.736	

TABLE A9.2 *Influence effects for effect of college degree on voting for Trump*

	LPM		Logit		PSM		CEM	
	Effect	% change	Effect	% change	Effect	% change	Effect	% change
Democrat	0.056	-49%	0.060	-50%	0.060	-57%	0.055	-43%
Income	0.010	-8%	0.010	-8%	0.026	-25%	0.000	0%
Male	0.001	-1%	0.000	-1%	0.004	-4%	0.000	0%
Age	0.000	0%	0.000	0%	0.006	-6%	-0.003	2%
Age squared	0.000	0%	0.000	0%	0.005	-5%	0.000	0%
Marital status	-0.001	1%	0.000	2%	-0.002	2%	-0.003	3%
Nonwhite	-0.018	16%	-0.020	14%	-0.023	22%	-0.030	24%
Average estimate	-0.114		-0.113		-0.104		-0.126	
N	128		128		127		127	
R^2	0.940		0.938		0.874		0.847	

Application II: Voting for Trump in the 2016 Election

In Application II, many of the $\Delta\beta$ estimates are similar across functional forms. For example, conditioning on democratic party affiliation reduces the effect of college on voting for Trump by 49 percent in LPM, 50 percent in logit, 57 percent in PSM, and 43 percent in CEM. One could debate whether party affiliation ("Democrat") is a posttreatment endogenous control in this case. In any event, this variable clearly has shared explanatory power with college degree.

The largest difference across functional forms is seen when conditioning on income. In both LPM and logit, controlling for income reduces the coefficient of interest by 8 percent. However, in PSM, controlling for income reduces the effect size by 25 percent, and in CEM controlling for income has no effect on the estimate of interest. This illustrates how different functional forms can adjust for controls in different ways.

10

Data Processing

Invisible Decisions That Matter

A large portion of statistical science and researcher judgment happens prior to regression. From a programming perspective, data processing can be understood as the coding that happens before running a regression command. The inherent vagueness of theory allows a one-to-many mapping of social theory to empirical test – any one theory could be tested in many different ways. Theories ride into battle with a host of auxiliary assumptions, which can defend a theory from being wrong and can be invoked discreetly to generate supporting evidence.

One category of auxiliary assumptions is data processing: What is the best way to prepare the data for a compelling empirical test? High-quality analysis can be hampered with flawed coding and categorizing of variables, cleaning strategies that add to rather than reduce data errors, and mishandling of missing data, among other problems. This chapter will focus on three core elements of data processing: (1) coding and categorizing data into variables, (2) addressing anomalous and/or outlier observations, and (3) deciding when or whether to use sampling weights. Data processing is part of the analysis, and analytic choices on this front are characterized by "invisibility, uncertainty, heterogeneity, and reliance on tacit knowledge" (Leahey 2008: 605).

Social theories aim to describe and explain *phenomena*, not *data per se*. Data are intended to capture or reflect phenomena but are not the phenomena itself. Sensors and survey instruments used for measurement could be flawed. Converting raw observations into "variables" involves many assumptions and potential errors. The degree of correspondence between data and the phenomena it aims to measure is often aspirational rather than known: Researchers propose measures but often do not know how well they capture the truth. As a result, whenever a theory fails to gain empirical support, one can always blame the measurement for being wrong rather than the theory. This move is sometimes known as "saving the hypothesis" – blaming anything other than the theory for a failed empirical test. Sociologists should feel familiar with the "saving" dynamic: Weber/Marx/Durkheim wasn't wrong; rather, a researcher implemented a flawed test of their theory. When evidence fails to validate a theory, researchers can save the theory by invoking problems with the data or measurement. By the same token, researchers can also revisit the data processing and measurement assumptions when the results *disagree* with a theory.

Raw data typically require a great deal of cleaning, wrangling, coding, and categorizing of variables and observations. Vague standards for this processing mean it can be troublingly ad hoc. Data processing choices are often invisible in the sense that they face little scrutiny – rarely do readers know exactly what was done, as this can only be accurately described by the actual code used to preprocess the data. Processing involves uncertainty as there are few conventional norms or standards of practice and it is often unclear what is the best way to preprocess (defining and coding variables, cleaning erroneous data, addressing outliers, and the like) – many times there is no single correct answer or practice. Indeed, processing often requires relatively intimate familiarity with both the subject area and the dataset – a tacit knowledge that is difficult to convey in the space of the "Data" section of a journal article.

Data processing is often not very analytically interesting, and decisions rarely attract much interest from reviewers, editors, or readers. It tends to be seen as a nuisance issue, rather than a subject of curiosity or an opportunity for productive discourse and the demonstration of rigor and excellence. Processing is often not regarded as "methodology" proper, and few readers or reviewers find it interesting to reflect on or critically engage with processing choices. Many reviewers see their essential role as a skeptical evaluator of analytical merit, challenging the authors to justify their analysis in greater depth than what is presented in the paper. Indeed, sniffing out logical and analytical flaws is what many reviewers are "good at" and find intellectually rewarding. In contrast, double checking the details of how data are cleaned and coded is not generally how reviewers see their job. In interviews, journal editors said that data cleaning is rarely discussed in reviews (Leahey 2008). As one editor noted, "unless there is some obvious indicator that [data were manipulated] … we operate largely on faith" (Leahey 2008: 620).

Indeed, the processing details are often "explained" only in the statistical code, which is not generally included in the journal review process and, at least in sociology, rarely provided for any other person to inspect once an article is published.

While many elements of analytical strategy and model specification may be fiercely contested when research is presented or reviewed, such debates often take for granted that the data were managed and processed with sound judgment and integrity – as if the working datasets were prepared by a disinterested expert; in short, the data are treated as "given." It is deep in the training of social statistics that datasets are created by "someone else": "In methods and statistics courses and in textbook examples, students are presented with cleaned data, predetermined measures, and flawless examples of analysis, so researchers do not typically learn about [data processing] … until they conduct research on their own" (Leahey 2008: 622).

Yet experienced researchers know this processing is often intensive and time-consuming, with many opportunities to make mistakes.

Crowdsourcing studies offer insight into the puzzles of data processing. Huntington-Klein et al. (2021) asked multiple authors to start from raw, noncleaned data to replicate a research design, requiring the replicators to make their own best decisions of how to clean and prepare the data for analysis. Two research designs were replicated by seven replicators each. No two researchers ended up with the same sample size, and in some cases the differences in N were enormous (e.g., 830,000 versus 4.3 million). Many of the differences across researchers were difficult to explain, often being coding decisions that "would likely go unmentioned in an eventual publication" (Huntington-Klein et al. 2021: 946).

In short, in the area of data processing, there is (1) uncertainty about best practices, (2) wide variability in possible methods, and (3) limited transparency to understand what authors have done. This generates much potential for authors to "improve" their preferred result in ways that are invisible to readers. Processing choices and assumptions are not often seen as part of the model, but they can influence the result just as much as control variables or functional form assumptions. Imagine if every data cleaning choice was made with a subconscious goal of finding or increasing an effect size. The researcher degrees of freedom involved in data cleaning seem high.

A classic example of uncertainty over data cleaning comes from data on the frequency of having sex (Jasso 1985; Kahn and Udry 1986). If a respondent reports having sex eighty-eight times in a month, is this simply a vigorous level of sexual activity? A data entry error? Is the respondent pranking the survey instrument? If a researcher drops or down-weights such observations, are they correcting implausible data to minimize the influence of outliers or are they sex shaming respondents and introducing new biases of their own?

These kinds of concerns are becoming more common. The quality and response rate of social science survey data have declined over time; response rates are dropping and people seem to take surveys less seriously (e.g., Kennedy and Hartig 2019). Researchers are using new sources like Mechanical Turk that tap a low-wage labor pool to routinely complete online surveys for pay as low as $2 an hour. It sometimes seems obvious that some respondents are not giving serious answers, producing an errors-in-variables problem; however, identifying insincere responses and deciding what to do with them are challenges (Sherkat 2012).

THE DARK MATTER OF RESEARCH DESIGN

Focusing on the invisibility of many research decisions, Camerer (2022) calls these issues the "dark methods" of research design. This term draws an analogy with physics where there is "dark matter which cannot be directly seen because it does not reflect light, but which is evident from its other effects" (Camerer 2022: 1). Here, we consider a compelling example of dark matter/methods driving a research result.

A classic sociological study by Weitzman (1985) featured a striking and influential empirical finding about the inequalities of marital separation: After divorce, women's standard of living fell precipitously, dropping by about 75 percent. Meanwhile, the standard of living of men *increased* by 40 percent. Previous research had shown this basic pattern of inequality – that women experience financial losses from divorce while men see gains – but these findings were far larger than other estimates and became widely cited in both academic and policy spheres. Reanalysis of the original data, however, could not reproduce these findings (Peterson 1996). Many data preprocessing decisions – especially treatment of missing data, imputation for partial information, and sample weighting strategies – were not precisely documented in the original study, and the original programming files that contain these details were lost (as the author changed jobs and computers over time). Reanalysis produced estimates that were only one third to one quarter of the original magnitudes: –27 percent for women and +10 percent for men. Moreover, a range of alternative methodological assumptions could not come close to the original estimates; Peterson (1996: 534) concluded, "I have been unable to discover how Weitzman's results could have been obtained." In response, Weitzman agreed that recreating the original estimates was not possible – their own extensive efforts to do so were described as "a very sad, time consuming, and frustrating experience" – and agreed that "it is likely ... that the gender gap is less than I reported" (Weitzman 1996: 538).

On one hand, the signs of the estimates are stable and so the basic conclusion was not contested. However, the difference in magnitudes is remarkable: Do women lose three quarters of their standard of living, or one quarter, following divorce? The difference is nearly 50 percentage points, and no one could explain how these estimates came out so different. Anyone who thinks this difference is not important should submit half of their annual income in perpetuity to an institute for methodological training. In general, the magnitude of an effect is no less important than the conclusion that it exists.

Moreover, if we consider the absolute difference in effects for men and women, the original estimate showed a gap of 115 points, while the revised gap was 37 points. If this range of outcomes is possible purely due to unknown differences in cleaning and processing a dataset, this has troubling implications for how much any one study can be believed. There was a lot of dark matter in this research design, which only becomes apparent when anyone – including the original author – attempts to reproduce the estimates.

MULTIVERSE ANALYSIS OF DURANTE ET AL.: "THE FLUCTUATING FEMALE VOTE: POLITICS, RELIGION, AND THE OVULATORY CYCLE"

While data processing decisions can greatly affect empirical results, the decision trees involved are not always very algorithmically tractable. Any element of data processing can be questioned, but the specification of alternatives usually requires a lot of field-area and data-specific knowledge – something that few general readers have. If a reader/reviewer thinks a control variable is questionable, the easy advice is to drop that control and see what difference it makes to the results (i.e., conduct and report an influence analysis). But when data processing decisions seem wrong, it usually requires exhausting hours working through the details of the problem before one can propose a better alternative. Without easily defined alternatives, a combinations algorithm has little to work with. Computational solutions are greatly limited by the availability of intelligent human inputs for data processing.

There are unique challenges in addressing data decisions in a computational multiverse framework. At the same time, these challenges provide some of the best illustrations of why multiverse thinking is important to social science.

Before proceeding further, we provide a proof of concept that multiverse analysis is a fruitful and informative way of understanding data processing decisions. We reanalyze a study titled "The Fluctuating Female Vote: Politics, Religion, and the Ovulatory Cycle," by social psychologist Kristina Durante and coauthors (Durante, Rae, and Griskevicius 2013) and its criticism by Steegen et al. (2016).[1] The article was controversial for its implication that women's core beliefs about religion and politics rise and fall with their monthly fertility cycle.

Women's ovulatory cycles, according to Durante et al. (2013), affect their day-to-day conservatism in matters of religion and politics. They find that women at their peak monthly fertility become more religious, more conservative, and more republican – but only if they are in committed relationships; single women, in contrast, become more liberal and less religious. The shift occurs, the authors argue, because ovulation can "nonconsciously alter women's reproductive goals" and their mate-seeking behavior (1008). For women in committed relationships, the stronger reproductive drive at peak fertility leads to greater focus on their existing relationship and a desire to show commitment. For single women, ovulation leads to more liberal orientations in a wide-net search to attract a mate.

While Durante et al. analyzed the question using ANOVA, the analysis can be expressed in the following interactive regression model:

$$\text{Religiosity}_i = a + b_1 hi\_fert_i + b_2 coupled_i + b_3 hi\_fert_i \times coupled_i + \varepsilon_i$$

The coefficient of interest is the interaction term b_3: When women are at high fertility *and* in a committed relationship, are they more religious? The coefficient in the Durante model is +2.30, with a standard error of 0.95. The estimate is statistically significant and is a clear empirical vote for the theory.

However, in multiverse analysis, almost all alternative processing decisions yield a weaker estimate. Each data processing assumption

---

[1] The replication package for this example is available online at https://osf.io/45ft2/files/osfstorage.

matters at least a little bit, and it seems that Durante et al. (2013) made nearly every decision in a way that favors their hypothesis. Methodological critics reexamining the data found that the results are highly sensitive to mundane choices in the classification and coding of the key variables (Steegen et al. 2016). There is ambiguity in how to exactly classify a woman's time of peak fertility, and seemingly arbitrary coding decisions were made that favor Durante et al.'s conclusion. Null results can be found with equally credible data processing decisions – alternative choices that Durante et al. (2013) themselves have made in other publications (Steegen et al. 2016). These results hinge on very narrow classification decisions that few readers would notice – such as whether peak fertility occurs on cycle days 6–14 or 7–19. The data also have a strange ambiguity in relationship status: Does dating "only one person" mean a respondent is single or in a relationship?

Estimating all combinations of the data processing uncertainties provides 120 regression estimates for the key parameter of interest: effects of peak fertility on the religiosity of married women (relative to single women). More details on the processing decisions are given later, but what stands out is that the Durante et al. specification provides the single most extreme and favorable estimate available in this multiverse of data processing (Figure 10.1). Other ways of processing these data generate estimates that either weaken these conclusions or say the opposite. Only 4 percent of these models report a statistically significant effect, while 96 percent do not.

Figure 10.1 shows how these different data preprocessing assumptions affect the results. The original Durante et al. estimate is shown by the vertical line – an interaction showing that women in a relationship are more religious during peak fertility. The shaded area shows the 95 percent confidence interval for that estimate. The multiverse distribution shows what happens when other reasonable data processing decisions are made – including many alternate decisions made by Durante et al. in different publications.

As Figure 10.1 emphasizes, the Durante et al. estimate is essentially the most extreme result that the data could support. Most of the estimates are somewhere close to zero. The modeling distribution is a textbook "crisis in science" case – an extreme tail estimate reported as the researcher's preferred result. Here we see again how an underlying theory involves a host of auxiliary assumptions – about how best to code and classify data – in order to test that claim. Making different assumptions about the best way to classify the data produces very different results.

Data Processing: Invisible Decisions That Matter

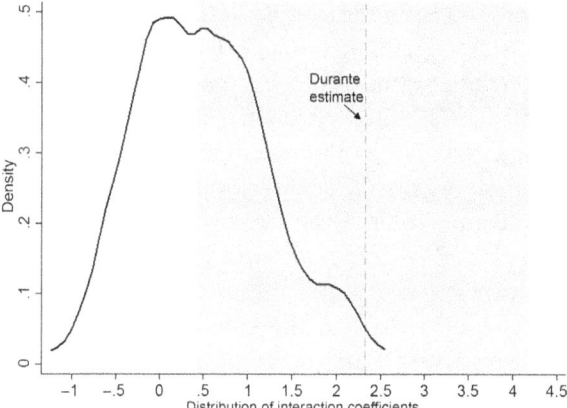

FIGURE 10.1 Effects of peak fertility on the religiosity of women in relationships
Note: One hundred and twenty regression estimates. N = 275. Shaded area represents the 95 percent confidence interval for the estimate from the Durante et al. (2013) model.

Interestingly, the 95 percent confidence interval of the Durante et al. specification is quite reasonable in its width; were it centered near the data processing mean, the 95 percent confidence interval would provide good coverage of what other authors using different data assumptions might find. But, in practice, the original estimate and its standard error are highly misleading about what can be found in repeated study.

ACCOUNTING FOR AMBIGUITY: DATA PROCESSING ASSUMPTIONS

Let's dig into the multiverse to see exactly what is driving these results (Table 10.1). The two explanatory variables in this study are "peak fertility" and "relationship status," both of which turn out to involve ambiguity in classification and coding. First, determining women's ovulation status (as high fertility vs. low fertility) is complex, is uncertain, and could be coded in many different ways based on the data. While the fertility cycle is an underlying biological reality, knowing where any respondent locates in that cycle is difficult. Indeed, fertility status is measured across five variables. Respondents are asked to report (1) the start date of their last menstrual period, (2) the start date of the menstrual period before that, (3) the typical length of their cycle, and (4 & 5) how sure they were about each of the previous two start dates. By distilling information from these variables, each respondent is assigned to either high- or low-fertility status. Steegen et al. (2016) identify five unique ways fertility status could be sensibly coded. Durante et al. (2013) have used these different coding definitions in other publications on the topic – showing that they themselves were uncertain about how best to classify women's fertility status and were willing to adopt different classification rules. Cycle days themselves depend on identifying cycle length and deciding what to do with respondents who are uncertain about their cycle.

If a reader already feels tired thinking about these data processing details, it only gets worse. The survey question measuring relationship status – the second part of the interaction term – had some ambiguous, overlapping categories. Participants were asked to choose one of four relationship categories:

(1) Not romantically involved with anyone
(2) *Dating or involved with only one partner*
(3) Engaged or living with my partner
(4) Married

Durante et al. (2013) counted people in the first two categories as "single" and the second two as "in a committed relationship." Category (2) is odd because "involved with only one partner" sounds like being in a relationship but is coded as "single." Did the original authors not notice this inconsistency when designing the survey instrument? Category (3), "engaged or living with" their partner, is clearly in a relationship but couples can be committed without living together, especially if they are "involved with only one partner." Steegen et al. (2016) identify three ways through this ambiguity: Treat category (2) as single, or treat it as in a relationship, or exclude it altogether to focus on clear categories. These three options can be used in combination with the five ways of categorizing fertility, providing 120 unique processing methods. As it turns out, the processing of the ambiguous category (2) has the single largest influence on the results. Table 10.1 shows the influence of modeling decisions in this multiverse.

While it may be true that fertility cycles influence religious and political leanings in some way, these data do not demonstrate the effect. The original study reported a knife-edge estimate – essentially the most extreme estimate available from the multiverse of possible results. It is always possible that the Durante et al. model shows the true effect, but believing that depends on assumptions that are very difficult to defend. At the

TABLE 10.1 *Multiverse options and influence analysis, Durante et al. study*

	Mean interaction coefficient	Percent difference from overall mean
All models	0.49	
Durante et al. estimate	2.30	369%
Definition of fertility status		
High = cycle days 7–14, low = 17–25	0.62	27%
High = cycle days 6–14, low = 17–27	0.90	84%
High = cycle days 9–17, low = 18–25	0.61	24%
High = cycle days 8–14, low = 1–7 and 15–28	0.24	−51%
High = cycle days 9–17, low = 1–8 and 18–28	0.08	−84%
Relationship status		
"Dating or involved with only one partner" = single	0.98	100%
"Dating or involved with only one partner" = in relationship	0.02	−96%
"Dating or involved with only one partner" excluded	0.47	−3%
Calculation of next menstrual onset		
Computed cycle length	0.74	51%
Reported cycle length	0.24	−51%
Exclusion due to unusual cycle length		
No exclusion	0.51	5%
Exclude women with unusual cycle length	0.47	−5%
Exclusion due to start date uncertainty		
No exclusion	0.59	21%
Exclude women who are uncertain of at least one start date	0.39	−21%

same time, declaring a large degree of modeling uncertainty is also an unsatisfying conclusion for a study. But science advances not by burying uncertainty but rather by converting uncertainty into empirical questions for further research. If more research is to be done testing this theory, it must advance our knowledge about the auxiliary assumptions – better measurement of relationship status and empirical clarification of how to define high fertility. Every form of model uncertainty invites a new line of research. Every time a scholar thinks "the best method or decision is unclear," that is a new research horizon.

TYPES OF DATA PROCESSING DECISIONS

Before going further with applied multiverse analysis, we discuss three central aspects of data processing: (1) variable construction, (2) the treatment of outlier and anomalous observations, and (3) the use of sampling weights. This does not encompass all the coding that occurs prior to running a regression, but it captures some key issues that come up in virtually any research project.

THE DIVERSITY OF VARIABLE CONSTRUCTION

Many studies chose a single preferred definition of their key variables and proceed as if rival measures and definitions either did not exist or were not available. But there are usually many credible ways of conceptualizing, measuring, calculating, and coding core variables. The Durante et al. multiverse discussed earlier demonstrated that measures like "peak fertility" can sound straightforward in a research article but turn out to be complex constructions with multiple credible alternatives that change the results. Even a simple measure like being in a committed relationship was not always very clear, but it strongly influenced the conclusions.

Most studies today could do far more to demonstrate the robustness of the ways they choose to define their core variables, and good examples of this are readily available. In a study of how globalization affects the welfare state, Brady, Seeleib-Kaiser, and Beckfield (2005: 928) note that "the measurement of globalization is contested and … the literature has yet to converge on a single measure"; embracing this uncertainty, they test seventeen different measures of globalization (including trade openness, foreign direct investment, migration, and the like). In studying how parental incarceration leads to behavioral problems in children, Wildeman and Turney (2014) examine twenty-one distinct measures of children's problem behavior (such as aggression, withdrawal/depression, attention problems, poor social skills, rule-breaking, and whether the problems were reported by teachers or parents). These two studies each addressed an important source of uncertainty: Wildeman and Turney addressed uncertainty about their outcome variable (behavioral problems), while Brady et al. focused on uncertainty about their treatment variable (globalization). While the authors no doubt have their own views on which would be the most informative metrics in each case, they give a host of other metrics equal standing. Research like this helps bring the literature together by showing what is at stake in using different measures and helps us understand why different researchers may get different results.

The literature on inequality shows growing interest in understanding different core conceptualizations. Economic wellbeing – and thus inequality – could be measured by income, consumption, or wealth. Income has long been the default metric of economic wellbeing. However, income fluctuates year to year and does not take into account that people can borrow, save, and receive transfers from others. Some argue that *consumption* better reflects real wellbeing, especially at the lower end of the distribution, and consumption metrics can distinguish between inequality in necessities versus inequality in luxuries (Attanasio and Pistaferri 2016). Wealth is a subject of growing interest for inequality researchers and is a compelling measure of economic capacity, especially at the top (Pfeffer and Waitkus 2021). But wealth also has key conceptual problems: (1) As much as half of all households have zero net wealth but still have income and consumption – making it a flawed measure of wellbeing; (2) most people's net wealth is not liquid but rather tied up in the value of their primary home – meaning they have it but mostly just use it for living in. So there are good reasons why there are multiple ways to conceptualize and measure economic wellbeing and inequality. Income, consumption, and wealth are all interrelated but may show different trends and patterns of association in different research areas. Interestingly, as research on inequality expands, we may see increasingly divergent conclusions depending on how authors chose to define economic inequality.

There is nothing wrong with focusing on one conceptualization of inequality, and today, the literatures on income, consumption, and wealth inequality all stand as distinct lines of inquiry. But one purpose of multiverse analysis is to help researchers envision ways to engage with different perspectives, either showing the generality of their findings or identifying the assumptions that serve as methodological scope conditions.

CODING AND CLASSIFYING VARIABLES

There are many ways to code any particular variable that is selected for research interest. Even once we settle on income inequality (rather than consumption or wealth inequality), consider the many ways that inequality could be coded: the top one percent share, the 90/10 ratio, the interquartile range, the Gini coefficient, or even just the variance or standard deviation as measures of dispersion. These all provide valid, sensible metrics of the distribution of income (or other continuous variables like lifespan [van Raalte and Caswell 2013]). Hirschman (2021) has discussed how different research traditions may come to favor one calculation of income inequality, leaving other metrics "out of focus" and unmeasured for long periods and missing important aspects of reality. There is no single best way to calculate inequality in income. The true income distribution is recorded in the raw data; different summary measures of that distribution may capture unique aspects of inequality, but no single measure reports all details of the distribution.

Most variables – given their conceptual measurement – can be constructed and coded in different ways. A study of the effect of education on mortality examined thirteen distinct ways of coding educational attainment, each of which map on to unique hypotheses of how education affects mortality (Montez, Hummer, and Hayward 2012). At one end of the spectrum, education could be coded entirely nonparametrically as a large set of dummies for each year of education completed. In this format, each year of educational attainment is treated as unique and its effects are separately estimated. At the other end of the spectrum, education could be coded as a linear count of years of education. In this case, every year is constrained to have the same effect as every other year; for instance, if there is something special about completing high school (12 years vs. 11) or completing college (16 years vs. 15) a linear measure of education will fail to capture the effects of these milestones. In between treating education as linear or nonparametric are a host of semiparametric coding strategies involving various splines and step functions. Testing them all, Montez et al. (2012) found that the best fitting specification of education – which led to the highest adjusted R^2 – was a relatively complex nonlinear function: "a linear decline in mortality risk from 0 to 11 years of education, followed by a step-change reduction in mortality risk upon attainment of a high school diploma, at which point mortality risk resumes a linear decline but with a steeper slope than prior to a high school diploma" (315).

Research on educational mobility has also highlighted the importance of how coarsely or finely educational levels are coded. This research examines a child's educational attainment relative to that of their parents. When education categories are coded very finely – say when each year of attainment is its own category – there will be more mobility in and out of each category. Even when children "inherit" the general education level of their parents, rarely do they have exactly the same years of education. Moreover, finer categories face greater problems of measurement error, since milestones like high school completion are better recorded in family memory than exact years. So, mobility research tends to focus on fairly broad categories – such as three categories (less than high school, high school, and college+) or five categories (adding "grade 10 or less" at the bottom and "MA+" at the top). Karlson (2021) shows that international comparisons and rankings of educational mobility can vary greatly depending on how coarsely or finely the education levels of parents and children are defined. For example, does the US have high or low educational mobility compared to other western countries? The answer depends, because some countries look much better on the three-category scale but worse on the five-category scale, and vice versa. Until this research area has a stronger consensus on the single best way to code educational mobility, robustness testing is essential for credible conclusions (Karlson 2021).

To reflect on another, seemingly mundane, variable construction question, consider research on political influence in America. In a widely cited study, Gilens and Page (2014) found that when the rich and the middle class disagree on policy preferences, policies mostly end up reflecting the preferences of the rich. "When a majority of citizens disagrees with economic elites … they generally lose" (Gilens and Page 2014: 576). This dominance of elite interests, they argue, challenges "America's claims to being a democratic society" (577).

Follow-up research, however, has produced conflicting findings. It turns out, as Bowman (2020) notes, many different authors are using different definitions of "class disagreement" over policy. If a slim majority (51 percent) of the elite favor a policy while a slim majority of the middle class oppose it, should this be coded as a policy disagreement? What if both groups support a policy but the elite favor it more strongly than the middle class? Bowman's (2020: 1018) study asks: "What kind of differences in preferences constitute policy disagreement? What criteria should be used to define disagreement?" He uses twenty-two different measures of disagreement based on combinations of preference thresholds and preference gaps: five- and ten-point preference gaps at different thresholds of support. The results vary substantially: By some definitions, the middle class "win" more policy disagreements than the elite – meaning that policy is more closely aligned with the views of the middle class than of the elite, while by other definitions the elite win by large margins. For example, the middle class "win rate" ranges from as high as 64 percent to as low as 6 percent, depending on the data definition (Bowman 2020: Figure B1). While Bowman concludes that the weight of the data support the conclusion that the rich have more influence over policy than the middle class, the evidence is much less stark than in the original Gilens and Page (2014) study.

A recent commentary emphasized how general is this issue of ambiguity. Addressing a research question about how immigration influences public support for social policies, Camerer (2022: 2) wrote that the question "seems to allow a lot of freedom to measure almost every scientific word in the hypothesis differently (immigrant, public support, social policies)."

Finally, it should be appreciated that any way of coding and classifying core variables could go wrong in implementation – opening up another dimension by which data processing can affect the results. Greater attention to and transparency about the multiple ways variables can be coded should help everyone understand what a researcher has actually done. For example, an article about police violence published in the journal *Science* by Joscha Legewie (2019: 1) was retracted when, as the author wrote, "a reader discovered classification errors in the data openly shared as part of the publication. After learning about these errors, I conducted a thorough investigation focusing on a larger sample of cases that revealed further classification errors."

The exact nature of these classification errors was not revealed, but they were sufficient to entirely overturn the results of the study. This example shows both the invisibility problem – most studies in sociology do not provide their data and code for close inspection – and the problem of uncertainty: Legewie was evidently confident in his original coding, and only after critical engagement postpublication did he come to recognize the flaws in data processing. We discuss many more similar examples in Chapter 12.

PROCESSING ANOMALOUS AND OUTLIER OBSERVATIONS

A second key element of data processing is the treatment of anomalous and outlier observations. Some researchers never consider outliers or at least never mention them in publications. Other authors routinely preprocess for outliers but may be extremely vague about what they did and why: for example, by simply reporting their sample size "after accounting for outliers."

Anomalous observations "by virtue of being different from other cases ... usually exert disproportionate influence on substantive conclusions" (Aguinis, Gottfredson, and Joo 2013: 271). At the same time, it is unclear whether that influence is warranted or not – whether outliers are misleading or enlightening. "Outliers can be legitimate data points and removal may cause loss of useful information … Sometimes outliers may reflect unusual but substantively meaningful aspects of the intended study" (Liao, Li, and Gordon 2016: 454). So, a priori, it is not clear if outliers are good or bad. Are they problems to be corrected or interesting cases that deserve extra attention?

When a researcher confronts an anomalous-seeming observation, there are three basic options: Live with it (do nothing), correct it (edit to make a more credible number), or discount it (or in some cases observations can be weighted by data quality). There is no single best method among these three; which is best depends on the underlying reason for the anomaly.

Consider the relationship between economic growth (gross domestic product, GDP) and population health. For most countries there is a strong positive association – a growing economy is good for public health. But there are some clear outliers in the data: Some places achieve remarkable gains in longevity despite low GDP. Costa Rica and the Indian state of Kerala are classic examples (Sen 1999); more recently, Ethiopia and Brazil have made surprising health gains relative to their economic growth (Freeman et al. 2020). These exceptional cases weaken the relationship between GDP and health. Some researchers are tempted to discount unusual cases, assuming them to be noisy distractions from the "real" pattern. Others would say that unusual cases like Ethiopia are especially interesting – pointing to alternative pathways to population health that are viable for poor countries – and should not be diminished simply because they are rare.

In a classic sociological study of sexual frequency among married couples, Jasso (1985) used large-N data to show that sexual activity was declining over time, to the detriment of marriages. However, it was later shown that these results depended entirely on the inclusion of 4 out of ~2,000 observations. These four couples, in the first wave of data, were coded as having had sex exactly eighty-eight times in a month – an anomalous frequency that was numerically similar to the missing data code of ninety-nine (Kahn and Udry 1986). In response, and to the amusement of many, Jasso (1986) defended those values as simply energetic, scolded the critics for sex shaming, and argued that dropping them induced sample truncation bias. Drawing a line between plausible and implausible data points is not a simple matter.

Data are often messy and not produced with as much care and attention as a researcher would like. Many anomalous observations are simply mistakes, errors, or insincere responses. Some countries with autocratic regimes do not honestly report their health data. Some survey respondents act as pranksters, saying for example that they are seven feet tall and weigh eighty-two pounds or had sex eighty-eight times last month. In these situations, researchers who do not apply a skeptical filter to their data – simply believing everything they are told – are being made the fools of untrustworthy narrators.

In contrast, some see data editing as inherently wrong, especially when done after a preliminary analysis. "Researchers," as one scholar put it, "should not remove unusual observations simply because they fail to conform to their beliefs" (Andersen 2008: 5). But there is limited consensus on this. In a vignette survey of 160 professors, respondents were presented with a case where a researcher edited messy data after being disappointed with their preliminary results. Many scholars strenuously objected to the practice, making comments like "a researcher is never at liberty to change respondents' answers" (quoted in Leahey et al. 2003: 72–73). However, others thought the practice was reasonable, stating that data collection is difficult, requires interpretation, and often calls for some "common sense" cleaning (73).

TREATMENT OF OUTLIERS

In a review of applied research practices for handling outlier observations, Aguinis et al. (2013) wrote that outliers are "typically not acknowledged or discussed openly in published journal articles," and when they are, "researchers often implement idiosyncratic, nontransparent, and difficult-to-replicate practices" (297). For example, some articles simply report their sample size "after accounting for missing data and outliers" without explaining how they identified said outliers or providing a rationale for why they deleted them (274). In their review, Aguinis et al. counted "14 unique and mutually exclusive outlier definitions, 39 outlier identification techniques, and 20 different ways of handling outliers" (270). In fairness, many of these unique methods are variants on a common approach, but even the core set of approaches presents a methodological cornfield.

HOW DO WE DEFINE AND IDENTIFY AN OUTLIER?

What do we mean by the term "outlier" and what is an observation "outlying" from? There are four main definitions in the literature, each of which are reasonable perspectives. First, outliers can be values that are outside the possible range for a variable (e.g., age coded as 150 or –20 [both of which we've seen in administrative data]) or that otherwise appear highly anomalous for some substantive reason (number of children reported as fifty). To identify such outliers, one would simply scatterplot the data and visually inspect for outliers. Second, and more generally, outliers could be any value at the extreme tails of the distribution, say below the fifth percentile or above the ninety-fifth. Third, outliers can be observations with large residual values, as shown from regression output – that is, observations that poorly fit the model. To identify these, the residual of each observation (its divergence from the regression line) is divided by the standard deviation of the outcome variable – the higher the standardized residual, the more likely an observation is an outlier. Fourth and finally, outliers can be any observation that substantively affects the parameter estimates if it is included or excluded. Such outliers are identified by a Cook's D analysis, which calculates for each observation i how much regression coefficients change when the ith observation is dropped. In short, there are multiple criteria and methods by which an analyst could challenge the validity of their observations – and could indeed use all of these methods or any combination of them at once.

WHAT DOES ONE DO WITH OUTLIERS ONCE THEY ARE IDENTIFIED?

Suppose everyone agrees that an observation qualifies as an outlier. What should be done with it? We see three core sets of options. The first is not to do anything to the outlier, providing a baseline analysis of unaltered data. This is the "clean hands" approach that dogmatically insists on at least one specification that takes the data entirely as given. The second option is to limit the extreme tails via truncation or winsorization. Truncation defines a believable range for a variable and removes all observations beyond that range. An arguably better method than truncation is winsorization: converting extreme values to a set point in the distribution, so that all observations above (say) the ninety-fifth percentile are set to the value of the ninety-fifth percentile. The third approach is to discount or down-weight influential observations, using either least absolute deviation (LAD) regression or the method of "robust regression." LAD is very similar to ordinary least squares but is less sensitive to large residuals; ordinary least squares method squares the residuals to compute a regression coefficient, which blows up large residual values;

LAD takes the absolute value of residuals rather than squaring them, which down-weights residual outliers. An arguably better approach than LAD is to use "robust regression," an iterative form of weighted least squares in which the most influential observations with a large Cook's D are dropped and remaining observations with large residuals are down-weighted (Andersen 2008). The terminology of "robust regression" is intended to mean "robust to outliers."

In our view, a multiverse analysis that incorporates concern for outliers should report all three of these approaches: (1) do nothing (unaltered data analysis[2]) as the baseline, (2) truncate or winsorize to address extreme values, and (3) use LAD or robust regression to address influential outliers. These are three separate specifications, each of which could be taken in combination with any other aspect of the model such as the choice of control variables or functional form assumptions (Klau et al. 2023).

A review of organizational science journals found that winsorizing is the most commonly used method of addressing outliers – used in some 600+ articles, or roughly one in four articles that address outliers (Sullivan, Warkentin, and Wallace 2021). Robust regression closely followed; a similar number of articles mentioned checking for outliers but were unclear in the method of detection or treatment. They concluded that "articles published in top journals have widely varying (or non-existent) approaches to outlier detection" (531). Incorporating these decisions into a formal multiverse analysis can help us routinely understand how and when outliers are influencing our empirical conclusions.

SAMPLING WEIGHTS

The use of sampling weights in regression analysis is a vexing source of uncertainty, confusion, and inconsistency. In the article "What Are We Weighting For?" Gary Solon, Haider, and Wooldridge (2015: 301) write, "Top-notch empirical scholars make conflicting choices about whether and how to weight and often provide little or no rationale for their choices." In *Mostly Harmless Econometrics*, Angrist and Pischke (2009: 91) add that "few things are as confusing to applied researchers as the role of sample weights. Even now, 20 years post-PhD, we read the section

---

[2] That said, retaining observations with strictly impossible values, such as negative years of education, is a waste of attention space. But readers should know when data have these kinds of errors in them and at what frequency.

of the Stata manual on weighting with some dismay." Econometricians advocate caution about the use of sample weights, and if used, they recommend a multiverse-style approach: Estimate models both with and without sample weights, and be clear about what difference it makes (Winship and Radbill 1994; Solon et al. 2015; Bollen et al. 2016).

In descriptive statistics, the importance of sampling weights is clear. When a sample is unrepresentative of the target population, perhaps by design, sample weights correct for bias in a descriptive statistic. Consider the poverty rate estimated from Census Bureau data – the official rate – and from the Panel Study of Income Dynamics (PSID). In a comparison by Solon et al. (2015), the official poverty rate was 12 percent, but the unweighted rate in the PSID was 26 percent – more than twice as high. This discrepancy occurs because the PSID deliberately oversamples low-income households. Using weights to account for the sample design, the *weighted* PSID estimate was 13 percent – essentially the same as the official poverty rate. This gives the impression that if a sample is unrepresentative, analysts should use sample weights to correct for any non-representativeness. Yet as Winship and Radbill (1994: 231) emphasized, "it is less obvious whether these weights should be used when estimating regression equations."

When estimating a regression coefficient or marginal effect, $\Delta y/\Delta x$, it is not necessarily important that the sample means of x or y match their distributions in the population. Indeed, sampling strategies that increase the variance of x are common and improve estimation (generate more reliable estimates with smaller standard errors), even though oversampling methods by definition make the sample less representative of the population. Under classical regression assumptions, estimator consistency does *not* require a representative sample. Moreover, the use of sample weights generally results in less efficient estimation – meaning larger standard errors. Sample weighting "can substantially inflate the variance of the model parameter estimates, even when the unweighted analysis produces essentially the same estimates. In that case, efficiency of the estimators and statistical power are improved by *not* using weights" (Bollen et al. 2016: 376, emphasis added). In other words, the conceptual need for weighted regression is not obvious and the weighting comes with a cost of less precise estimates.

Of course, there are reasons to use sample weights. Sample representativeness may be important in the context of effect heterogeneity, such as if the causal effect on an oversampled group is different than effects on the undersampled groups. In cases of strongly heterogeneous effects, the overall marginal effect may change substantially based on sample composition. Representativeness can also matter for regression when there are *unmodeled* nonlinear effects of x on y, such as a missing interaction effect or if a treatment variable is modeled as linear when the true relationship is log-linear. There are other unique scenarios where the sample composition could matter for regression, discussed in Bollen et al. (2016) and Solon et al. (2015). In all these cases, one can infer that sample weights matter by observing the difference between weighted and unweighted regression estimates. If the estimates change when the sample weights are applied, it suggests either effect heterogeneity or model misspecification.

The use of sample weights should not be a default, and it always requires justification beyond the goal of representativeness. The fact that a sample is demonstrably unrepresentative does *not* mean that sampling weights are needed or beneficial. Weighted regression is justified only if it changes the parameter estimates relative to unweighted regression. This leads to a Hausman test for sampling weights. The logic of a Hausman test is if two estimators generate the same parameter estimates, one should prefer the estimator with the smallest standard errors (in relative terms, choose the best unbiased estimator). Under a null hypothesis that sample weights do not matter, weighted ($\widehat{\beta_w}$) and unweighted ($\widehat{\beta_u}$) regression estimates will be the same in expectation, but the standard errors of $\widehat{\beta_w}$ will be larger. The Hausman test is $H = \dfrac{\widehat{\beta_w} - \widehat{\beta_u}}{\text{Var}(\widehat{\beta_w}) - \text{Var}(\widehat{\beta_u})}$ and is distributed chi-square (Bollen et al. 2016: 383). If the test is significant, it means that the weights make a nontrivial difference to the parameter estimates and deserve consideration. If the test is not significant, it indicates the weights are unnecessary and would not justify the loss of statistical efficiency from using weighted regression.

In our view, the Hausman test provides clear guidance on whether sampling weights should be considered as a plausible model ingredient. However, there is much diversity in research practice. Thoughtful advice comes from Jeffrey Wooldridge and colleagues: Econometric theory is built on imperfect assumptions and provides only "inexact … guidance about how to do empirical research" (Solon et al. 2015: 311) Some researchers always use weights while others never use them, and methodological knowledge is not yet settled enough to establish one single standard of practice. Absent a clear consensus today on sample weights, methodologists advocate a multiverse-style approach: Whenever weights are in question, readers should see results from both weighted and unweighted models. In our view, this means that when sample weights are considered, they should never be assumed but rather always subjected to multiverse analysis.

CONCLUSION

A central part of statistical modeling is data processing. Data processing decisions can shape statistical results just as much as choices about controls or functional form. Concepts such as inequality, poverty, educational attainment, religion, globalization, immigration, public policy, and the like could be operationalized in many different ways, even within one given dataset. Bowman (2020) for example, highlighted twenty-two distinct and reasonable ways that the idea of "policy disagreement" could be coded in a public opinion dataset. In many studies, there are multiple variables (the outcome, the treatment, and key controls) that each could have been coded in multiple different ways. Multiverse analysis of Durante et al. (2013) illustrated a case where seemingly every possible processing choice was made in favor of the authors' preferred result.

The many details of data processing are a core part of a model specification but are often buried or hidden in the background. Treatment of outliers, for example, is rarely discussed in an article: Authors often report a sample size "after accounting for missing data and outliers" but do not explain how outliers were defined or what was done with them. Some research articles invoke sample weights without any analytical criteria or appreciation of the downside risks of weighted regression. When two different authors analyze the same dataset, it seems they almost never end up with the same sample size.

Despite all these challenges, data processing decisions are often the nearly invisible "dark matter" of a research article. Most authors treat processing decisions as tiresome distractions from the "real" methodological questions and rarely explain in any detail what they did. Most readers seem to agree that these are the boring details of an analysis. This means that processing decisions are often just "waved by" in journal review ("these aren't the droids you're looking for") and rarely face critical inspection. But many articles have crashed on the rocks of data processing, and numerous prominent sociological articles have been retracted over these kinds of errors (Legewie 2019, and many more as Chapter 12 will highlight).

Many more null results in social science are hidden by weakly justified data processing decisions that have not yet been questioned. Researchers rarely justify their decisions in any detail, but often processing choices have a large impact on the results. Moreover, the role of processing decisions comes to light only when a replication package is available (which should be required of every publication) and at least one knowledgeable critic takes the time to question every detail of a study.

Critics are often the ones who lay bare the reality that almost any coding and processing decision has a credible alternative, leading to a large multiverse even before any control variables are selected. In the next chapter, we conduct a detailed multiverse analysis of data processing decisions in a fiercely contested sociological study.

11

Data Processing Multiverse Analysis of Regnerus and Critics

Now we put together many dimensions of data processing into a comprehensive multiverse analysis. We reanalyze a now infamous study by Mark Regnerus, which was subjected to many criticisms that have featured centrally in Chapter 10: data processing and the potential for dark matter in the research design to be driving the empirical findings.

Is it harmful for children to grow up with gay or lesbian parents? Publishing in the journal *Social Science Research*, Regnerus (2012a) found that the children of lesbian, gay, bisexual, and transgender (LGBT) parents, compared to those raised in "intact biological families" (IBFs), were worse off in many sociodevelopmental ways: They were more likely to be unemployed, be on public assistance, have drug abuse problems, have contemplated suicide, and more. Others have reanalyzed the data and argued that the results depend on analytic choices – particularly on data processing decisions (Cheng and Powell 2015; Rosenfeld 2015).

This article is one of the most hotly contested studies in twenty-first-century sociology. It has been invoked in Supreme Court debates and rulings on same-sex parenthood and adoption rights. An external review at *Social Science Research* considered retracting the article (Sherkat 2012). Many scholars have questioned nearly every detail of the study's data, assumptions, and analysis. We draw on this postpublication discourse to develop a multiverse analysis of the original study.

A widely debated study like Regnerus (2012a) is ideal for this analysis, because a compelling data processing multiverse requires a great deal of specific input from expert analysts – who both identify contested aspects of processing and propose alternative specifications that may be equally or more credible. We construct two distinct multiverse analyses: a control variable multiverse and a data processing multiverse. This allows us to address a central question for this chapter: How do "researcher degrees of freedom" from data processing compare to those stemming from choice of controls? How much variation in results do each of these sources of uncertainty generate?

Our baseline model specification is replicated from Regnerus (2012a), and we draw on two published articles for criticism and alternative specifications (Cheng and Powell 2015; Rosenfeld 2015). We add to this additional processing alternatives we identified through close replication of all three articles. Our full multiverse includes over 2.6 million unique model specifications.[1]

THE STUDY

Regnerus's study collected a new dataset called the New Family Structures Study (NFSS), using an online survey administered by the data company Knowledge Networks. About 15,000 people took a screening survey, answering the question "Did either of your parents <u>ever</u> have a romantic relationship with someone of the same sex?" Response choices were "Yes, my mother had a romantic relationship with another woman," "Yes, my father had a romantic relationship with another man," or "No." The full survey was taken by 2,988 people, including all of the 236 people who indicated in the screener question that one of their parents had been in a gay/lesbian relationship.

Regnerus's original regression was approximately

$$y_{ij} = \alpha + b_{1j}\text{gay\_father}_i + b_{2j}\text{lesbian\_mother}_i$$
$$+ [\text{other family types}] + [\text{controls}] + \varepsilon_{ij} \qquad (11.1)$$

for i individuals and $j = 1, \ldots, 40$ unique outcome variables. The reference category is the IBF – people who grew up with both biological parents and whose parents were still alive and still married at the time of the interview. Other family types include single parents, stepparents, divorced parents, and other departures from the two biological parents reference group. The forty outcome variables include educational attainment, economic wellbeing, health outcomes, mental health outcomes, civic engagement, substance abuse, family arrangements, and criminal activity. Some are "positive" outcomes (closeness to biological mother/

---

[1] The replication package for all of the analyses presented in this chapter is available online at https://osf.io/45ft2/.

father) while others are "negative" (unemployment). Others are not obviously positive or negative, such as being in a homosexual relationship or frequency of TV watching. For each outcome, effects were estimated for lesbian mothers and gay fathers separately. This original formulation produces an unwieldy amount of regression output. With forty outcomes and two categories of LGBT parents there are eighty coefficients of interest, before conducting any robustness tests. We take two steps to streamline this output down to one summary coefficient.

First, following Rosenfeld (2015), we combine the many outcome variables into a single index. Rosenfeld used nineteen outcomes that were unambiguously positive or negative and did not have large numbers of missing values. To create the index, he reverse-signed the positive variables to make an index of negative outcomes, then standardized the variables so they were on the same scale (in which positive values correspond to more negative outcomes, counterintuitively). We rebuilt this index so that (1) the index is correctly signed (positive values indicate better outcomes), (2) we include more outcome variables (twenty-nine versus nineteen), and (3) we more flexibly account for missing data.[2] Compared to Rosenfeld's index construction, this increases the number of outcome variables by 10 and increases the sample size by nearly 500 (including 45 treatment cases – which is 19 percent of the total – and 454 control cases). We believe this outcome index significantly improves on Rosenfeld's construct, but we include both as multiverse options so readers can see what difference it makes to the results.

Second, we pool together lesbian mothers and gay fathers into one group of those with an LGBT parent. Pooling together gay fathers and lesbian mothers in one model provides a weighted average of the separate effects while increasing statistical efficiency (i.e., producing smaller standard errors), as in Mazrekaj, De Witte, and Cabus (2020) who simply report results for those in same-sex parent families.[3] Through these

---

[2] Rosenfeld (2015) drops all respondents who are missing on *any* of the nineteen outcome variables he used (17.5 percent). In contrast, we use all available responses on the twenty-nine outcome variables we include and afterward check for missingness. We require respondents to have responses for at least ten outcome variables. With this rule, we drop only 0.77 percent of respondents. Following Rosenfeld, we continue to exclude outcomes that are normatively neutral (such as being in a same-sex relationship).

[3] We note that in the baseline model, both these effects are negative and the effect of lesbian mothers is larger in magnitude than that of gay fathers. However, this heterogeneity is not analytically important for our reanalysis, and indeed none of the studies we reviewed in this debate actively discussed or interpreted the different effects of having a lesbian mother versus having a gay father.

two steps, we summarize the eighty coefficients into a single model that provides one summary estimate of the effect of having an LGBT parent. Hence, our reference model is

$$\text{index}_i = \alpha + b_1 \text{LGBT\_parent}_i + [\text{other family types}] + [\text{controls}] + \varepsilon_i \quad (11.2)$$

CONTROL VARIABLES

Regnerus (2012a) had selected six control variables : age, mother's education, family-of-origin income, and dummy variables for female, white, and having been bullied while growing up.[4] Cheng and Powell (2015) identify five additional controls: mother's and father's age at birth, region, metropolitan status, and a dummy for the family having received welfare while growing up. This constitutes the eleven-variable "controls only" multiverse with $2^{11} = 2{,}048$ models.

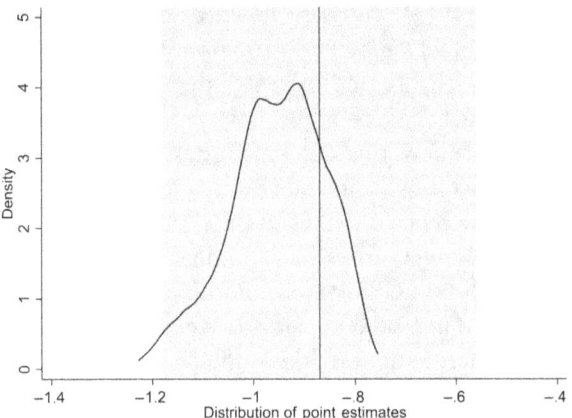

FIGURE 11.1 Distribution of gay/lesbian parenting effects in control variable multiverse
Note: Data from the NFSS, $N \approx 2{,}466$, depending on the specification. Shown are the coefficients from 2,048 models defined by eleven possible control variables. All models estimated using ordinary least squares (OLS) using sampling weights. The vertical line shows the estimate from a close approximation of the preferred model in Regnerus (2012a) and the shaded area shows the conventional 95 percent confidence interval for that estimate.

---

[4] The original study also included a state-level gay-friendly score, which we cannot include since the public version of the NFSS data does not include state.

Note that Rosenfeld rejects one of these controls, bullied as a child, as endogenous and does not include it. This does not affect our analysis as the default multiverse assumption is that any control could be endogenous and thus potentially excludable.

Figure 11.1 shows the control variable multiverse. The original results are highly robust to the choice among these control variables, with all of the estimates positive and statistically significant. Indeed, the "Regnerus model" (i.e., using just the six controls from that study) yields an estimate that is on the low end of this distribution. None of the control variables have notable influence. The most influential control suggested by Cheng and Powell (2015) is family receipt of welfare while growing up, and including it reduces the multiverse mean by only 11 percent (from –1.0 to –0.9). The modeling standard error is 0.09, which is smaller than the sampling standard error in the Regnerus model (0.16). Thus, the conventional 95 percent confidence interval has wider bounds than the control variable multiverse. Uncertainty about the choice of these controls has little impact on the conclusions: Using all, none, or any combination thereof produces similar results.

DATA PREPROCESSING DECISIONS

From the beginning, criticisms of this study focused not on control variables but rather on many aspects of the data and the processing strategies. Thus, our focus is on two core types of data processing: (1) treatment of anomalous observations and (2) construction of the explanatory and dependent variables.

ANOMALOUS OBSERVATIONS IN NFSS DATA

Many critics have commented on the anomalous observations that can be easily gleaned from the NFSS codebook. "Some number of respondents were likely just having fun filling out the survey"(Perrin, Cohen, and Caren 2013: 333). For example, "20 male respondents have had sex with more than 100 women, while 16 female respondents have had sex with more than 100 men ... Ten respondents have been pregnant a dozen or more times" (Sherkat 2012: 1348). One man who said he was raised by a gay father also reports being seven feet and eight inches tall, weighing eighty-eight pounds, and having been married eight times (Cheng and Powell 2015).

A number of scholars have suggested that the structure of the screening survey – which asked 15,000 people if their parents had a gay/lesbian relationship – attracted pranksters to the survey. The screening survey was an economical way of identifying a sample of respondents who are rare in the general population. But a drawback is that it also informed respondents upfront that the survey would focus on a topic that is both highly personal and politically heated (at the time of the survey in 2011 marriage equality was intensely debated in national politics).

Regnerus (2012a) did not exclude any anomalous observations, leading to criticism that "data cleaning was apparently not something in the research agenda" (Sherkat 2012: 1348). Yet this echoes the debate over Jasso (1985) and how to deal with observations that seem implausible or respondents who seem unserious. Should analysts delete or down-weight these observations, or is doing so a way of filtering the data through one's own beliefs and inducing bias through sample truncation? We have argued earlier that the raw data should be included in the baseline analysis, alongside the postcleaning results, so we can understand what impact, if any, data cleaning has on the estimates.

For data cleaning decisions, we follow the close inspection by Cheng and Powell (2015), who argue that roughly 44 percent of the respondents coded as raised by an LGBT parent are misclassified or borderline cases – a substantial error rate if their assessments are correct. Specifically, they identify twenty-nine people with an LGBT parent who gave unreliable or inconsistent responses across different parts of the survey (considered misclassified). They flagged six other cases where information was plausible but suspicious (borderline cases). They also argue that in order for LGBT parents to causally influence a child's upbringing one expects them to have lived with the children. Many of those having LGBT parents co-resided with them only for short time periods. They consider fifty-three people who lived with their LGBT parent for a year or less (in twenty-four cases, never lived with them at all) as misclassified. They also flag fifteen people who lived with an LGBT parent for only two to four years as borderline cases. From this data review, we see three processing options: (1) use all data, (2) drop the cases Cheng and Powell code as misclassified, and (3) drop the borderline cases. In a response to his critics, Regnerus presented models that dropped cases where the respondent had never lived with the parent's same-sex partner, without making any adjustments for people with unreliable and inconsistent responses. We add this as a fourth processing option.

Finally, we consider a method for addressing outlier observations in the NFSS data. The outcome index follows a nonnormal distribution largely due to a long left tail: some people reporting extremely negative outcomes. We include as a multiverse option winsorizing the outcomes index and running OLS on that dataset.

VARIABLE CONSTRUCTION

A key source of disagreement between the author and critics is how to operationalize the comparison of the "treatment group" to the reference group: the family types that people grew up in. The study is a comparison of children growing up in IBF versus those raised by an LGBT parent. Those growing up in other family types fill out the classification: single parents, divorced parents, stepparents, adoptive parents, and "other." Coding up these other family types is needed to restrict the comparison to be between LGBT families and IBFs. Yet there are a host of problems with this construction.

Outside of the reference category of IBF, the family types are not mutually exclusive. People coded as growing up with an LGBT parent "may quite plausibly have been in any one of the other categories as well, and indeed most of them probably were" (Perrin et al. 2013: 331). However, the family type variable sums to one for every individual; anyone with an LGBT parent is coded as LGBT only, even if they also fit into the other categories. Treating these categories as mutually exclusive is confusing and potentially biasing if those with gay/lesbian parents also went through divorces, spent time in single parent families, or had step- or adoptive parents.

Cheng and Powell (2015) relax the constraint that IBFs still be married at the time of the survey. In effect, they argue that people raised by gay or lesbian parents ought to be compared to all people raised by their biological parents, regardless of whether the parents divorced after age eighteen. This expands the size of the reference category (IBF) from 919 to 1,191 people, and Group 3 (divorced after the respondent came of age) is absorbed into the reference group.

Rosenfeld (2015) proposes a fundamental change to how family types are modeled. He dispenses with Regnerus's categories entirely and focuses on the concept of *family transitions*. A family transition is any change in the adult members of the respondent's household while growing up. If one parent moves out of the household, it counts as one transition. If a grandparent moves into the household and then later moves back out, it counts as two transitions. And so on. Rosenfeld replaces the categorical family structure coding with a count of the number of family transitions during childhood. Thus, while the Regnerus coding strategy sets up a comparison between LGBT families and IBFs, the Rosenfeld strategy compares LGBT families with those with the same recorded number of family transitions. Table 11.1 shows the regression structure of these two approaches. Rosenfeld's coding substantially reduces the effect of an LGBT parent in this model, though the effect is still statistically significant in Model 2.

However, measurement error problems frustrate this coding structure as well. People who grew up in IBF were not asked their detailed family history. Hence, for the IBF group, we do not know if grandparents, aunts, or uncles moved into or out of the household at any point in their lives. For non-IBF respondents, these extended family members count for family transitions. If we assume that IBFs had unmeasured transitions of adult family members, then the analysis is biased. What would be the direction of bias? IBFs appear as perfectly stable households, when some of them likely were not. So, IBFs would look *even better* if we could measure and remove the (negative, as shown in Table 11.1) effect of these family transitions.

Model 3 in Table 11.1 shows the effect of splitting LGBT parents into two groups. Both lesbian mothers and gay fathers have similar effect estimates (–0.27 and –0.40) as in the pooled Model 2 (–0.31); however, estimated separately, they have larger standard errors and do not achieve statistical significance. This is a classic case when subgroups should be pooled together for statistical efficiency: The within-group differences are not of interest, and pooled together the results are more informative. Keeping the gay father/lesbian mother estimate separate does not meaningfully affect the coefficient; it only serves to reduce statistical significance. Model 3 does not indicate a null effect; rather, it shows that the analysis runs out of statistical power when the LGBT group is split.

The differences between the Regnerus model structure and the Rosenfeld structure leads to an important debate (and as the multiverse will show, one's stance on this debate is critical in shaping one's conclusions about the research question). Regnerus's main comparison is between LGBT families and IBFs, and many have pointed out the flaws in calling this comparison an "LGBT effect." It is surely an unfair standard to compare LGBT parents to perfect, stable, intact families. Indeed, LGBT are not the only family type that compares unfavorably to IBFs; every other family type compares unfavorably to IBFs, regardless of whether a same-sex couple is involved. To truly estimate an LGBT effect, one would need to disentangle it from the "not-IBF"

TABLE 11.1 *Regression models for effect of family structure on positive outcomes index, Regnerus versus Rosenfeld definitions*

	Model 1 Regnerus	Model 2 Rosenfeld	Model 3	Model 4 Regnerus + Rosenfeld
Family type				
IBF	(ref.)			(ref.)
Gay/lesbian parents	-0.87*** (0.16)	-0.31* (0.16)		-0.50** (0.17)
Lesbian mother			-0.27 (0.15)	
Gay father			-0.40 (0.35)	
Divorced later	-0.43** (0.15)			-0.43*** (0.08)
Adoptive	0.23 (0.17)			0.23 (0.17)
Stepfamily	-0.50*** (0.10)			-0.23* (0.10)
Single parent	-0.28*** (0.07)			-0.11 (0.07)
Other family type	-0.40*** (0.09)			-0.31** (0.10)
Other controls included?	Y	Y	Y	Y
Family transitions (broad)		-0.07*** (0.01)	-0.07*** (0.01)	-0.06*** (0.01)
Constant	-0.47**	-0.56**	-0.56***	-0.43*
R^2	0.26	0.26	0.26	0.28

Notes: N = 2,466. ***$p < 0.001$, **$p < 0.01$, *$p < 0.05$. Weighted regressions predicting positive outcomes index. Other controls are age, biological mother's highest level of education, origin-family income, and dummy variables for female, white, and having been bullied as a child.

effect. Rosenfeld's coding strategy achieves this disentangling, by comparing children of LGBT families to children of non-LGBT families with the same level of instability.

On the other hand, Regnerus pushed back against this critique by arguing that LGBT parents tend to have less stable relationships, and this is one of the reasons why LGBT parenting is bad for children. In other words, he argues that family transitions are on the causal pathway from LGBT parent to child outcomes and thus serve as a bad control

(Regnerus 2012b: 1370). There is no clear winner in this debate; both Rosenfeld and Regnerus make reasonable points.

Rosenfeld argues against the endogeneity interpretation – which is central to his preferred analysis. He notes that while LGBT families indeed have more family transitions than other family types (say, stepfamilies) in the NFSS data, this is frequently because of lesbian parents losing legal custody of their children – something that rarely happens to straight mothers who are divorced or otherwise single (Rosenfeld 2015: 495). Rosenfeld thus argues that the higher family transitions of LGBT parents is caused by a legal system biased against them, rather than being endogenous to LGBT status itself, and thus constitutes an appropriate control. This is a compelling argument as far as it goes, though it is not clear that the legal system fully accounts for potential endogeneity in family transitions.

Another detail in Rosenfeld's coding is the types of family transitions that he includes. He presents two different measures of transitions. His preferred measure includes any adult transition, so some transitions are extended family members (such as grandparents) or unrelated adults entering or exiting the child's household. His second measure includes only transitions involving the loss (or return) of a parent, since parental transitions are likely more important in the lives of young people. Rosenfeld favors the broad "any adult" coding on the basis of an R^2-type test, but in the absence of a theoretical motivation, the R^2 is not necessarily a strong reason to favor a model specification. We include both measures in the multiverse to see how the model choice influences the results.

Rosenfeld presents his coding structure as a complete alternative to Regnerus, but these approaches could be combined: retaining the full family types and simply adding family transitions as an additional element. Rosenfeld (2015, fn. 7) suggests this would not be possible due to a collinearity problem, but that is incorrect. Within family types (other than IBF) there is plenty of variation in the number of transitions, and models with both family types and family transitions readily estimate. This is shown in the final column of Table 11.1, which is a hybrid of the Regnerus and Rosenfeld coding. There is shared variance between family types and family transitions, and retaining family types, at least in this simple model, reduces the effect of transitions and increases the effect of LGBT parent. This suggests that family types are needed for more accurate estimation of the effect of transitions.

Together, there are three broadly different ways of constructing and coding family type – the central explanatory variable in this study. In

Table 11.1, we label these the Regnerus approach (full categorical coding), the Rosenfeld approach (dummy coding with transitions), and the Regnerus + Rosenfeld approach (full categorical with transitions). None of the approaches are perfect given the underlying data problems, and each have different strengths and weaknesses.

There are other details in the data processing multiverse. But in the interest of getting to the results, we will report the remaining data processing alternatives in Table 11.3 of the influence analysis that shows their impact.

FULL MULTIVERSE RESULTS

Figure 11.2 shows three distinct details: (1) the Regnerus estimate, indicated by a vertical line, (2) the controls-only multiverse, previously reported, and (3) the full controls-plus-data processing multiverse. The full multiverse contains all 2,048 models from Multiverse 1, and it also incorporates all combinations of those controls with all the other data processing and modeling choices: (1) alternative coding strategies for four control variables and the outcomes index, (2)

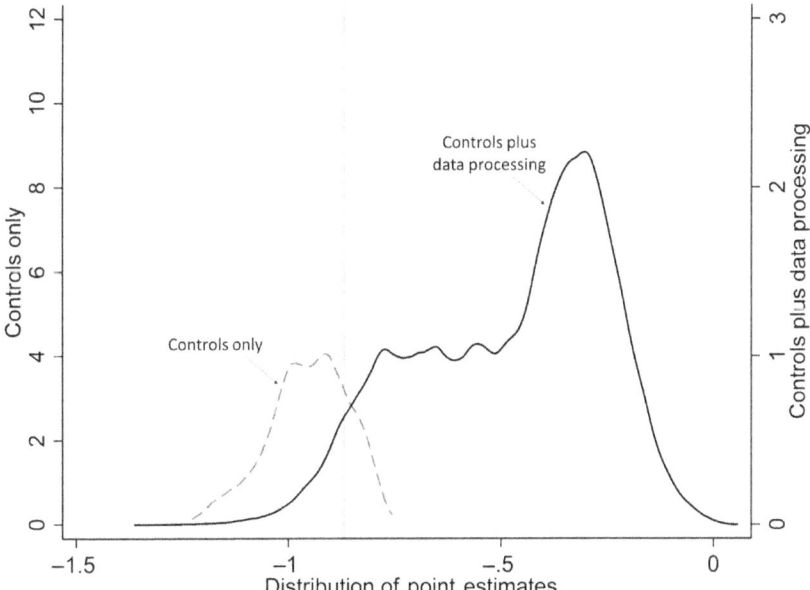

FIGURE 11.2 Distribution of gay/lesbian parenting effects in full multiverse
Note: Data from the NFSS, $N \approx 2,466$, depending on the specification. Results from 2.65 million models. The vertical line shows the Regnerus estimate.

alternative ways of dealing with outliers, (3) corrections for misclassification of LGBT parent, (4) alternative definitions of the comparison group, and (5) alternative weighting strategies. This multiverse expands to roughly 2.7 million models.

The full multiverse distribution is much wider and is substantially shifted toward zero compared to the control variable multiverse. The modeling standard error in the full multiverse is more than twice as large as that for the controls only. A wider range of estimates is possible in the full multiverse, and 95 percent of estimates are smaller than the Regnerus estimate (which falls at the fifth percentile of the modeling distribution). Data processing decisions have much more influence on these results than the choice of controls. This is both because there are many more alternative specifications for data processing and because some of those processing decisions are much more influential than the control variables. Our central conclusion is to affirm that data processing decisions deserve a central place in multiverse analysis. While the choice of control variables is much more tractable in a combinatorial multiverse analysis, controls may not be the most important decisions in the overall analysis, nor do they adequately account for the potential variability of findings across different analysts using the same data.

In terms of substantive conclusions, the full multiverse analysis shows that critics were only partly successful in challenging the results. Clearly, very few of the 2.65 million estimates are zero or opposite-signed. Table 11.2 shows the summary statistics. Only 992 models report a positive coefficient for LGBT parent, which is 0.04 percent of the models, and none of those positive estimates are statistically significant. In practical terms, the estimated effects are strictly negative. Some 76 percent of the models are both negative and statistically significant. In the full multiverse, the Regnerus estimate appears more extreme than most alternative models, but both the sign and significance are very stable. The robustness ratio in the full multiverse is 3.14 – easily robust by conventional rules of thumb.

The Regnerus estimate is a borderline tail estimate that depends on multiple contested assumptions. But a conclusion of "no effect" is not supported by these data, either. The most reasonable conclusion is that there is some negative effect of gay/lesbian parenting on children's outcomes in these data, but it is probably smaller than suggested by Regnerus's original study.

To be clear, we do not view the mean of any multiverse as the best estimate. The purpose of multiverse analysis is to show what estimates are

TABLE 11.2 *Multiverse results, gay/lesbian parenting effect*

	Controls only	Controls plus data processing
Number of models	2,048	2,654,208
Mean estimate	−0.95	−0.48
Minimum coefficient	−1.23	−1.36
Maximum coefficient	−0.76	0.06
Positive	0	992
Positive and significant	0	0
Negative	2,048	2,653,216
Negative and significant	2,048	2,022,745
Percent negative and significant	100%	76%
Modeling standard error	0.09	0.22
Sampling standard error	0.16	0.16
Total standard error	0.19	0.28
Robustness ratio	4.66	3.14

plausible given the data and a rich set of modeling assumptions. But other things being equal, estimates closer to the center of the distribution are technically easier to justify as they are supported under more bundles of assumptions, while tail estimates are harder to justify because they require a larger set of exact assumptions to be true.

In Table 11.3, we document every data preprocessing decision included in the multiverse and show how each decision affects the empirical conclusion. Column 1 shows the average coefficient for all models invoking that assumption. The "all models" average is −0.48, meaning an effect size of about one half of a standard deviation in the outcome index. Column 2 shows the average standard error for all models invoking that assumption. Column 3 shows the percent change in the average coefficient, relative to the "all models" average. This column indicates the relative influence of the model assumption specified in each row. So, the "Regnerus model" has an estimate of −0.87, which is 82 percent larger than the overall mean. In this last column, a positive percent change means the specification choice leads to a larger absolute estimate, while a negative percent change means it pushes the estimate toward zero. As the table documents, our multiverse considers many different dimensions of an empirical analysis. As the table shows, many factors contribute in small ways to the diversity of possible results. The central specification issues are how to structure the comparison group for LGBT families (options C.1 to C.6) and how to deal with potentially misclassified or borderline cases (options M.1 to M.4).

TABLE 11.3 *Influence effects for gay/lesbian parenting effect*

		(1) Average coefficient	(2) Average standard error	(3) Percent change from "all model" average
All models		−0.48	0.15	
Regnerus model		−0.87	0.16	82%
Comparison group	C.1: IBFs	−0.76	0.15	59%
	C.2: Both parents until 18, may have divorced later	−0.71	0.14	49%
	C.3: All families with same number of "any adult" transitions	−0.26	0.14	−44%
	C.4: All families with same number of parental transitions	−0.29	0.15	−40%
	C.5: IBF, with "any adult" transition and other family types	−0.38	0.15	−21%
	C.6: IBF, with parental transitions and other family types	−0.47	0.15	−2%
Misclassification of people raised by gay father/lesbian mother	M.1: Raw data	−0.55	0.14	16%
	M.2: Exclude misclassified cases	−0.47	0.13	−1%
	M.3: Exclude misclassified/borderline cases	−0.38	0.14	−20%
	M.4: Exclude cases where respondent never lived with gay father's/lesbian mother's same-sex romantic partner	−0.50	0.18	5%
Positive outcomes index	P.1: 19 component variables; exclude cases with missing values on any component variable	−0.51	0.16	7%

Category	Specification			
	P.2: 29 component variables; exclude cases with missing values on more than 19 component variables	−0.44	0.14	−7%
Weights	W.1: Sampling weights	−0.46	0.19	−3%
	W.2: No sampling weights	−0.49	0.11	3%
Outliers	U.1 No adjustment for outliers	−0.47	0.15	−1%
	U.2 Winsorize outcome index	−0.48	0.15	1%
Coding of income	I.1: Categorical, missing kept as category	−0.49	0.14	3%
	I.2: Categorical, missing treated as missing	−0.45	0.15	−6%
	I.3: Continuous, log income	−0.44	0.15	−7%
	I.4: Drop income	−0.53	0.15	10%
Coding of age	A.1: Age	−0.47	0.15	−1%
	A.2: Age and age squared	−0.47	0.15	−1%
	A.3: Drop age	−0.48	0.15	1%
Coding of race	R.1: Dummy for white vs. nonwhite	−0.48	0.15	0%
	R.2: Five categories	−0.48	0.15	0%
	R.3: Drop race	−0.48	0.15	0%
Coding of mother's education	E.1: Missing kept as category	−0.49	0.14	2%
	E.2: Missing treated as missing	−0.47	0.15	−1%
	E.3: Drop mother's education	−0.47	0.15	−1%

Notes: All models run using OLS. In addition to those shown, the multiverse analysis also considers the following possible controls: female, bullied as youth, origin-family welfare receipt, mother's age at birth, father's age at birth, region, and metropolitan status. Replication package at https://osf.io/45ft2/.

An interesting result involves the use of sampling weights (options W.1 and W.2). All the researchers contributing to this analysis used sample weights to render the NFSS data representative of the general population in terms of observable demographics like age, gender, and race (all analysts agreed that the raw data were highly unrepresentative of the US population). However, a priori it is not clear that weights are needed for regression and none of these authors based the decision to use weights on a Hausman test (Bollen et al. 2016). Hence, our data processing multiverse also includes unweighted models. At first glance, the use of weights doesn't seem to matter much: the unweighted results (–0.49) are slightly larger in magnitude than the weighted estimates (–0.46). However, the use of sample weights in this analysis leads to standard errors that are nearly twice as large – reflecting the concern that weighted least squares can be very inefficient (Solon et al. 2015). The unweighted models have an average standard error of 0.11; the weighted models have an average of 0.19. This loss of efficiency has a big impact on the significance level of many models: Among unweighted models, 95 percent have a significant LGBT effect. Among the weighted models, with their slightly smaller effect sizes and much larger standard errors, only 58 percent have a significant effect. Even though the weights change the modeling distribution very little, they have a tremendous impact on the vote count.

A smaller but noticeable processing choice is how to construct the outcomes index: Rosenfeld's approach (P.1) included only nineteen of the outcomes and dropped observations that were missing on any one of those outcomes (i.e., listwise delete before constructing the index). Our alternative (P.2) included twenty-nine outcomes and only dropped respondents that were missing on a large portion of the outcomes. We developed this alternative because we believed the Rosenfeld index resulted in an unnecessary loss of information. Our method results in smaller estimates (–0.44) than the Rosenfeld index (–0.51) – moderate influence in the context of this study.

Many processing choices had only small effects, if any, on their own. Winsorizing the outcomes index had little effect on the results. The coding of race, or even to include race in the analysis, had no influence in these data (options R.1–R.3). Critics had objected to Regnerus's specification of race as a white/nonwhite dummy, but estimates are generally the same if race is coded as a dummy, coded as five categories, or not included at all. The literature also has some disagreement over the coding of income, either (I.1) as income categories, with one of the categories being "income not reported"; (I.2) as income categories, with missing income coded as missing rather than a separate category; (I.3) convert the categories to continuous log income; or (I.4) drop income entirely (as per a control variable multiverse). Among these options, dropping income leads to the largest LGBT effect (−0.53), while log income gives the smallest effect (−0.44). The important point here would be that there is little difference in results between continuous log income and categorical income.

One last data processing choice not included in Table 11.3 is the general treatment of missing data using listwise delete (adopted here, with some noted exceptions) or using multiple imputation. Our main conclusion is that multiple imputation is not computationally feasible within a large multiverse analysis. Because multiple imputation is itself computationally intensive, implementing it as an alternative data processing choice of each one of over 2.5 million models had an unacceptable runtime using a conventional computer – potentially several months. In smaller scale testing, however, we found that multiple imputation had little influence relative to listwise delete in these data.

TWO MULTIVERSES: REGNERUS VERSUS ROSENFELD

A central debate comes down to whether "family" should be operationalized as the types laid out in Regnerus or as the history of transitions advocated by Rosenfeld. In practice, there are many permutations of the two approaches, including combinations of both that are hard to rule out. Nonetheless, Figure 11.3 shows what is at stake in the two core approaches.

The key distinction between these two sets of models is that all models in the "Rosenfeld multiverse" include a control for family transitions (all of options C.3 through C.6), and the models in the Regnerus multiverse do not (options C.1 and C.2). The two approaches yield strikingly different results: The Regnerus models have an average coefficient of −0.74, and 99.9 percent of models have a negative, significant LGBT parent effect. The Rosenfeld models have an average of −0.35, and only 64 percent of models have a significant effect. That's a difference of about four-tenths of a standard deviation on the outcomes index; it is not trivial. If one favors the Regnerus coding, then the LGBT parent effect is negative, large in magnitude, and fully robust. If one supports the Rosenfeld assumptions, the effect is still negative but much smaller and only modestly robust.

The division between the "Regnerus models" and the "Rosenfeld models" reflects fundamentally different conceptions of what constitutes

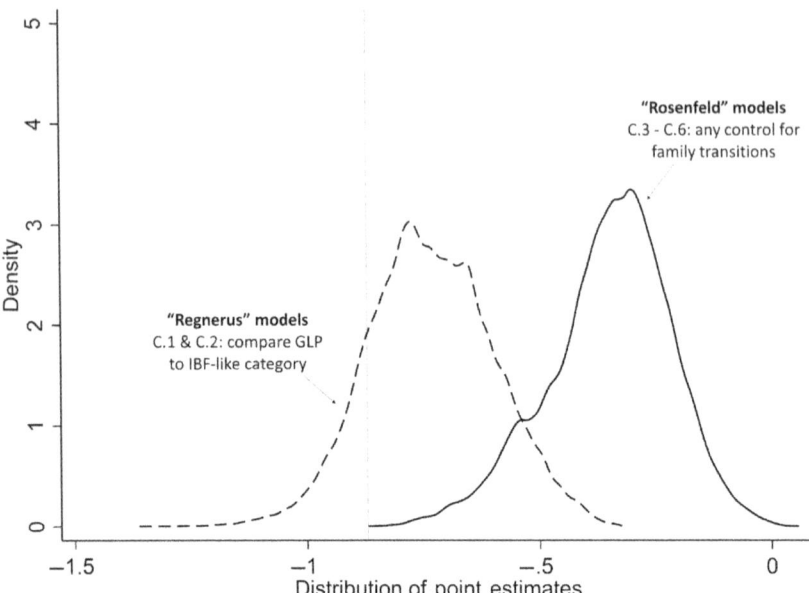

FIGURE 11.3 Distribution of gay/lesbian parenting effects in Regnerus multiverse versus Rosenfeld multiverse
Note: Data from the NFSS, $N \approx 2,466$, depending on the specification. Results from 2.65 million models. The vertical line shows the Regnerus estimate.

an LGBT parent effect, and both conceptions have weaknesses. The Regnerus models compare people with LGBT parents only to people from the most stable families, which probably conflates a true LGBT effect with a more general "not-IBF" effect. On the other hand, the Rosenfeld models may be biased downward if family transitions are one of the pathways through which LGBT parenting affects adult outcomes (as Regnerus argues is the case). If one prefers Rosenfeld's conception of an LGBT parent effect, one probably thinks the true effect is closer to the Rosenfeld curve; if they prefer Regnerus's conception, they look at the Regnerus curve.

For those looking to discredit Regnerus's findings, we point to one more critical result: In order to reject those findings, it becomes necessary not only to prefer the Rosenfeld model structure but also to defend the use of sample weights in this analysis. Among the Regnerus models, over 99 percent have a significant effect, regardless of whether weights are used. But among the Rosenfeld models, the weights make a critical difference: 92 percent of the Rosenfeld/unweighted models have a significant result, compared to only 37 percent of the Rosenfeld/weighted models. If this difference occurred because the weights led to smaller point estimates, then the weighted models would surely be more defensible (Solon et al. 2015; Bollen et al. 2016). But that is not the case: Using weights only moves the average coefficient (among Rosenfeld models) from –0.36 to –0.34. The difference in significance levels is driven almost entirely by the widening of the standard errors in the weighted models (from 0.11 to 0.19). The weighted models have about the same effect estimate but are much less precise.

CONCLUSIONS

In our experience of replicating this original study and the two replications of it, we were continually surprised by how much more we learned about the research through replication than through reading alone. We thought we understood each article quite well by reading its methodological descriptions and published results, but in practice, we almost never did and were often surprised by things we learned through replication. This project took much more time and effort than we expected, but we highly recommend the experience to others. Only through replication can one fully embrace the spirit of scholarly skepticism, in full knowledge of how the estimates were produced. To replicate is to appreciate the assumption-laden nature of empirical claims.

We opened the discussion of data processing with the Durante et al. (2013) multiverse, which starkly rejected the claims of that original study: The authors' preferred estimate was the single most extreme finding available in the data; only 4 percent of multiverse estimates were statistically significant, and half of all estimates were opposite-signed – amounting to an overwhelming null result. In contrast, we were surprised by the robustness of the Regnerus finding. Prior to examining the data directly, we accepted the conclusions written by the critics and expected that a comprehensive multiverse analysis would drive their point home in a powerfully conclusive way. Rosenfeld (2015: 478) had written that in reanalysis "same-sex couple parents ... are weakly or not at all associated with negative adult outcomes." Cheng and Powell (2015: 615) concluded that the Regnerus results are "so fragile that they appear largely a function of ... possible misclassifications and other methodological choices." It is certainly true that in multiverse analysis – recognizing the data processing questions raised by the critics – the estimates become much smaller. Our surprise was discovering that in these data a negative effect is nonetheless still robust and that there are essentially no opposite-signed results.

This multiverse of estimates all derive from one underlying dataset. Regardless of the analysis, there are undeniable problems in the data themselves that have no postcollection analytical solution. Whether one prefers to specify the comparison group for same-sex parents using family types or family transitions (or both, as seems most sensible), both these variables are substantially mismeasured. Transitions are mismeasured since IBFs were never asked about any extended family transitions, and types are mismeasured because a family is falsely restricted to being only one type when in fact the categories are overlapping (Perrin et al. 2013). We do not know how these errors in measurement affect the results because the needed information was not collected. Nevertheless, both critics offer at least partial praise for the data: saying that the collection effort was "certainly impressive" (Cheng and Powell 2015: 617) and had "advantages over other data sources" (Rosenfeld 2015: 479). We defer to this expertise on evaluating the relative quality of the data at the time but remain disappointed that the key measures central to this research have obvious and unresolvable errors in measurement.

We have other reservations about the data. We see it as bad practice to prescreen a survey with the question "are either of your parents gay?" and then include everyone who responds "yes." It has been easy to document that some of the respondents "were having fun with the survey," but the underlying selection mechanism into this kind of politically charged (at the time) prescreened survey is very difficult to understand or adjust for. The problem of nonserious survey respondents is greatly compounded when studying small subsets of the population. For small populations, even small rates of misclassification error can create large amounts of noise and bias in results (Cheng and Powell 2015). In the screening survey of the NFSS data, only 1.7 percent of the respondents indicated that a parent had been in an LGBT relationship. If pranksters are especially drawn to survey questions about sexuality – which seems to be the case – then many more of the respondents might be misclassified.

Social theory seeks to predict and explain *phenomena*, not *data* per se. Theory need not apply to data when they are collected through poor proxy measurements of the phenomena of interest. Scholars hope that data are closely coupled with the underlying phenomena that matter, but measurement systems have many flaws. For this reason, we strongly favor big administrative data for the analysis of small, hard to reach populations. Using such data in the Netherlands, Mazrekaj et al. (2020) find that the children of same-sex parents do better than average at school, implying a supportive and successful home environment. Acknowledging that no dataset is flawless, we hope the literature going forward will aspire for bigger and better quality data.

Finally, we emphasize that critics and replicators can and should be subject to criticism themselves. Publication and replication are a back-and-forth debate in which, it is hoped, the best arguments ultimately win. Replicators should be held to a high standard, as they have the benefit of the original authors' thinking, and should be expected to only improve the quality of evidence. In this view, there are some flaws in the critics' work that deserve mention.

A key mistake that both critics make is to focus exclusively on significance testing, particularly as they drop substantial portions of the data. Neither Rosenfeld nor Cheng and Powell ever report a substantive estimate or regression coefficient for their LGBT effects but instead report only the significance tests. Regnerus's regression tables are themselves unconventional, but readers can at least look at a table and see what is the difference in outcome between any family type on any outcome variable. Readers cannot retrieve this information from either of the critics, who just report whether a regression yielded a "star." A focus on significance testing alone, to the exclusion of effect sizes, is bad statistical practice in any context (Gelman and Stern 2006). It is especially flawed here, as the critics provide new specifications that cut the sample size and greatly reduce the treatment group. Whenever one imposes a sample exclusion – especially from an already small treatment group – this must be evaluated by the change in the parameter estimates, not by a drop in statistical significance. It is not a fair assessment of the data to report that significance levels fall after dropping as much as 44 percent of the treatment group: Of course statistical significance will be lower when the sample is smaller. Our multiverse modeling distribution (Figure 11.2) and influence analysis (Table 11.3) correctly put the focus on effect sizes across different specifications. This is not a criticism of the decision to drop misclassified cases, but it is a reminder of the importance of looking at the change in effect sizes rather than significance levels whenever imposing a sample restriction.

A second problem in this literature is a weakly theorized subdivision of the treatment group: splitting LGBT parents into separate specifications for gay fathers and lesbian mothers. Regnerus originally coded LGBT parents separately in this way, and critics have followed suit in their own statistical models. The separate coding is not wrong but is unnecessary, was not given substantive justification, and dilutes statistical power. Since the effect sizes for gay father and lesbian mother are similar, there is no reason to split up LGBT groups by sex. Indeed, none of the authors ever interpreted or discussed as meaningful the difference between gay fathers and lesbian mothers, leaving it unclear why the separate coding was used. Our models pool LGBT parents rather than splitting by sex, which preserves statistical power and increases the statistical significance of the results.

Critics of the Regnerus study have challenged the data and analysis in many ways that, when implemented, reduce the effect size. But the remaining debate is over the magnitude of the LGBT parent effect or over the quality of the data but not over the existence of an LGBT parent effect *in this dataset*. To the extent that modeling decisions matter, data processing features are more important than the control variables in this analysis.[5]

The fundamental principle of multiverse analysis is open and transparent social science. In the debate around the Regnerus study, we provide three distinct contributions: (1) the distribution of results across over 2.6 million model specifications, with model ingredients from both the original study and from its critics; (2) an influence analysis documenting how different data processing decisions affect the results; and (3) a new replication package (https://osf.io/45ft2/) that combines all this work including all analyses to date so that others can question, learn from, and expand on this multiverse.

---

[5] Admittedly, debates about how to structure the variable of interest could partly be framed as a debate about control variables, just as questions about, say, selection bias could be framed as an omitted variable problem.

12

Retractions in Social Science

Misadventures in Data Processing

Often, we learn about data processing issues only when a study fails to replicate – another scholar looks closely enough at the analysis to attempt an exact reproduction of it and discovers the kinds of errors or problems that routinely escape attention at the journal review phase. We review a series of retractions and rebukes that involved data processing errors in high-profile social science publications. As noted earlier, Legewie (2019) voluntarily retracted his article in the journal *Science* after a reader, upon examining the data and code, discovered classification errors in the analysis. The precise nature of these classification errors was never publicly disclosed, but it was sufficient to void out the article entirely.

This chapter only touches on the inventory of fatal replications and retractions published in social science in recent years. Our goal is not to embarrass these authors – mistakes in statistical analysis are easy to make – but rather to learn from their mistakes. Each case involves a successful social scientist making fatal errors in data processing and along the way offering instructive lessons and cautionary tales. Without careful attention to these big mistakes, we will never come to appreciate the central importance of data processing in our model specifications. This chapter provides some "typologies of error" that we hope increases sensitivity and attention to the mundane details of coding that can be devastating to a study.

Each one of these cases is also a call for open code and (when ethically and legally possible) open data – none of these errors would have been caught without transparency in the statistical code.

EXHIBIT A: GROWTH, AUSTERITY, AND EXCEL ERRORS

A highly cited study by Harvard economists Carmen Reinhart and Ken Rogoff (2010) found that when government debt reaches a threshold of 90 percent of GDP, the result is macroeconomic stagnation and decline. This finding drove policy debates and supported budget-cutting austerity agendas. On close inspection, however, it turned out that Reinhart and Rogoff had inadvertently excluded countries like Australia and Canada which had high government debt and strong economic growth. Moreover, the study equally weighted countries in the analysis, even though the number of years each country contributed to the analysis varied dramatically. For example, Belgium's twenty-five years of experience with high government debt was given equal weight to New Zealand's single year of high debt – a baffling decision. Partly because of this weighting strategy, one year of data from New Zealand (in 1951) became a powerful outlier that strongly skewed the results (Herndon, Ash, and Pollin 2014). None of this was visible to readers until the underlying data and code – in this case an Excel spreadsheet – was made available to other researchers.

EXHIBIT B: POLICE VIOLENCE AND EXTREME OUTLIERS

A prominent study published in the *American Sociological Review* explored the theory that high-profile cases of police violence have harmful spillover effects on communities – creating distrust of legal authority and reducing public willingness to report crimes to the police (Desmond, Papachristos, and Kirk 2020). The study used data on 911 calls from the city of Milwaukee before and after a brutal police beating of an unarmed black man which was widely covered in local media. With a dataset of 1.1 million 911 calls, Desmond et al. (2020: 870) found that the episode of police violence had a large dampening effect on 911 calls – an effect that "persisted for months, resulting in a net loss of more than 20,000 911 calls." They conclude, compellingly, that episodes of "police violence not only threaten the legitimacy and reputation of law enforcement; they also – by driving down 911 calls – thwart the suppression of law breaking, obstruct the application of justice, and ultimately make cities ... less safe" (870).

Yet this study also shows that a single outlier can have a surprisingly large effect on research results. In replicating the study, Zoorob (2020) finds that the results "depend entirely on a statistical outlier" that appears forty-seven weeks after the violent incident was reported. This is striking since the analysis draws on a total of ninety-five weeks including the before and after periods – each week contributes scarcely more than 1 percent of the data. "Dropping this single week at the periphery of the data" changes the negative effect on police reporting to a positive and nonsignificant effect (178). The replication also emphasizes that in the initial months following the police violence, there is no visual or "raw" evidence of a change in 911 calls – the result is driven by structural modeling of a nonlinear time trend that is heavily influenced by the outlier week. Zoorob concludes that while police violence may well have negative effects on police–community relations, data from the Milwaukee incident do not demonstrate the effect.

The original authors acknowledged the issue only so far as to say that "Zoorob identified a potential outlier that should be scrutinized when evaluating our findings" (Desmond et al. 2020: 184). They also add new variables to their model to help support the original result – namely, controlling for average weekly temperature. This approach of discovering new models, after one's core published analysis falls apart, deeply lacks credibility. While this was intended to help demonstrate robustness, it only emphasizes another dimension of model uncertainty: The results depend not only upon outliers but also on control variables that the experts in this research (the original authors themselves) had not previously thought of. In effect, Desmond et al. (2020) double down on errors in their analysis; they report new errors of omission that they hope will be seen as offsetting the errors that their critic identified. This kind of response really just shows that no strong conclusions can be derived from the data. The broader methodological lesson from this case is that bias or skew from outliers can show up in surprising places, even when the sample size appears very large.

EXHIBIT C: MARITAL INFIDELITY AND THE CODING OF INFINITY

In a study of marital infidelity published in the *American Sociological Review*, Munsch (2015) coded infidelity as the combination of (1) having the same spouse in consecutive years and (2) reporting more than one sexual partner in that time. In a later correction, the author acknowledged a coding error that treated missing data as evidence of cheating and explained how the mistake happened. Noting that "Stata treats missing values as positive infinity," Munsch explained that when respondents declined to report their number of sexual partners they were treated as having infinite sexual partners – which is greater than one, so they were coded as having been unfaithful. This mistake accounted for almost 40 percent of the cases of adultery (Munsch 2015: 833). Such errors are easy to make, and clean coding requires limiting the analysis to values less than infinity. Correcting such coding errors overturned one of the main conclusions of the study and weakened support for others; the findings "are not as robust as initially reported," the author concluded (838). In general, both readers and reviewers take it for granted that these kinds of mistakes are avoided.

EXHIBIT D: PANEL ATTRITION AND GRAY DIVORCE

In a panel study of elderly couples, authors mistakenly treated survey attrition (one spouse not responding) as marital separation (Karraker and Latham 2015a). For a couple to be coded as "intact" both spouses had to respond to later waves of the survey; if one spouse did not respond for any reason, the couple was accidently coded as divorced. This had a large impact on the results, since divorce is very rare among elderly couples while survey attrition is common. The authors explained the magnitude of the error: "Whereas the original [study] reported 859 divorces, the corrected number is 161; correspondingly, the number of marriages lost to follow-up increases from 21 (originally reported) to 939 (corrected)" (Karraker and Latham 2015b: 418). In short, the coding error was many times greater than the number of true divorces.

The error was identified only when Karraker and Latham shared their code with another sociologist who was perplexed by the findings. Although "gray divorce" is known to be a rare event, the original study reported that 32 percent of elderly marriages end in divorce – more than five times the corrected rate of 6 percent. Obviously, something was wrong; reading the code, their friendly critic found the error and explained it to the authors. It turns out the whole error happened entirely in "one line of code" (2015b: 417). Of course, it scarcely matters that only one line of code was wrong, because it was a very important line: As the authors concluded, "This miscoding alters all results and invalidates the previously published results" (2015b: 417).

The article was retracted but not entirely and not transparently. For some reason, after a retraction notice *The Journal of Health and Social Behavior* allowed the authors to replace the article with a "corrected version," and as of 2022, the corrected article does not indicate that it was retracted and replaced with a new version with sharply curtailed claims and no acknowledgment of any error. Only the 2015b retraction notice acknowledges what went wrong, and the article continues to accumulate citations.

EXHIBIT E: MISSING DATA ON MORALIZING GODS

In a social science study published in the journal *Nature*, it was discovered that much of the data were in fact missing values that the authors had improperly recoded (Whitehouse et al. 2019; Beheim et al. 2021). The study was part of a debate over the role of "moralizing gods" in historical human civilizations. For most ancient societies the historical record does not indicate whether their gods were moralizing or not, and this variable is often coded as missing in the original archeo-historical database. For example, for around the period 1000 to 500 BC, the historical record does not reveal whether civilizations of the Niger Inland Delta or the Yellow River Valley believed in gods that would punish them for moral transgressions. Nevertheless, Whitehouse et al. (2019) recoded all missing/unknown observations to be zeros, indicating the *absence* of moralizing gods. Given that 61 percent of the observations (490 of 801) were missing/unknown, this is a dramatic rewriting of human history prior to running a regression. The processing decision was not reported in the original article, and Beheim et al. (2021) show that when the analysis is limited to known cases, the results are opposite-signed and statistically significant, completely reversing the original conclusion.

EXHIBIT F: BOWLING ALONE OR INTERVIEWER FATIGUE?

An influential 2006 study found that Americans' social ties shrank dramatically over the previous two decades (McPherson et al. 2006). The percent of Americans reporting no close confidants in the General Social Survey (GSS) – no one to talk to about important matters – rose from 9 percent in 1985 to 25 percent in 2004. Contributing to a prior narrative of Americans "bowling alone" (Putnam 2000) the authors concluded that "the ties that bind are fraying" (McPherson, Smith-Lovin, and Brashears 2008). However, a number of empirical anomalies were quickly noted, such as that other data sources on social networks did not support this growing isolation, and within the 2004 GSS even married people showed a dramatic increase in having no one to talk to, despite living with a confidant (Fischer 2009). Further inquiry eventually traced the anomalous result back to a small subset of interviewers that worked for GSS in 2004. Interview staff, who are often low-wage workers, were evidently bypassing a portion of the survey because of its heavy load of follow-up questions whenever a confidant is named and because of the placement of these questions at the end of the 2004 GSS instrument when interview fatigue was setting in (Paik and Sanchagrin 2013).

In updated analysis, Paik and Sanchagrin (2013) identify interviewers who generated anomalously high numbers of completed interviews with no confidants listed. Specifically, there were "a number of interviewers who obtained highly unlikely or extreme values for social isolation across all of their interviews" (Paik and Sanchagrin 2013: 350). Ultimately, they conclude that the 2004 GSS design generated "fatigue effects among interviewers and that some interviewers were unskilled, unmotivated, or worse, intentionally avoided collecting egocentric network data" (354).

Few researchers consider the possibility that data are erroneous simply because surveys interviews are conducted by low-wage workers who find the job tedious and seek out shortcuts to recording real data. At the same time, discovering these data problems required more researcher effort and publications than it took to produce the original study. Few studies ever receive this level of scrutiny, which suggests that even serious flaws in data – when present – often go unnoticed.

EXHIBIT G: LATIN AMERICAN LAND REFORM AND DUPLICATED DATA

A study of land reform and inequality in Latin America published in the *Journal of Political Economy* was discovered by replicators to be mostly comprised of duplicate observations (Montero 2022, 2023; Kjelsrud, Kotsadam, and Rogeberg 2023). The study focused on radical reforms in El Salvador, where the military government expropriated many large private sector farms (haciendas) and reorganized them as worker-owned cooperatives. Montero (2022) found that in the long term, cooperatives had higher wages and less internal inequality than at haciendas. However, these results did not hold after correcting the data error. The author acknowledged the mistake and explained how the error occurred (and showed the erroneous code he used): The survey data were originally separated into multiple modules and had to be merged together by the analyst: "The identifiers I used to join the modules together were not unique in all modules. This mistakenly created incorrect, duplicated observations ... and I did not notice these duplicates" (Montero 2023: 1). It turns out that three quarters of the workers in the data were duplicates. One reason this was so fatal to the results is that inequality among duplicated observations is obviously zero! Moreover, after excluding the duplicates, many farms were left with data from only one worker – again rendering nonsensical estimates of inequality among workers at the farm. Montero (2023: 1), to his credit, concluded, "As correctly noted in Kjelsrud et al. (2023), once the data are corrected, there are no longer enough individuals ... to confidently examine differences in income and income inequality across properties." The risk of accidentally duplicating observations while merging data is a processing error that, we expect, few social scientists even realize could happen. This is a risk all scholars should be humble about, and we admire Montero for explaining to his readers exactly what went wrong.

CONCLUSIONS

Data preprocessing mistakes are a common cause of article retraction in social science. In (almost) all of these cases, the original authors conceded they made data processing choices that were wrong. These are not cases of reasonable debate in the face of analytical uncertainty, and their original methods – as acknowledged errors – do not belong in a proper multiverse analysis. Nevertheless, these cases should give pause to researchers who believe their data processing decisions are correct, and they highlight the centrality of data processing for getting the analysis right. Focusing more attention on processing decisions, as well as subjecting them to the logic and practice of multiverse analysis, is central to improving the rigor and reliability of social science research. At the minimum, greater attention to processing choices and their alternatives will help identify and avoid these types of outright errors.

It is rare that readers or reviewers engage with data processing decisions, but they should. Any number of troubling data processing details may be lurking in prestigious publications. This is part of the dark matter of research design – nearly invisible aspects of the research that shape the results (Leahey et al. 2003; Leahey 2008; Camerer 2022). These mistakes are easy to make, but they are also entirely avoidable and in a world of cumulative science should always be acknowledged, corrected, and explained when they are discovered. The reality, however, is that these kinds of errors are almost never discovered unless the authors make public their data and code. By the same token, a norm or obligation to make code and (when possible) data available to readers is a powerful incentive to make sure the code is clean and correct prior to publication – an essential guardrail for scientific practice that all social science journals should embrace.

When obvious errors in analysis are discovered, authors evidently have several types of responses available to them. Some try to reframe a devastating error as merely an issue of concern. This is an understandable instinct but something only the powerful can get away with. This approach also often comes with efforts to bury their mistake – and their astute critic – under new rounds of analysis that attempt to save their hypothesis. When journals publish "responses to critics," in our view, this should be limited to addressing the merits of the criticism and defending the models that were used and should not allow the original authors to take a fresh walk down the garden of forking paths.

A second approach of authors, when errors are discovered, is to acknowledge a mistake, and even willingly retract the article, but never explain what they did wrong or how the mistake happened. This is a great improvement over denial and obfuscation but still does a disservice to readers. If a finding turned out to be so wrong that it was corrected or retracted, the article can still make a contribution to understanding how mistakes are made. The authors, the peer reviewers, and the journals editors all believed the result enough to publish it. In our view, it is not enough to say "whoops, never mind" and delete the article. Cumulative science requires that we learn from these mistakes and improve our "mental models" of how errors in research happen, so that everyone gets better at catching these mistakes before publication. Without an accounting of how mistakes happen and get published, we never improve our defenses against bad science and set ourselves up to be fooled over and over again.

In this chapter, we've focused on examples of objective errors in data processing – where authors mistakenly conducted analyses that were different from what they intended. Social scientists need the humility that comes from seeing accomplished scholars make serious mistakes – because anyone can make these mistakes. However, modeling errors are far more general than accidental mistakes in data processing and coding. Modeling error occurs whenever an exact specification is not equal to the true (unknown) data generation process. It occurs whenever an assumption is incorrect in a way that influences the results. Because models are only approximations of how the world works, modeling error is ubiquitous and inherent in the scientific process – just like sampling error. Once we recognize it is easy to make mistakes in simply coding one's *intended* analysis, we need to step back and accept that our entire framework can be wrong. Science is a human enterprise where we muddle toward the truth as best we can using noisy data and simplifying assumptions. Projecting undue confidence in this process – refusing to acknowledge the many potential sources of modeling error – leaves a cloud of doubt over the merits of science in the twenty-first century.

13

Weighting the Multiverse

In this chapter, we tackle the tricky topic of weighting the multiverse. The default multiverse analysis uses uniform weighting, in which all plausible models receive the same weight. If a model is deemed "plausible," then it counts the same as any other plausible model. This default reflects the reality that when two different researchers analyze the same data, they essentially never use the same model – and factors like statistical training and research experience do not account for modeling differences (Silberzahn et al. 2018; Schweinsberg et al. 2021; Breznau et al. 2022). Methods and modeling assumptions are not simply random, but each author does take their own walk through a garden of forking paths. Within the bounds of a plausible model framework, there seems little consensus on which specification is best. Researchers working with data come to form strong model preferences, but they greatly overestimate the chance that another researcher will independently arrive at the same model.

Nevertheless, when estimating a large computational multiverse, it is inevitable that some models will be more plausible than others. Some scholars worry that multiverse methods may go too far in embracing model uncertainty (O'Brien 2018; Slez 2018; Western 2018; Robitzsch 2022; Cantone and Tomaselli 2023). Can we improve on uniform weighting and give some models more weight in the final analysis than others? In the process of estimating many diverse specifications, can we also down-weight the least-credible models and assign greater weight to the best specifications? Can we develop a credible metric of model plausibility, so that we weight models by the probability that they are true?

This chapter opens the door to more complex weighting methods and aims to clarify the major issues at stake. Scholars who criticize uniform weights and favor more "active" weighting point to Bayesian model averaging (BMA) as either inspiration or as an exact framework to adopt. We discuss the core principles of this method, show how it works in practice, and compare it to other reasonable and arguably better weighting approaches. Different weights can generate very different sets of results, becoming its own kind of researcher degree of freedom. BMA turns out to be an extreme form of weighting that comes very close to selecting one estimate – a method of model selection, rather than model robustness. Moreover, BMA does not take into account omitted variable bias, and it systematically favors biased models. Finally, there is an inherent trade-off between model transparency and model weighting, defined by the degree of nonuniform model weights. We show all these problems using an applied dataset on the effects of air pollution on student attention span. As we will see, weighting is a hard topic with no easy answers. We offer this chapter as an introduction to model weights and as a caution about the challenges of easily adopting model weights.

BAYESIAN MODEL AVERAGING

Bayesian statisticians were among the first scholars to embrace multi-model analysis, and multiverse analysis comes from this central lineage (Leamer 1983; Raftery 1995; Western 1996). At the same time, multiverse analysis is very different from BMA. Essentially, BMA estimates many different models and then weights those models by an exponential transformation of model fit (Raftery 1995). Consider a multiverse model space with j models. BMA generates weights ω_j for j models using the posterior probabilities, divided by a normalizing constant, given by the formula

$$\text{BMA weights:} \quad \omega_j = \frac{\exp(-0.5 \times \Delta \text{BIC}_j)}{\sum \exp(-0.5 \times \Delta \text{BIC}_j)} \quad (13.1)$$

The term ΔBIC_j is the Bayesian information criterion (BIC) for model j minus the maximum BIC in the model space. For readers less familiar with the BIC, it is very similar to the adjusted R^2: a measure of model fit, with some penalty for the numbers of variables in the model. The effect of ω_j is that estimates from models with a higher model fit are assigned higher weight while those from models with a lower R^2 are given a lower weight.

This approach seems reasonable on the surface, but it has two fundamental flaws. First, BMA assumes that model fit statistics like the R^2 or the BIC are indexes of model quality and measure proximity to the true model. However, when the goal is to understand and estimate unbiased relationships, they are not. Model fit statistics do not take into account simple criteria like the omitted variable bias formula (Belloni et al. 2014; Robitzsch 2022). Moreover, there are many types of "bad" controls that can improve model fit while adding bias to a treatment effect estimate. For these reasons, social scientists rarely assign much interest or attention to the fit statistics of a model.

Second, the BMA weight function exponentiates differences in model fit between specifications (ΔBIC_j). This blows up small differences in model fit to be very large differences in weight. Recall that, with exponentiation, a difference of 5 becomes $e^5 = 148$ and a difference of 10 becomes $e^{10} \cong 22,000$. BMA weights use a 0.5 constant to arbitrarily "slow down" the exponentiation of small differences in model fit, but it still comes out as an extreme weighting function. Most estimates are assigned roughly zero weight, while one model receives the overwhelming majority of the weight. As Yao, Simpson, and Gelman (2018: 2) note, BMA "will asymptotically select the single one model" that maximizes the fit statistic. In finite samples, BMA typically gives nonzero weight to a handful of models, as we will see. But to be clear, typically 95 percent or more of models are given zero weight and essentially deleted from the analysis. While BMA technically averages over all models, it does so only after weighting most of the candidate models to zero. This means that BMA is more a method for model *selection* rather than robustness. The BMA weighting method essentially rejects the mission of multiverse analysis, which is to show the range of estimates that can be plausibly supported by the data.

BMA is a formula for model weights that exists, and thus serves, as a starting point for further thinking about weights. Sensible alternatives also exist. For example, even if model fit is one's central criterion for weights, there is no need to exponentiate differences in model fit. Weights could be proportional to model fit, rather than exponentials of it. We will show the dramatic difference between weights that are proportional to model fit and weights that are exponentials of that fit. We also consider weights that incorporate the omitted variable bias – the double lasso weights. And finally, we consider weights based on multiverse model influence metrics.

BMA methods are built on criteria for predictive rather than inferential modeling. To understand and appreciate this problem, we need to take a significant detour into these rival worlds of analysis: prediction versus explanation.

PREDICTIVE MODELS, TREATMENT EFFECTS, AND THE RELEVANCE OF MODEL FIT

Regression models are "designed and estimated for a purpose," and that purpose should be central to how models are evaluated (Hansen 2005: 63). Multiverse analysis is developed to be used in a "treatment effects" analysis, where the goal is to understand the relationship between a focal variable (the treatment) and an outcome, using controls (and other aspects of specification) to improve the quality of inference.

Machine learning methods widely used today are generally designed and estimated for a different purpose: predictive modeling. The distinction between predictive modeling and inferential or "treatment effects" research has been a long-standing source of confusion. There is a common belief that efforts at "prediction" and "explanation" should converge on the same answers (Shmueli 2010; Hofman, Sharma, and Watts 2017). In practice, prediction and treatment effects explanation are different kinds of questions, and they do not converge on the same model nor answer each other's questions except under special conditions. Inferential analysis uses substantively different criteria for selecting variables and for evaluating models than does predictive analysis – the focus is on reducing omitted variable bias rather than on *predicting* per se.

Consider an analysis of an outcome of interest (y) focusing on a key treatment variable (x) and a set of possible controls (z_k):

$$y_i = \alpha + \beta x_i + \{\delta_1 z_{1i} + \delta_2 z_{2i} + \cdots + \delta_k z_{ki}\} + \varepsilon_i \qquad (13.2)$$

In predictive modeling, the goal is to find a prediction of the outcome $\hat{y}$ that is as close as possible to the true outcome, y. In treatment effects analysis, the goal is to find an estimated effect $\hat{\beta}$ that is as close as possible to the true treatment effect, β. Predictive analysts define bias as the difference $\hat{y} - y$. In contrast, bias in a treatment effects analysis is defined quite differently as the difference $\hat{\beta} - \beta$. Both approaches use the same basic regression model as a starting point, but they differ in the questions they are asking from it, their focal point of success, and how they select the set of z_k variables to address their respective concepts of bias.

Predictive analysis calls z_k "predictors" while the treatment effects analysis calls them "controls" or "potential confounders." Significant predictors are not the same as influential controls. Predictors are defined by the δ_k coefficients that show their correlation with y (and thus their contribution to the BIC or R^2 of Eq. [13.2]). In contrast, controls are defined by the omitted variable bias formula, which involves the δ_k coefficients from Eq. (13.2) as well as the relationships between the treatment variable x and the z_k controls (correlations which are not estimated in Eq. [13.2]). In other words, predictive analysts are concerned with how z_k changes the prediction $\hat{y}$. Treatment effects analysts are concerned with how z_k changes the parameter estimate $\hat{\beta}$. Treatment effects analysis is asking a more specific question and requires more information (at the minimum, the correlations between x and z_k) than predictive modeling. Often, the two approaches do not converge on the same model and do not give answers that the other finds useful.

In prediction problems, it makes sense to judge the quality of a model by a measure of fit, such as the BIC or the R^2, because these measures accurately reflect the purpose of a predictive model (to minimize the difference $\hat{y} - y$). (Note that BMA uses the BIC, which generally has a near-perfect correlation with the R^2 in linear models: The correlation between them in the pollution and learning data used in this chapter is -0.99. In short, the BIC can be understood as simply a rescaling of the R^2.) But the purpose of an inference analysis is to achieve conditional independence between treatment and control conditions, and success in meeting this goal is much more difficult to evaluate since the true control condition – the counterfactual – is inherently unobservable (Holland 1986). In the vast literature on this subject in econometrics, the model fit of a regression, by itself, is not how models are evaluated.

When considering a possible predictor variable, z, the only question the fit statistic considers is the strength of the (partial) correlation $r(z, y)$. Anything that is significantly correlated with y will generally improve the BIC, and any variable *not* significantly correlated with y will not. But in a treatment effects analysis, the correlation $r(z,y)$ is only half of the concern. A confounding variable, by definition, is not just correlated with y but also correlated with x. As shown in the traditional omitted variables bias formula, bias is driven by the product $r(z,y) \times r(z,x)$ (Greene 2012: 54–56).[1] In a treatment effects analysis, it is somewhat misleading to think of the "model fit" as the R^2 of Eq. (13.2). Our goal is to reduce omitted variable bias, not simply to predict y. The model we are trying to

---

[1] Note that when there are multiple omitted variables, and only some are included, bias is driven by a much more complex set of multiple correlations (see Clarke 2005).

fit involves both Eq. (13.2) and an additional "treatment equation." The treatment equation treats x as an outcome and estimates the relationship between x and each z_k control variable:

$$x_i = \mu + \{\theta_1 z_1 + \theta_2 z_{2i} + \cdots + \theta_k z_{ki}\} + \omega_i \qquad (13.3)$$

The model fit from this treatment equation can be denoted R_x^2, to distinguish from the model fit of the outcome Eq. (13.2), denoted R_y^2. When estimating treatment effects, both equations are important. In fact, ordinary least squares regression can be written as involving an outcome Eq. (13.2) and treatment Eq. (13.3) in a process that strips out the effect of z from both equations, and this better reflects the intuition of adjustment for omitted variable bias (Morgan and Winship 2015: 136–137). Methods like propensity score matching also make explicit that inference involves two separate equations: one for the outcome and one for the treatment.

To make the distinction between prediction and treatment effects more intuitive, consider an analysis of migration: Why do people move? Some explanations focus on life-course events like high school or college graduation, changing jobs, and having children. Other explanations highlight place-based push and pull factors like urban amenities, school quality, local tax rates, and the location of friends and family. Now consider a predictive model which asks: Which households are most likely to move? The aforementioned explanatory factors *might* be useful variables. But especially powerful predictor variables would be renting a moving truck, purchasing a lot of boxes, and filing a change-of-address form with the post office. These variables give no insight into why people move but are almost guaranteed markers that a move will happen. For inferential research, a variable like "rented a moving truck" should never be included in an explanatory model: It is an endogenous variable that is caused by the decision to move, not an exogenous determinant or explanation of migration. Predictive models, in contrast, do not care about these distinctions. Indeed, models that try to simply predict migration will include as many endogenous predictors as possible.

This kind of predictive modeling is very common in the business sector. Often analyses focus on variables that give accurate predictions without any meaningful explanatory value. The retail chain Target developed a "pregnancy prediction" model to help it identify expecting mothers (Duhigg 2012). Parents with new babies are especially valuable customers, as they have a lot of expenses and are often too busy to shop around for the best deals. Sending tailored advertising, incentives, and offers to pregnant women is a key marketing objective – but how can they tell which women are pregnant? Target's analytics division used its massive in-house data to build a predictive model: Individual purchases are tracked via customer ID numbers, and customers who sign up for the baby shower registry provide a test sample of pregnant moms. Target analyzed how shopping habits evolved as women in the baby shower registry approached their due date: Which consumer purchases are the strongest early predictors of pregnancy? Simple examples are increased spending on unscented lotion and vitamin supplements like magnesium and zinc; Target found twenty-five products that were strong pregnancy predictors. Applying the model to all purchases generates a list of tens of thousands of customers at any moment who are likely pregnant. Accuracy in predicting pregnancy, however, can have almost nothing to do with social science theories of fertility and childbearing. Indeed, the term prediction itself is perhaps a misnomer, and data science often simply uses the term "classification": The task is trying to tell who is already pregnant, rather than predict who will be in the future. Understanding the markers of pregnancy is a form of social knowledge, but that is very different from *explaining* why some women, but not others, are having children.

Variables that matter for explanation can be very different than those that matter the most for prediction or classification. Newer methods have attempted a blending of methods for prediction and explanation, known as the double lasso (LASSO stands for least absolute shrinkage and selection operator, but is no longer capitalized).

MODEL FIT AND THE DOUBLE LASSO

The double lasso was introduced by Belloni et al. (2014) as a model selection algorithm designed for treatment effects analysis when there are many possible controls. In this chapter, we explain the method in simple, intuitive terms and refer to the original articles for more detailed accounts (Urminsky et al. 2016: Chernozhukov et al. 2018). The algorithm can be produced in three steps: (1) Select controls that best predict the outcome y_i by optimizing R_y^2; (2) select controls that best predict the treatment variable x_i by optimizing R_x^2; and then (3) estimate the treatment effect of x_i on y_i (i.e., β) using all the controls selected in the two variable selection steps.

If one uses R_y^2 alone to assign weights in a multiverse, it excludes a class of controls that matter for omitted variable bias: controls that have a low correlation with y but a high correlation with x. This is often a serious error; variables with a low correlation with y can still cause substantial bias in the parameter estimate if they are strongly correlated with x. Intuitively, rather than focusing on the R_y^2 (or, equivalently, the BIC_y) we evaluate how well a set of controls address omitted variable bias using the metric $R_x^2 + R_y^2$. These are the model fit statistics from *both* the outcome equation and the treatment equation.

APPLIED DATASET: AIR POLLUTION AND STUDENT ATTENTION IN CLASS

To illustrate these metrics, we use a dataset on over 1,000 primary school children attending forty-nine schools with differing degrees of ambient air pollution (Sunyer et al. 2017).[2] Different schools and classrooms, due to their location and proximity to dense traffic, recorded a wide range of environmental air pollution (nitrogen dioxide levels). Urban air pollution is known to affect respiratory health and may also have behavioral and developmental effects on children. The study measured whether pollution levels influenced cognitive attention span. The outcome variable comes from a computer-based test designed to measure student attention to tasks; very low performance could be indicative of attention deficit disorder.

Table 13.1 shows the single and double lasso selection methods. Column 1 shows the outcome equation used by both. All controls are regressed against the outcome variable (student reaction time). The coefficients in this model capture the partial correlations $r(z,y)$ but not the correlations $r(z,x)$ and therefore reflect only one half of the omitted variable bias formula. The single lasso selects all controls that are significant in the outcome equation, yielding an inference equation (column 2) with four controls. The single lasso estimate is 1.6, with a standard error of 0.4: Air pollution leads to significantly higher student reaction time, meaning poorer student attention. As we will see, BMA produces exactly the same estimate as the single lasso and uses the same criteria for selecting controls.

Next, we move to the double lasso. Column 3 shows the treatment equation, in which the controls are regressed against the treatment variable (pollution), which captures the partial correlations $r(z,x)$. As we

---

[2] The replication package for the analysis presented in this chapter is available at https://osf.io/45ft2/files/osfstorage.

TABLE 13.1 *Single and double lasso demonstration*

	(1) Outcome equation	(2) Single lasso inference equation	(3) Treatment equation	(4) Double lasso inference equation
Pollution (treatment variable)	n/a	1.6*** (0.4)	n/a	2.2*** (0.5)
Age (years)	−23.6* (11.2)	−23.2* (11.0)	1.0 (0.7)	−25.8* (11.1)
Age started school	5.6 (3.1)		−0.1 (0.2)	
Home SEI	−57.1* (22.3)	−33.6 (20.1)	−3.4* (1.4)	−48.1* (21.7)
Green home	27.7 (57.4)		−45.9*** (3.5)	123.3* (60.3)
School noise levels	0.9 (1.0)		0.8*** (0.1)	−0.9 (1.0)
School SEI	29.6 (21.1)		8.0*** (1.3)	8.3 (21.2)
Number of older siblings	−1.5 (6.7)		−0.6 (0.4)	
Number of younger siblings	10.5 (6.5)		−0.6 (0.4)	
Female	52.4*** (8.0)	52.9*** (7.9)	0.3 (0.5)	53.5*** (7.9)
Grade (ref. = 2nd)				
3rd	−64.0*** (15.0)	−64.7*** (14.7)	0.7 (0.9)	−62.1*** (14.7)
4th	−92.0*** (25.3)	−91.8*** (24.8)	−0.6 (1.6)	−87.8*** (24.9)
Low birth weight	−16.8 (14.5)		0.1 (0.9)	
Parents smoke	−16.7 (20.7)		1.2 (1.3)	
Constant	933.1***	945.0***	−1.4	963.8***
R^2	0.203	0.206	0.337	0.210

Notes: *$p < 0.05$, **$p < 0.01$, ***$p < 0.001$. N = 1,084. SEI = socio-economic index. "Green home" is a measure of green space near the child's home.

can see, a very different set of controls are significant in the treatment equation compared to the outcome equation. Only one variable, home SEI, is significant in both. Three variables that are significant for the outcome (age, gender, and grade level) are not significantly associated with the treatment variable. And three variables significant in the treatment equation (green space near home, school noise levels, and school SEI) are not significantly correlated with the outcome. Thus, the outcome equation alone is insufficient to capture the correlations $r(z,y) \times r(z,x)$ that are needed for the omitted variable bias formula. Thus, the double lasso selects the *union* of controls that are significant in *either* the outcome or the treatment equation. The double lasso inference equation includes seven controls (four from the outcome equation and an additional three from the treatment equation). The double lasso estimate is 2.2 – about 35 percent larger than in the single lasso. In short, the double lasso selects different controls and obtains a different estimate than the single lasso.

The double lasso still relies on modeling assumptions to claim it is the best model or yields an estimate equal to the true population parameter. It relies on the assumption that all these control variables are confounders rather than mediators, colliders, or intermediate outcomes. It also requires an assumption that there are no other omitted variables that belong in the models – that is, that, if measured, would be selected by the double lasso criteria. If those assumptions hold, we can say the double lasso estimate (2.2) is approximately correct and the single lasso estimate of 1.6 suffers omitted variable bias.

One might be tempted to ask why any controls are being dropped by these selection algorithms. Why not just include everything? By the criteria of omitted variable bias, it would be better to include all these controls than to use the single lasso. Though not reported in Table 13.1, the "full" model that includes all controls gives an estimate of 2.2 – exactly the same as the double lasso. So, the short answer is that the double lasso has selected all the controls that matter for reducing omitted variable bias. The second answer is that the double lasso was developed for use with high-dimensional data: cases when there are more potential control variables than observations and thus not possible to estimate a model that includes all controls (Belloni et al. 2014). Suppose there are 1,000 observations, but 10,000 possible Z controls (some datasets have this structure). The double lasso provides an exploratory analysis of which controls are most likely to belong in the model, according to the omitted variable bias criteria. While "variable selection methods are no substitute for thinking" about the causal relationships between the variables, the double lasso "can provide an empirical basis for determining which variables to think hard about" (Urminsky et al. 2016: 18). The single lasso – like BMA – systematically misses some of those variables that deserve careful attention.

TABLE 13.2 *Regression models of student reaction time on in-school air pollution, with three types of model weights*

	(1)	(2)	(3)	(4)	(5)	(6)	(7)	(8)
NO_2 level	1.7***	1.6***	1.7***	1.6***	2.1***	2.0***	2.1***	2.0***
	(0.4)	(0.4)	(0.4)	(0.4)	(0.5)	(0.5)	(0.4)	(0.4)
Home SEI		−38.3		−33.6		−49.8*		−44.1*
		(20.2)		(20.1)		(20.7)		(20.6)
Grade (ref.: 2nd)								
3rd			−66.0***	−64.7***			−64.7***	−62.7***
			(14.7)	(14.7)			(14.7)	(14.7)
4th			−94.5***	−91.8***			−93.2***	−89.2***
			(24.8)	(24.8)			(24.8)	(24.8)
Green home					115.6*	148.2*	103.4	132.6*
					(58.5)	(60.0)	(58.2)	(59.6)
R^2	0.189	0.191	0.203	0.206	0.191	0.196	0.206	0.209
BIC	13,673	13,676	13,667	13,671	13,676	13,677	13,671	13,673
R^2x	0.002	0.029	0.007	0.032	0.209	0.212	0.211	0.213
$R^2x + R^2y$	0.191	0.220	0.210	0.238	0.401	0.407	0.417	0.422
Weighting strategies								
Uniform weights	0.125	0.125	0.125	0.125	0.125	0.125	0.125	0.125
R^2 weights, proportional	0.118	0.120	0.128	0.129	0.120	0.123	0.129	0.131
BMA weights	0.032	0.006	0.722	0.089	0.007	0.004	0.107	0.032
Double lasso weights	0.076	0.088	0.084	0.095	0.160	0.163	0.166	0.169
Influence weights	0.000	0.039	0.011	0.050	0.200	0.239	0.211	0.250

Notes: *$p < 0.05$, **$p < 0.01$, ***$p < 0.001$. $N = 1,084$. All models control for age and sex. "Green home" is a measure of green space near the child's home. Data from Sunyer et al. (2017).

MODEL ROBUSTNESS VERSUS MODEL SELECTION

A further problem with BMA is that it works primarily as a model selection procedure. It is called model "averaging," but in practice only a tiny fraction of the multiverse is assigned nonzero weight; a handful of models receive nearly all of the weight, while other models are essentially deleted. This kind of weighting scheme bypasses the question of model robustness and engages in biased model selection. The goal of multiverse analysis is for authors to defend their preferred model *in full light of what other reasonable estimates can be found in the data*. It is not a method for choosing a preferred model.

We illustrate how the BMA weights work with a small number of models: eight specifications examining the pollution and student learning data. After showing how specific models are weighted using different methods, we scale this up to the full multiverse. For now, let us think about a handful of simplified models and the different ways they could be weighted.

Table 13.2 shows a small multiverse of eight models estimating how air pollution affects student reaction time. The model set shows all combinations of three controls: grade level, home SEI, and a measure of green space near the child's home. The bottom half of the table shows several methods of weighting the models. First, consider uniform weights: Each of the eight models receives 1/8 = 12.5 percent of the weight. The next row uses weights proportional to the R_y^2; since the fit of these models are fairly similar – ranging from 0.189 to 0.209 – the proportional model fit weights range from 11.8 to 13.1 percent – all very similar to uniform weights. Weighting simply by model fit, without exponentiating fit statistics, makes very little difference for the modeling distribution. BMA weights, in contrast, dramatically favor a single model, with Model 3 receiving 72 percent of the weight.

Double lasso weights, in general, favor any model that includes home greenness, which is significantly correlated with the treatment variable.

INFLUENCE WEIGHTING

Another proposal for weighting the multiverse, suggested by Muñoz and Young (2018b), is called *influence weighting*. Rather than weighting based on predictive model fit, models receive weight when they include control variables (or other model inputs) that are highly influential for the results. The intuition is that *noninfluential* variables or inputs do not matter for the parameter estimate and therefore can be included or excluded with little harm. However, *influential controls* have important consequences for the results and therefore deserve the most analytical attention. Specifications that *exclude* influential controls should not be allowed to carry too much weight, unless the exclusion has already been analytically justified. The main motivation of influence weighting was the concern that BMA and R_y^2 methods systematically exclude certain kinds of influential variables (Belloni et al. 2014). As we showed in Chapter 6, influence and correlation with y are different matters – some of the strongest predictors of y are not influential controls, and some of the most influential controls are not strong predictors of y.

With influence weighting, the weights are proportional to the sum of absolute influence score of each variable included in a model. In a sense, models are evaluated and weighted based on how well they incorporate influential control variables. Influence scores come from a meta-regression of estimated coefficients for the variable of interest across all specifications in the model space. From Chapter 5, recall the influence regression is

$$b_j = \alpha + \theta_1 D_{1j} + \theta_2 D_{2j} + \cdots + \theta_P D_{Pj} + \varepsilon_j \qquad (13.4)$$

in which b_j is the regression estimate from the j-th model. The influence coefficient θ_1 shows the expected change in the coefficient of interest (b_j) if the model ingredient corresponding to D_1 is used in the j-th model.

For each specification, Mj, the model weight is the sum of the absolute influence score, $\sum_P^1 |\theta_p D_{pj}|$, divided by the sum of the absolute scores for all models. If control variable D_1 is included in a specification, then $D_{1j} = 1$, and the absolute value of its associated influence statistic θ_1 is included in the model weight. Otherwise, $D_{1j} = 0$, and its influence score is excluded from the weight. Models with more of the influential controls will have higher weights, and models omitting those controls will have lower weights.

$$\text{Influence weights}: \qquad \theta_j = \frac{\sum_P^1 |\theta_p D_{pj}|}{\sum_j^1 \sum_P^1 |\theta_p D_{pj}|} \qquad (13.5)$$

The last row in Table 13.2 shows the influence weights for the eight models of the pollution effect on student reaction time. In this case, models are weighted by whether they include the influential control variable "green near home." This variable has only a modest effect on student reaction time – its impact on R^2 is trivial, but it has a big influence on the pollution effect. The influence weights give the four models that include this influential control between 20 percent and 25 percent of the weight, and the four models that don't include it get 5 percent or less.

Our main goal with this simplified example has been to illustrate how different approaches generate very different model weights. Weighting multiverse estimates has intuitive appeal, but different weighting methods can generate very different results. Weighting itself becomes a powerful researcher degree of freedom. If these model weights are used to determine what estimates are reported to readers, different methods can reveal very different information. Applied researchers should proceed very cautiously with model weights and be very clear to readers what, if any, nonuniform weights they have used.

WEIGHTING THE FULL MODELING DISTRIBUTION

Now we apply these weighting methods to the full empirical distributions from the pollution data. Figure 13.1 shows the weighted distributions. Panel A shows uniform weights; this is simply the unweighted modeling distribution of 4,096 models with every combination of the twelve controls. Panel B shows the BMA weights compared to the uniform distribution. BMA gives one model 36.5 percent of the weight, and then gives seventeen other models between 1 percent and 7.5 percent. (BMA's "winning" estimate is 1.63, compared to the single lasso estimate of 1.61.) This graph makes clear the transparency versus selection tradeoff: Does one desire an algorithm to select a single result or a framework for showing what estimates the data can support?

The next three panels show the proportional weights – first the R^2 weights, then the double lasso weights, and finally the influence weights. These offer "nudged" distributions that are close to the uniform distribution; neither the raw model fit statistics (R^2 or BIC) nor the influence scores of models are different enough across specifications to dramatically shift the uniform distribution. All sets of proportional weights shift the distribution toward the higher estimates of the pollution effect. They do not eliminate the range of possible estimates, but smaller results are down-weighted for failing to include the strongest predictors of y (R^2 weights), x (double lasso weights), or the most influential controls (influence weights). While the exponential weights transform the distribution into a spike around basically one result, these proportional weights "nudge" the distribution. The double lasso and the influence weights in this empirical case turn out nearly identical.

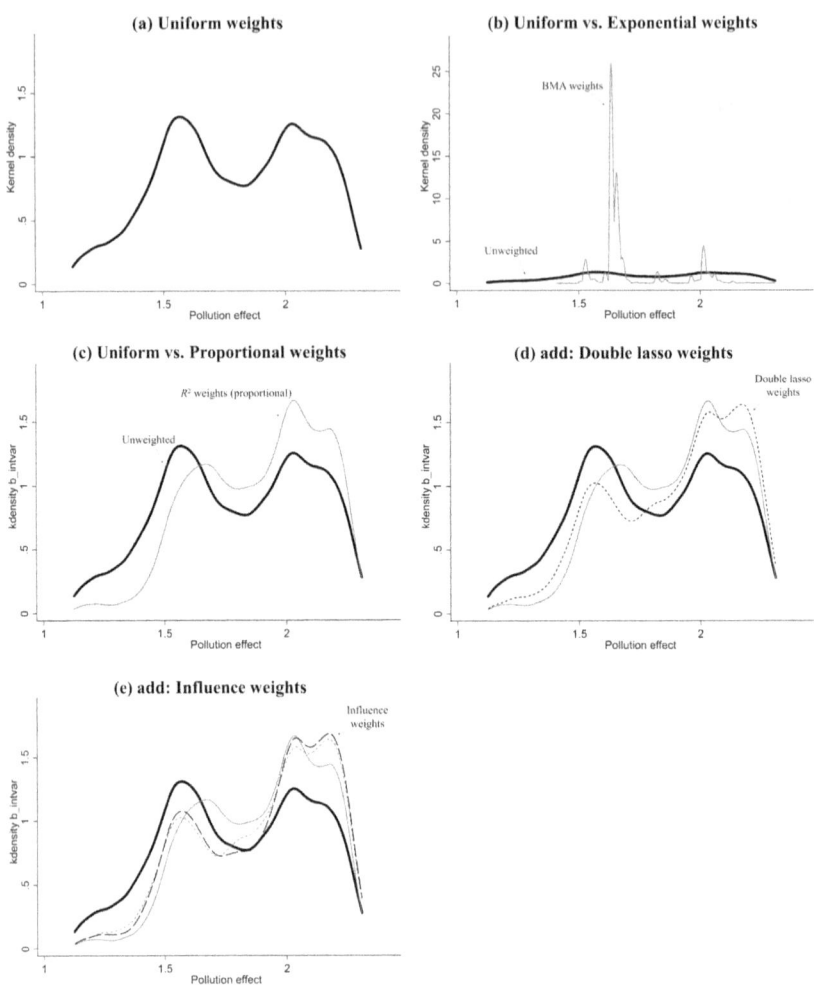

FIGURE 13.1 Weighted modeling distributions, air pollution effect on student reaction time
Note: Estimates from 4,096 model specifications. Data from Sunyer et al. (2017).

These different modeling distributions do not say which estimate is closest to the truth. All of these weighting methods still rely on untested assumptions that there are no bad controls in the model space – no endogenous, posttreatment, or collider variables. They all assume there are no additional omitted variables – unknown unknowns – that could bias a model in unexpected ways. These are not assumptions that should be made without careful consideration. Posttreatment controls, for example, tend to be very influential and can introduce large degrees of bias (Rosenbaum 1984; King 1991; Gelman and Hill 2006; Montgomery et al. 2018; Elwert and Winship 2014).

The BMA graph issues a confident conclusion, but that conclusion is misleading and based simply on exponentiating the model fit. The R^2 has *something* to do with the truth of a model; it is one element of model truth but ignores other, equally important, aspects of a model that matter for inference. BMA weights are so extreme that they almost entirely undo the transparency of a multiverse analysis. Rather than relying on the BMA method, researchers could simply report the model with the highest R^2 if they think that is important for readers. However, there is nothing Bayesian about favoring the model with the highest R^2 or the smallest BIC: Such an approach ignores the omitted variable bias formula. Better practice is to simply be clear about which model an analyst prefers on the basis of prior theory.

CONCLUSIONS

Developing credible, nonuniform weights for the multiverse is a difficult challenge. To be credible, the weights need to reflect the chance that the models are true. But in a treatment effects scenario, there is no statistic that can be calculated from the data themselves that would provide this information. For example, correlations do not distinguish between confounder, mediator, and collider variables. The sorts of issues that affect plausibility require theory and judgment. O'Brien (2018: 7) suggests that the models might be weighted by the "proportion of diverse social scientists who think that a particular independent variable should be included in a model." This is a useful way to think about weights in the multiverse: Ideally, weights would reflect the degree of scientific consensus around the best way to analyze the empirical question at hand. In practice, this information is not readily available. We consider several practical methods for developing weights: BMA, proportional R^2 weights, double lasso weights, and influence weights. If a researcher favors nonuniform weights, we recommend either the double lasso or the influence weights. They gently weight the results, favoring models using omitted variable bias criteria. BMA is systematically biased for inference (as are the R^2 weights) and should not be used.

We also stress again that multiverse analysis is not intended to be used as a model selection procedure. Authors use theory and existing evidence for model selection, and we are not attempting to turn this task over to an algorithm. The mean of the modeling distribution does not need to represent the "best" estimate. Many weighting schemes seem designed to make the mean match the most plausible estimate, but this is not necessary. Analysts should select the best estimate using their own judgment and expertise, guided by prior research and theory, just as they have always done. In choosing that preferred estimate, they can favor an estimate from any part of the modeling distribution they think is most defensible. The multiverse analysis is a separate and different task, where the analyst shows how the preferred estimate compares to the rest of the modeling distribution. If the author has selected an extreme tail estimate, it does not mean that the estimate is wrong. It simply means that they have to work hard to convince the reader that their estimate is the best one. Multiverse analysis does not simplify life for researchers: It asks them to defend their preferred model in light of what other plausible models show.

We also emphasize that analysts have a lot of tools to craft a sensible modeling distribution without needing to rely on any weighting scheme. We have encouraged users to show the full range of modeling assumptions that might be defended by serious scholars, even if they do not favor those assumptions themselves. But one could easily show both the full distribution and a more curated distribution of models that they themselves find most defensible. For instance, in the Regnerus example that we discussed at length in Chapter 11, we showed the full range of plausible estimates of the lesbian, gay, bisexual, and transgender (LGBT) parenting effect and then we showed two smaller distributions, one based on Regnerus's conceptualization of family structure and one based on Rosenfeld's (Figure 11.3). These authors have different ideas about how to measure an LGBT effect, and the modeling distribution looks very different based on whose assumptions you believe. We should not allow generic and poorly understood weighting algorithms to overshadow or replace detailed evaluation of methods. It is crucial to be transparent about how varying assumptions can lead to differing results, clarifying that analysts are engaged in a debate about methods rather than providing definitive results.

We need to guard against naive enthusiasm for more complex methods (Glaeser 2008). Uniform weighting of the multiverse can strike some readers as too simple. But weighting models involves a complex trade-off between transparency and model selection. Many weighting schemes involve opaque weights that are inconsistent with the goals of inference, much less the goals of multiverse analysis. We have illustrated the problems with BMA weights and suggested a better method (influence weighting) that preserves the goals of inference but still serves to invoke, rather than relax, modeling assumptions. We are left with a strong warning that complex weighting schemes based on poorly understood criteria do not contribute to transparency or the goal of robust results. Methods which simply show the available estimates should not be discounted because they are easy to understand. As one philosopher put it, sometimes we can see a lot just by looking.

All that said, we recognize that in some empirical cases weighting the multiverse may be useful and instructive. We offer the following guidance on the use of weights. First, in a treatment effects framework, analysts should weight by either the double lasso or the influence scores, not by model fit, as these methods more accurately reflect the aims of a causal model. Second, for the purpose of a robustness analysis, we encourage analysts to weight the models proportionally, not exponentially, and this maintains transparency about the full range of plausible estimates. Finally, we encourage those who use weights to show readers both the weighted and uniform distributions.

14

Conclusion

Reliance on single-path analysis, where studies provide one empirical estimate and ignore alternative analytical approaches, is an outdated approach to social science that is rapidly losing credibility. Today's challenge is coming to terms with methodological abundance and computational power. With thousands of statistical models executable in seconds, researchers face a vast array of methodological choices including control variables, estimation techniques, functional form assumptions and data preprocessing strategies. While classical statistical theory assumes that a single "true model" is known prior to data analysis, in practice, researchers have only a faint idea of what the true model might entail.

Selective reporting of single-path estimates creates a profound problem of asymmetric information: Analysts know much more about the sensitivity and stability of the results than do readers. This basic asymmetry is known and undermines confidence in published results. We know that authors' analytic choices can have a big influence on the results of empirical studies, but readers cannot easily quantify that influence. A continual question is: "How would the results change if someone else (such as a critic) did the analysis?" The current norm of reporting a handful of ad hoc robustness checks is weakly informative and lags far behind the reality of modern computational power.

Since its earliest origins, science has sought to overcome the biases of its human practitioners – to have guardrails that prevent bias and allow the evidence to shine brighter than any ideology. Even the best of us are susceptible to motivated reasoning and the lure of a model that shows an exciting result. Multiverse analysis presents a way forward, with a rigorous and transparent method to address the problems of model uncertainty and asymmetric information. It gives researchers a tool to backtrack along the garden of forking paths and to systematically investigate and present to their readers the range of estimates that is available from plausible models. Multiverse analysis is a process for acknowledging that other reasonable modeling decisions could have been made and for making the impact of one's own decisions transparent.

THE MULTIVERSE ALGORITHM

In Chapter 4, we explained the basic process for conducting a multiverse analysis. We drew a conceptual analogy between the sampling distribution and the modeling distribution: The sampling distribution shows how an estimate varies in repeated sampling; the modeling distribution shows how the estimate varies in repeated modeling. Analysts have been intensely focused for over a century on quantifying and reporting the level uncertainty stemming from sampling, but a single-minded focus on sampling uncertainty ignores the second fundamental source of uncertainty: modeling uncertainty. A solid body of evidence from meta-analysis and many-analysts studies suggests that confidence intervals are a very poor guide to what future studies will find. In every empirical research area that we examined, the average reported standard error was smaller than actual variation across studies, and in most cases it was substantially smaller. It is clear that uncertainty about model specification is no less fundamental than uncertainty about sample data.

We showed some simple tools for incorporating measures of model uncertainty into an analysis. A model space is defined by identifying a set of plausible modeling options and estimating all combinations of those options. The distribution of estimates from that set of models can then be reported. We showed how to calculate the modeling standard error, as well as a total standard error that incorporates both modeling and sampling uncertainty. We also suggested simple "vote count" measures – the percentage of estimates that are positive/negative and the significance rate – that can aid in interpreting the distribution of results.

THE CONTROL VARIABLE MULTIVERSE

In Chapter 5, we took a deep dive into one foundational type of multiverse analysis: the control variable multiverse. It has become standard practice to include long lists of control variables in statistical models, but there are myriad ways that the overuse of controls can harm an analysis.

We showed examples of common types of bad controls – mediators, colliders, proxies – and we showed that even when there's nothing inherently bad about any particular control, analysts who look at many combinations of controls before selecting a final set risk modeling noise in the data. Telling the difference between good and bad controls is a difficult task, requiring careful scrutiny and well-honed judgment. Every control in a model deserves skepticism and requires substantive justification.

Multiverse analysis allows readers to see for themselves how the results would change if the author had used a different set of controls. Often the multiverse analysis will reveal that a control doesn't have much impact on the results one way or the other, and neither analyst nor reader need waste much time deliberating over its inclusion. Other times a result is highly sensitive to the inclusion of a particular control, and the control variable multiverse will draw attention to those cases and make it incumbent on the author to justify the variable's inclusion (or exclusion) from the model.

Sometimes control variables are regarded as necessary for obtaining a correct specification. When a control variable is well established in the existing literature, such that readers and scholars alike are already convinced the variable belongs in the model, it need not be subject to multiverse testing. Indeed, sometimes certain controls are necessary for defining the theoretic estimand. But any such control should be carefully justified and grounded in theory or prior research, ideally using a causal diagram showing the assumed relationships between the control, the treatment, and the outcome. To repeat our advice from Chapter 3: Justify it, or multiverse it.

INFLUENCE ANALYSIS

Chapter 6 described the second step in a multiverse analysis: the influence analysis. Influence analysis allows researchers to dig deeper into their model specifications and observe the influence of each model assumption on the key result. In standard regression tables, the influence of modeling decisions on the coefficient of interest is either opaque or completely unknown. For instance, regression tables show the effects that the control variables have on the outcome variable but not how the inclusion of each control influences the main result (the estimated effect of x on y). The statistical significance of control variables gives limited indication of their influence: In our empirical applications, the most significant controls sometimes have little or no influence on the coefficient of interest, and the nonsignificant and seemingly "unimportant" controls can have the strongest influence. An influence analysis makes it clear which controls (or other aspects of model specification) are critical to the results.

When a result is not fully robust, influence analysis provides methodological explanations for the failure of robustness. Sometimes, it may reveal that many arbitrary assumptions affect the results and that no credible conclusion is available. Other times, a conclusion may hinge on one or two important methodological decisions that need to be carefully justified. Here it can be helpful to think about the methodological scope conditions of a finding. In exposing these critical assumptions, the influence analysis can guide further deliberation and research about which assumptions are most credible.

Even when a result is robust, influence analysis plays an important role. The conclusion of a multiverse analysis is never infinite robustness but rather robustness to a specific set of factors. Influence analysis makes clear which parts of an analysis are being tested and highlights the methodological bounds of the conclusion.

FUNCTIONAL FORM ASSUMPTIONS

In Chapter 9, we extended the multiverse further by incorporating alternative functional form assumptions: ways of linking the left- and the right-hand sides of the model. Just as there are often many possible control variables, there are usually an abundance of estimation commands and strategies one could reasonably use in any particular study, such as ordinary least squares (OLS), logit, or matching. In our empirical examples, we found that the average estimate was often very similar across different functional forms, with little systematic shifting of the entire modeling distribution. Yet we also found that different functional form assumptions can greatly affect the stability or variance of the modeling distribution. In our applied cases, two forms of matching provided a much wider range of possible results than OLS or logit. In our results, none of the functional forms we considered improved on the estimate stability of linear regression: Alternatives like logit and Poisson could at best match the stability of OLS, but they did not improve it. We also introduced a method of estimand-consistent robustness testing, by transforming coefficients from different model types (such as OLS and logit) onto the same scale prior to comparing results.

DATA PROCESSING

Raw data typically require a great deal of cleaning, coding, and categorizing of variables and observations, and vague standards for this data preprocessing mean it can be troublingly ad hoc, with much temptation to "improve" one's preferred result. Data processing involves substantial uncertainty, and there are few conventional norms or standards of practice. An author's choices are often "invisible" – rarely do readers know exactly what was done. Indeed, processing requires strong familiarity with both the subject area and the dataset, and this kind of tacit knowledge is difficult to convey in the limited space of the typical data section in a journal article. Furthermore, data processing is often not very analytically interesting, and decisions rarely attract much interest or critical engagement from reviewers, editors, or readers.

But preprocessing decisions can influence the results just as much as the choice of control variables or assumptions about functional form. In Chapter 9, we discussed three types of preprocessing decisions that analysts routinely face: how to code and classify variables, whether or not to use sampling weights, and how to treat outliers. We showed with empirical examples how these sorts of decisions can have a critical impact on the results of an analysis and the importance of subjecting them to multiverse analysis.

EMPIRICAL EXAMPLES

In Chapter 3, we presented a multiverse analysis of the impact of a hurricane's name on its death toll. The authors of the original study reported that storms with female names had higher death tolls, in theory because these storms seemed to local residents to be less threatening and thus leading to fewer precautions. However, the multiverse analysis showed this result depends on a knife-edge specification and is supported by less than one in a hundred plausible models. The same is true of Durante, Rae, and Griskevicius's (2013) analysis of how women's ovulatory cycle affects their political beliefs, which we presented in Chapter 10. The authors reported that women at their peak monthly fertility become more religious, more conservative, and more republican – but only if they are in committed relationships. The multiverse analysis showed that only 4 percent of plausible models were consistent with that claim.

On the other hand, multiverse analysis also often shows a finding to be highly robust to a set of modeling options, as was the case in our analysis of the effect of race on mortgage lending. We did not show many examples of strong robustness, because they do not tend to make very interesting case studies: When results are highly robust, there is not much more to say. But our testing across different datasets suggests that a high degree of robustness to many modeling assumptions is not uncommon.

Somewhere in between these two extremes lie those findings with limited or mixed robustness, where one or two critical modeling judgments must be made in order to draw conclusions. One example is our analysis of gender and mortgage lending, where we found the result to depend critically on the inclusion of two specific control variables. The identification of those two variables led to informative follow-up analyses that ultimately gave a better understanding of the phenomenon. Another case with mixed results was the multiverse analysis of Regnerus's (2012a) study of the effects of same-sex parenting, which we discussed at length in Chapter 11. Given the amount of criticism that the study drew from other scholars, we expected this to be another knife-edge specification that was highly dependent on a particular set of modeling assumptions. In fact, the basic result was fairly robust – 76 percent of models had the same basic finding as what Regnerus reported: a negative and significant effect of same-sex parenting on the outcomes of adult children. Nevertheless, Regnerus's estimate was at the tail end of the modeling distribution and only 5 percent of the models had a result as large as what he reported. Most of the uncertainty is about the magnitude of the estimated relationship. The influence analysis revealed a critical assumption – the measurement of family structure – that largely determined whether the lesbian, gay, bisexual, transgender parenting effect was very large or more modest in size. We found that many of the problems with the analysis that critics pointed out did not end up having much effect on the key result; moreover, one factor that did have a fairly big impact (whether or not to use sampling weights) was not even questioned by Regnerus or his critics and was only revealed through routine inclusion of this modeling option in the multiverse. Overall, we find that the Regnerus result is "in the data" with remaining uncertainty about its magnitude. Our main reservations about the study, at this point, are more about the underlying data quality than the modeling assumptions. This is a clear example of how the multiverse influence analysis can help set aside issues that do not really affect the results and focus future efforts and scrutiny on assumptions that matter.

FINAL THOUGHTS

We believe that, in the future, multiverse analysis will be as important as statistical significance in the evaluation of empirical results, and reporting extensive and systematic robustness tests will be an important signal of research quality. In a world with growing computational power and increasingly broad menus of statistical techniques, multiverse analysis can make research results more compelling and less dependent on idiosyncratic assumptions. In the process, this will help restore trust in – and the trustworthiness of – published findings.

There is room for disagreement about the best form for a multiverse analysis to take and how exactly it should be implemented. The fundamental principle is that there should be greater transparency about how analytical choices affect the results. If a result depends on a very specific constellation of controls or other modeling decisions, this should be made clear to the reader, and it is incumbent on the author to make the case that the specific model specification is the most theoretically sound – in full view of what other estimates are possible.

Multiverse analysis simulates the process of repeated study and brings into the analysis what skeptical replicators might find. This, in turn, points to a key reason why authors tend to avoid this kind of robustness testing: there is a strong possibility that some models will have the "wrong" sign or fail to achieve significance. Authors prefer to report – and reviewers and readers often prefer to see – a wall of confirming evidence for a hypothesis that suppresses any doubts, ambiguities, or inconsistencies in the results. But this is bad practice. Along with rigorous multiverse analysis, we need greater tolerance for "imperfect stories" and more focus on the weight of the evidence. It is not "embarrassing" to show that an analysis depends on certain assumptions. On the contrary, social scientists should be open and transparent about what assumptions are necessary for their conclusions. Embracing transparency and showing what estimates are available – as well as which aspects of model specification affect the results – are central to thinking through the challenges of inference in regression analysis.

Similarly, we encourage a tone of modesty in conclusions about the robustness of research results. Empirical conclusions are provisional in nature because they depend on assumptions that may be called into question in the future (Heckman 2005). Multiverse analysis is similarly provisional. The potential model space is open-ended; new additions can always be considered. Researchers should aim for a multiverse analysis that is developmental and compelling but should accept that it will never be definitively complete. We should concentrate on robustness to specific methodological issues rather than asserting robustness against all possible alternative modeling strategies.

In an era when the authority of science is in doubt, embracing multiverse analysis and accounting for model uncertainty are central to making research findings credible and compelling. Embracing transparency and showing what estimates are available – as well as which aspects of model specification affect the results – are important to thinking through the challenges of data analysis in the twenty-first century.

Finally, multiverse analysis is a work in progress. The project will grow and improve over time as more researchers embrace the uncertainty of a specification and develop new tools for distinguishing the voice of the author from the voice of the data. We are excited to see how the next generation of scholars, and their new ideas, will advance this project in fresh and inspiring ways. Indeed, we already have some ideas of our own for the next edition.

Appendix: Coding with MULTIVRS in Stata

This appendix demonstrates how to use the MULTIVRS package that is available for Stata (Young and Holsteen 2021). Neither Stata nor the MULTIVRS package is required to do multiverse analysis, but the package makes the process very easy. From the Stata command line, MULTIVRS can be installed with the text:

`ssc install multivrs`

Here, we show examples that demonstrate the basic features of the program using an extract of data from the National Longitudinal Survey of Women. This dataset is included in Stata (`nlsw88.dta`) and can be loaded using the command:

`sysuse nlsw88`

We show some of the basic functionalities of MULTIVRS, and we also refer readers to the help file in Stata (`help multivrs`) for a quick overview of the syntax and options.

THE BASIC MULTIVERSE COMMAND AND OUTPUT

The basic form of the multivrs command is

`multivrs estimation_command depvar focal_var controlterm [controlterm ...] [if] [in] [, options]`

This follows the format of a standard Stata regression command, so that one simply adds "multivrs" to the beginning of the command. So, if the original regression command is a returns-to-education analysis using ordinary least squares (OLS), "reg wage college [list of controls]," the new command is simply "multivrs reg wage college [list of controls]."

Figure A1 shows the basic MULTIVRS command and its output for a simple multiverse in which the dependent variable is union membership (*union*) and the key variable of interest is hours of work (*hours*). There are nine possible controls, for a total of 512 models. By default, the command also produces a simple density graph showing the modeling distribution of the estimates (Figure A2).

Note that MULTIVRS automatically checks for missing data across models and imposes listwise deletion to ensure that the sample size is constant in all specifications. We see this as good practice in general, but

```
. multivrs regress union hours age grade collgrad married south smsa c_city
ttl_exp tenure
Note: sample size varies across model specifications.
Listwise deletion:  381 out of 2246 observations will not be used.

Calculating 512    models...
Estimated time is 85 seconds (1.4 minutes).

Linear regression;
Variable of interest        hours
Outcome variable            union        Number of observations    1,865
Possible control terms      9            Mean R-squared             0.04
Number of models            512          Multicollinearity          0.10

Multiverse Statistics:                   Significance Testing:

Mean(b)             0.0020               Sign Stability             100%
Sampling SE         0.0010               Significance rate           54%
Modeling SE         0.0004
Total SE            0.0011               Positive                   100%
                                         Positive and Sig            54%
Robustness Ratio:   1.8536               Negative                     0%
                                         Negative and Sig             0%

Model Influence
                    Marginal Effect         Percent Change
                    of Variable Inclusion   From Mean(b)
south                    0.0006                 27.5%
tenure                  -0.0004                -21.1%
married                 -0.0002                -11.8%
collgrad                -0.0002                 -9.8%
grade                   -0.0001                 -5.8%
c_city                  -0.0001                 -4.1%
ttl_exp                  0.0000                  1.8%
smsa                    -0.0000                 -1.7%
age                      0.0000                  0.8%

Constant                 0.0023
R-squared                0.8277
```

This command took **14.1** seconds (.2 minutes) to complete.

FIGURE A1 Basic multiverse output: union hours example

Appendix

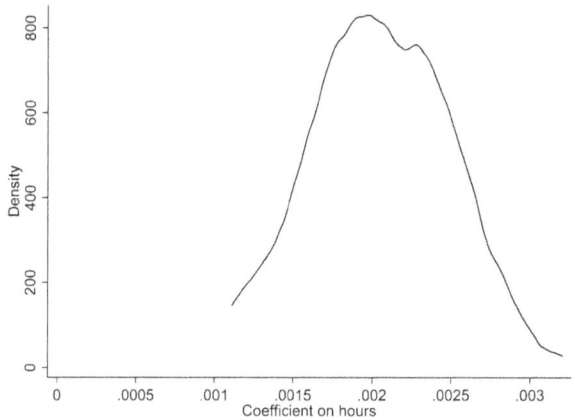

FIGURE A2 Density graph produced with MULTIVRS command

there are many situations where listwise delete may not be desired and it is informative to allow the sample size to vary. Automatic listwise deletion can be turned off using the option nolistwise, as we'll discuss later.

SAVING RESULTS

The results of the MULTIVRS command can be saved using the saveas option:

multivrs reg union hours age grade, saveas(union)

This command estimates a small multiverse with only four models – all possible combinations of the controls *age* and *grade*. It generates two new files in the working directory: a data file named union.dta and a do file named union.do. (Adding the option replace would permit saveas to overwrite existing files with the same names.)

Figure A3 shows a subset of the contents of the data file, union.dta. The dataset has four observations, one for each model. The variables *r_age* and *r_grade* are dummy variables indicating whether these controls are included in the model. Other variables include the sample size (n), the regression coefficient of interest (b_intvar), the p-value on the coefficient of interest ($pvalue$), and dummy variables indicating whether the coefficient of interest is positive and/or significant. (The dataset also includes many more variables not shown here.) These saved model results are useful for many purposes, such as making customized graphs, conducting supplemental analyses, or appending together the results of separate multiverse runs.

	r_age	r_grade	n	b_intvar	pvalue	sig	pos
1	1	0	1875	.0026058	.0088608	1	1
2	0	1	1875	.0022178	.0260402	1	1
3	1	1	1875	.0022291	.0253264	1	1
4	0	0	1875	.0025945	.0091338	1	1

FIGURE A3 Model results saved to data file using "saveas" option

```
1  * This file gives the code to replicate each of the models estimated in the multivrs command:
2  multivrs reg union hours age grade, saveas(union)
3
4  * Generate the indicator variable for observations to use (incorporating any listwise delete, [if]
5  tempvar touse
6  mark 'touse'
7  markout 'touse' union hours age grade
8
9  * The number preceding each model corresponds to the variable model_id in the results dataset.
0  * 1
1  regress  union hours age if 'touse'
2  * 2
3  regress  union hours grade if 'touse'
4  * 3
5  regress  union hours age grade if 'touse'
6  * 4
7  regress  union hours if 'touse'
```

FIGURE A4 Do file produced with "saveas" option

Figure A4 shows the full contents of union.do. This file shows exactly what the MULTIVRS command has done. Line 2 shows the multiverse command as it was entered. The next section – in this example, lines 5 through 7 – is for specifying the sample on which models are to be estimated. An indicator variable named "touse" is generated, and is coded as 1 if a case is to be included in the sample and 0 if not. When listwise deletion is used to deal with missing values (as is the default method), this variable will be coded 0 for cases with missing values on any variable. If the sample is restricted using "if" or "in" syntax (for instance, "multivrs reg union hours age grade if south==0"), then the touse variable will incorporate these sample restrictions. If automatic casewise deletion is turned off and there are no other sample restrictions, then this section does not appear in the file at all.

Next, every model in the multiverse is listed as a numbered regression – this shows the full list of models generated by the "all combinations" algorithm. Users should examine this list carefully to make sure it matches the model space they intended to estimate.

The model list provides flexibility for running more complex model types that are not directly supported by MULTIVRS. For instance, one could do a "find and replace" to change "regress" to "stcox" (for the Cox proportional hazard model, which is not implemented in MULTIVRS) or any other regression command available in STATA. We discuss this in more detail later.

GROUPING

It can often be useful to "group" variables so that they are treated as a set. If two control variables are put in parentheses, they will be considered one term, and they will be included or excluded from the model together. In Figure A5, the two education variables (highest grade completed and a dummy for college graduation) are grouped to be a single control term. No model can include *grade* if it does not include *collgrad*: the two variables are either both in the model or neither of them is in the model. This cuts the number of models in half, since it reduces the number of control terms from nine to eight.

Grouping can also be used to designate variables as necessary controls. For instance, we could designate the two education variables as

```
. multivrs regress union hours age (grade collgrad) married south smsa c_city
ttl_exp tenure
Note: sample size varies across model specifications.
Listwise deletion:  381 out of 2246 observations will not be used.

Calculating 256    models...
Estimated time is 85 seconds (.1 minutes).

Linear regression;
Variable of interest
Outcome variable              hours
Possible control terms        union          Number of observations    1,865
Number of models              8              Mean R-squared            0.03
                              256            Multicollinearity         0.10

Multiverse Statistics:                       Significance Testing:

Mean(b)              0.0021                  Sign Stability            100%
Sampling SE          0.0010                  Significance rate         59%
Modeling SE          0.0004
Total SE             0.0011                  Positive                  100%
                                             Positive and Sig          59%
Robustness Ratio:    1.8994                  Negative                  0%
                                             Negative and Sig          0%

Model Influence
                     Marginal Effect         Percent Change
                     of Variable Inclusion   From Mean(b)
south                0.0006                  26.6%
tenure               -0.0004                 -21.1%
grade                -0.0003                 -15.1%
collgrad             (Grouped with grade)
married              -0.0002                 -11.2%
c_city               -0.0001                 -4.1%
smsa                 -0.0000                 -2.0%
age                  0.0000                  0.8%
ttl_exp              0.0000                  0.6%

Constant             0.0024
R-squared            0.8471
```

FIGURE A5 Grouping control variables

necessary covariates by grouping them in parentheses with the variable of interest (*hours*):

```
multivrs regress union (hours grade collgrad) age married
south smsa c_city ttl_exp tenure
```

With this command, both *grade* and *collgrad* would be included in every model (and the number of models in the multiverse would again be cut in half).

CHANGING THE ESTIMATION COMMAND

To estimate the same set of models with logit instead of OLS, we could change the estimation command from `regress` to `logit`:

```
multivrs logit union hours age grade collgrad married
south smsa c_city ttl_exp tenure
```

MULTIVRS supports nine specific estimation commands: regress, logit, logistic, probit, poisson, nbreg, areg, rreg, and xtreg.

EITHER|OR SYNTAX

Either|or syntax can be used to mark some components of the MULTIVRS command as alternative options. For instance, we could use this syntax to assess functional form robustness:

```
multivrs (logit|probit|regress) union hours grade collgrad
age married south smsa c_city ttl_exp tenure, margins
```

This command would essentially estimate the original multiverse three times: once using logit models, once using probit, and once using OLS regression. Figure A6 shows the output.

Notice that we are testing across models that normally report results on a different scale: OLS reports marginal effects, which are not comparable to logit coefficients, odds ratios, or probit coefficients. For this reason, we used the option `margins`. This converts the logit and probit coefficients to average marginal effects for the variable of interest, saves these estimates (and the associated standard errors and p-values) rather than the regression coefficients, and summarizes and plots them. For more information, in Stata see margins (`dydx`).

When a command uses models with noncomparable estimates, and the `margins` option is not specified, multivrs defaults to "significance only" output, reporting only the sign and significance statistics. In this case, the influence statistics are reported as marginal effects on the probability

```
. multivrs (logit|probit|regress) union hours grade collgrad age married south
smsa c_city ttl_exp tenure, margins
Note:  sample size varies across model specifications.
Listwise deletion:  381 out of 2246 observations will not be used.

Calculating 1,536  models...
Estimated time is 4    minutes (.1 hours).
Each dot represents 1000 models calculated
.
Logit/Probit/Linear regression (displaying marginal effects):
Variable of interest         hours
Outcome variable             union          Number of observations    1,865
Possible control terms       9              Mean R-squared             0.03
Number of models             1,536          Multicollinearity          0.10

Multiverse Statistics:                      Significance Testing:

Mean(b)             0.0021                  Sign Stability            100%
Sampling SE         0.0010                  Significance rate          55%
Modeling SE         0.0004
Total SE            0.0011                  Positive                  100%
                                            Positive and Sig           55%
Robustness Ratio:   1.8659                  Negative                    0%
                                            Negative and Sig            0%

Model Influence
                        Marginal Effect     Percent Change
                     of Variable Inclusion   From Mean(b)
south                       0.0005              26.0%
tenure                     -0.0004             -18.4%
married                    -0.0002             -11.5%
collgrad                   -0.0002             -10.9%
grade                      -0.0001              -6.7%
c_city                     -0.0001              -4.4%
model:   regress           -0.0001              -3.6%
smsa                       -0.0000              -2.1%
ttl_exp                     0.0000               1.7%
model:   probit            -0.0000              -1.7%
age                         0.0000               0.7%

Constant                    0.0024
R-squared                   0.8077
note: logit is the reference model.
```

This command took 3   minutes (0 hours) to complete.
Type **multivrs, more** to see sign and significance results for each model type.

FIGURE A6 Either|or syntax to specify alternative estimation commands

of seeing significant (or positive) coefficients. This default aims to avoid outputting estimates that are not comparable. (This "significance only" output can be toggled on for any command using the sig_only option and turned off when not wanted using the nosig option.)

EITHER|OR SYNTAX FOR VARIABLES

Either|or syntax can also be used when alternative forms of a variable are available. Suppose, for instance, that we didn't want our model to include both of the education variables at the same time. We could specify:

242   *Appendix*

```
multivrs regress union hours grade|collgrad age married
south smsa c_city ttl_exp tenure
```

With this command, one third of models would include *grade*, another third would include *collgrad*, and the remaining third would include neither variable. No model would include both *grade* and *collgrad*. Either|or can be used for any variable in the equation, whether it is the outcome variable, the focal variable, or a control.

Grouping and either|or syntax can be combined for even greater flexibility. For example, ((x1|x2) x3) would specify that x1 and x2 will not be included in the same model, but that x3 will be included in all models that contain either of them. In the union membership example, suppose we wanted to incorporate a new *age_squared* variable, but only in models that also include *age*. We could use grouping and either|or syntax to accomplish this:

```
multivrs regress union hours grade collgrad(age|(age
age_squared)) married south smsa c_city ttl_exp tenure
```

With this command, one third of the models would have no control for age, another third would control for *age* alone, and the remaining third would include both *age* and *age_squared*. No models would include *age_squared* without also including *age*.

ALLOWING SAMPLE SIZE TO VARY ACROSS MODELS

By default, the MULTIVRS command constrains all models to be estimated on the same sample. Any case with missing values for any

```
. multivrs regress union hours grade collgrad age married south smsa c_city
ttl_exp tenure, nolistwise
Note:  sample size varies across model specifications.

Calculating 512   models...
Estimated time is 7 seconds (.1 minutes).

Linear regression;
Variable of interest          hours
Outcome variable              union         Number of observations     1,865-1,877
Possible control terms        9             Mean R-squared                    0.04
Number of models              512           Multicollinearity                 0.09

Multiverse Statistics:                      Significance Testing:

Mean(b)              0.0020                 Sign Stability                    100%
Sampling SE          0.0010                 Significance rate                  53%
Modeling SE          0.0004
Total SE             0.0011                 Positive                          100%
                                            Positive and Sig                   53%
Robustness Ratio:    1.8382                 Negative                            0%
                                            Negative and Sig                    0%
```

FIGURE A7   Allowing sample to vary across models with "nolistwise" option variable in the analysis is excluded from all models. In many practical applications, it will be preferable to allow the sample to vary across models, such that each model is estimated on the largest possible sample. This can easily be accomplished with the `nolistwise` option. Compare the output in Figure A7 with the output in Figure A1. With listwise deletion turned off (Figure A7), the sample size range across models from 1,865 to 1,877, which tells us that different variables have different amounts of missing data. In Figure A1, all models were estimated on the same sample of 1,865 cases, and sample size does not vary.

INCLUDING A PREFERRED ESTIMATE

If a user has a preferred estimate of the coefficient of interest, it can be incorporated into the display of results using the option `pref` (*estimate, SE*). With this option, the preferred estimate is plotted as a vertical line in the automatically produced density graph of the modeling distribution (as in Figure A9), and the table of results includes model robustness statistics relative to the preferred estimate. Figure A8 shows the output of the union membership example when a preferred estimate is specified. The output includes percentile of the modeling distribution at which the

```
. multivrs regress union hours grade collgrad age married south smsa c_city
ttl_exp tenure, pref(.0020818, .0010229)
Note:  sample size varies across model specifications.
Listwise deletion:  381 out of 2246 observations will not be used.

Calculating 512   models...
Estimated time is 8 seconds (.1 minutes).

Linear regression;
Variable of interest            hours
Outcome variable                union           Number of observations        1,865
Possible control terms          9               Mean R-squared                 0.04
Number of models                512             Multicollinearity              0.10

Multiverse Statistics:                          Significance Testing:

Mean (b)               0.0020                   Sign Stability                 100%
Sampling SE            0.0010                   Significance rate               54%
Modeling SE            0.0004
Total SE               0.0011                   Positive                       100%
                                                Positive and Sig                54%
Robustness Ratio:      1.8732                   Negative                         0%
                                                Negative and Sig                 0%

Statistics for Preferred Estimate:
Pref. est.             0.0021                   Percentile of modeling dist.    54%
Sampling SE            0.0010
Modeling SE            0.0004
Total SE               0.0011
```

FIGURE A8 Including a preferred estimate

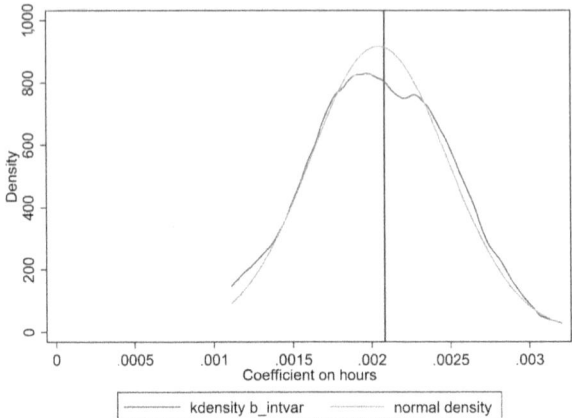

FIGURE A9 Modeling distribution with normal distribution and preferred estimate

preferred estimate falls, as well as modeling and total standard errors relative to the preferred estimate. For example, the output shows that the preferred estimate falls at the fifty-fourth percentile of the modeling distribution – nearly at the median and far from the tails.

GRAPHING OPTIONS

The option `normal` overlays a normal distribution on the graph of the empirical modeling distribution, as shown in Figure A9. This can be used to highlight departures from normality in the modeling distribution (which are modest in this example).

The option `nozero` relaxes the default constraint that the graph include zero. This is useful in cases where results are highly robust and none of the estimates approach zero.

A CATCHALL OPTION

Users may wish to use a Stata option that is not incorporated in the MULTIVRS program. The option `other(other_option)` is a fall-back, allowing users to attempt to input any optional syntax that the supported estimation commands allow. This is an advanced option for programmers, when they want to use more complex options than what are specifically supported in MULTIVRS.

Appendix

MODEL SPACE OPTIONS

When working with large numbers of controls or other modeling options, the model space can quickly become very computationally burdensome. For example, if there are twenty-five control terms, there are $2^{25} \cong 33$ million unique specifications, which starts to push the limits of regular use and can take a long time to run. MULTIVRS allows the option of defining the full model space but estimating only a sample of the specifications.

The option `sample(percent)` randomly samples the given percentage of possible models. The percentage may be any integer between 1 and 99. Our informal testing has found that when the model space is large, sampling down to 10 percent or even to 1 percent can yield results that are remarkably representative of the full model space.

Another option for reducing the size of the model space is `size(#)`. This option constrains the number of covariates in the models according to one of the following specifications:

Options	Description
size(#)	exactly # control terms
size(#min, #max)	between #min and #max control terms inclusive
size(#min,.)	greater than or equal to #min control terms
size(., #max)	less than or equal to #max control terms

For example, if there are twenty-five possible controls, then specifying `size(4,8)` estimates only moderate-sized models with between four and eight controls; this would reduce the model space from 33.5 million models to 1.8 million. Setting a maximum model size of seven with the option `size(.,7)` would reduce the model space to about 726,000. Subsetting to only models with exactly seven controls with `size(7)` would reduce the model space to 480,700. This method follows from Sala-i-Martin (1997), who tested two million models of size seven.

In Figure A10, we compare the two different ways of reducing the size of the model space. The figure is based on three multiverse commands:

(1) the full modeling distribution:
multivrs regress union hours age grade collgrad married south smsa c_city ttl_exp tenure

(2) a fifty percent random sample of models:
multivrs regress union hours age grade collgrad married south smsa c_city ttl_exp tenure, sample(50)

(3) all models with four or five controls:
```
multivrs regress union hours age grade collgrad
married south smsa c_city ttl_exp tenure, size(4,5)
```

The first command estimates the full modeling distribution, including all possible combinations of the nine controls (512 models). The second command runs a 50 percent random sample of the full distribution

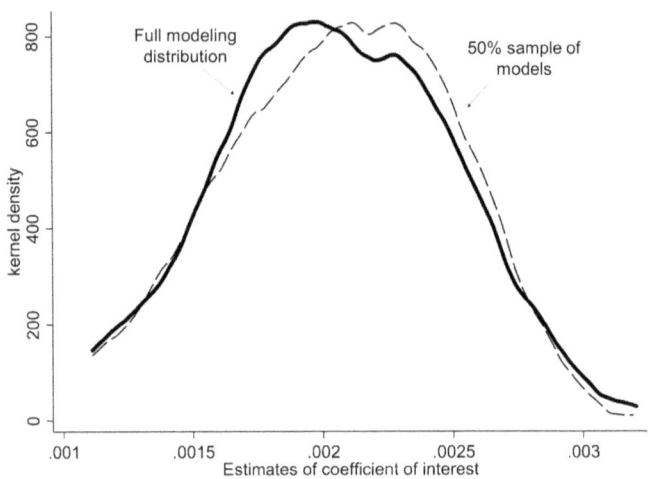

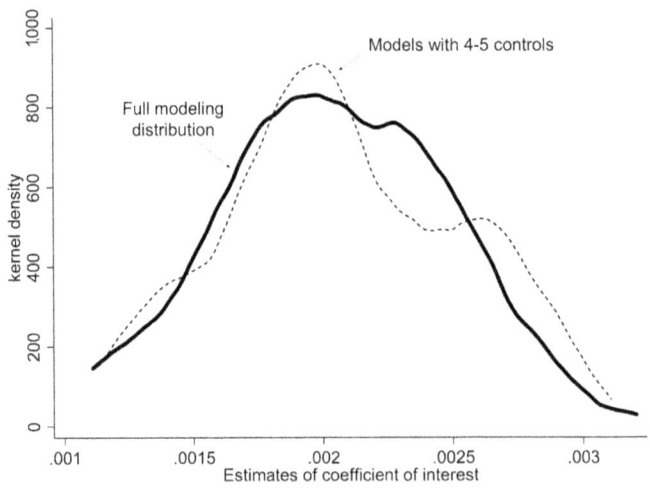

FIGURE A10 Options for reducing size of model space

(256 models). The third command runs all models from the full distribution that include either four or five controls (210 models). Panel A of Figure A10 shows the full modeling distribution against a 50 percent sample, and Panel B compares it to the size-restricted sample. As is evident in the graphs, using a random sample of models will generally yield a modeling distribution that is more similar to the full distribution; restricting the number of controls tends to distort the results in more substantive ways. If the only goal is to reduce the size of the model space in order to reduce run time and make the multiverse more tractable, then sampling is the better solution. However, in some cases there may be substantive reasons to prefer models with a certain number of controls, and in these cases it may be more sensible to reduce the model space by restricting model size.

When working with larger model spaces, even a 1 percent sample of models can be highly representative of the full model space. For instance, Figure A11 revisits the multiverse of the Regnerus analysis that we discussed in Chapter 11, which included more than 2.6 million models and took around eighty hours to run (more than three days). We compare the full modeling distribution (solid line) to a 1 percent sample of roughly 26,000 models that could run in less than an hour (dashed line). The distributions are virtually identical. While we would always favor reporting

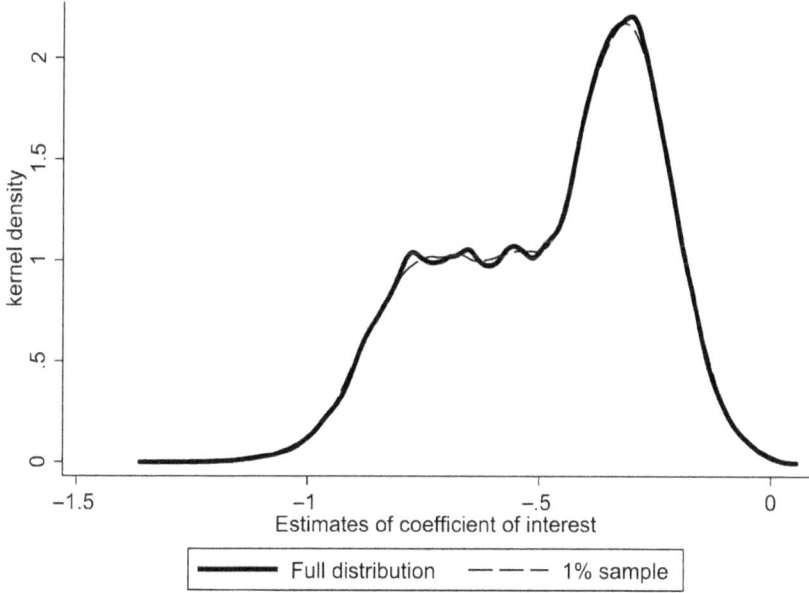

FIGURE A11 Full modeling distribution versus 1 percent sample, Regnerus multiverse from Chapter 11

the full modeling distribution when feasible, it is valuable to know how reliable the results from a random sample can be.

WEIGHTING THE MULTIVERSE

The option weights(weight_type) specifies the weighting method for summarizing the model results (i.e., calculating means and standard errors). The default method is uniform weighting, which assigns equal weight to each model. Alternatively, weight_type may be "bic" for exponential Bayesian information criteria (BIC) weighting (an approximation to the posterior probabilities), "inf" for weighting by model influence, or "r2" for weighting by R^2. By default, the results are unweighted (uniform weights), and each of the other three types of weights is saved in the results file (variables wt_bic, wt_inf, and wt_r2).

Making graphs that compare the different weighting strategies, as shown in Chapter 13, requires working with the SAVEAS data file. Here we show how to do this using some of the code from the pollution example in Chapter 13. The code opens, runs the multiverse, and saves the results; then it opens the saved data file and generates graphs of the unweighted and weighted modeling distributions. Figure A12 shows the graphs that are produced by the code.

```
* Open dataset
use https://www.stata-press.com/data/r16/breathe

* Recode variables
gen home_SEI = 1 - sev_home
gen school_SEI = 1 - sev_school

* Run multiverse and save results
multivrs reg react no2_class age age0 home_SEI school_SEI
green_home noise_school i.sex i.grade siblings_old
siblings_young i.lbweight i.msmoke, saveas(pollution)

* open the saved data file
use pollution.dta, clear

* density graph of unweighted modeling distribution
(i.e., uniform weights) vs. exponential BIC weights:

twoway kdensity b_intvar || kdensity b_intvar[aw=wt_bic],
legend(label(1 "Uniform weights") label(2 "BIC weights"))

* density graph of unweighted modeling distribution vs.
R^2 and influence weights:
```

Appendix

```
twoway kdensity b_intvar || kdensity b_intvar[aw=wt_r2]
|| kdensity b_intvar[aw=wt_inf],
legend(label(1 "Uniform weights") label(2 "R^2 weights")
label(3 "Influence weights"))
```

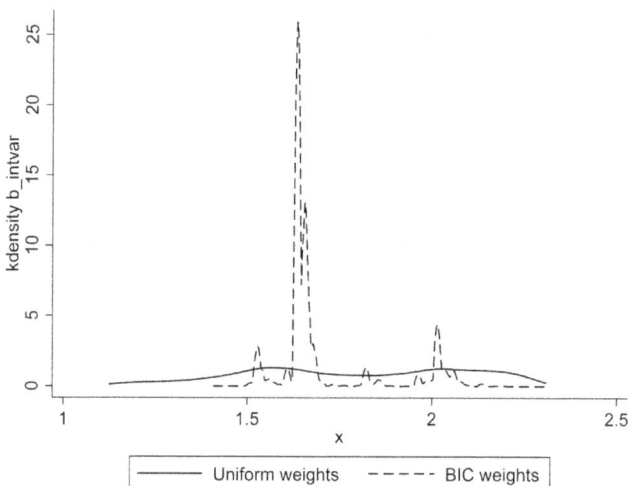

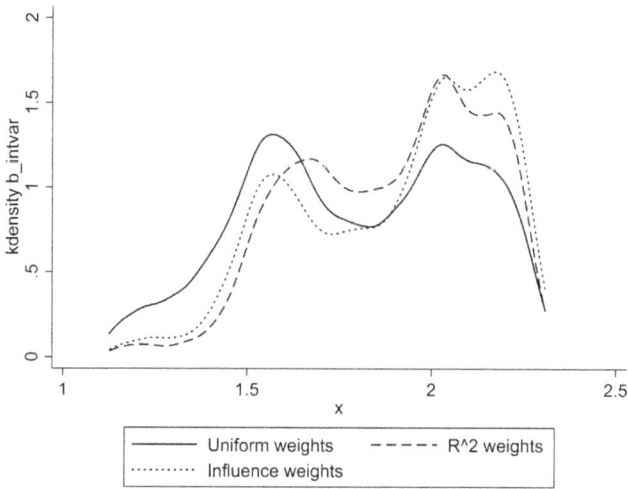

FIGURE A12 Unweighted modeling distribution (uniform weights) versus exponential BIC weights, R^2 weights, and influence weights

USING THE SAVEAS FILE FOR GREATER FLEXIBILITY

Sometimes a multiverse analysis is too complex to be captured in one run of the MULTIVRS command. For example, older versions of the command did not yet support the multiverse of estimation commands (item 5). So, a multiverse that included an outcome and a set of possible controls estimated with OLS, Poisson, and negative binomial would require three separate runs of the program (one for each model type), in which the results would be saved and then appended together (Young and Holsteen 2017). Now, this is handled simply with the either|or syntax discussed earlier, but users may encounter other situations where their model space cannot be easily captured in one run of MULTIVRS.

Consider the hurricane names example that we presented in Chapter 3. One of the modeling options was to restrict the sample to years 1979 onward, rather than using all years of data. One way to incorporate this kind of sample restriction into a multiverse is to (1) estimate a multiverse using the full sample, (2) estimate a second multiverse using the subsample, and (3) append together the two sets of saved estimates. Sample code for doing this is shown here:

```
# estimate models using all years of data
multivrs reg logdeaths zfem zdam zminpress popmil year,
saveas(hurricanes_allyears)

# estimate models using data for 1979 on
drop if year<1979
multivrs reg logdeaths zfem zdam zminpress popmil year,
saveas(hurricanes_post1979)

# append together the two sets of estimates and save
use hurricanes_allyears
gen post1979=0
append using hurricanes_post1979
replace post1979=1 if post1979==.
save hurricanes.dta
```

We hope that MULTIVRS is flexible enough that the append workaround is rarely needed, but the aforementioned example shows how it can be used. In practice, this particular example could be done in an easier way, by creating a second version of the outcome variable where pre-1979 hurricanes are recoded as missing:

```
gen logdeaths_post1979 = logdeaths if year>=1979

multivrs reg (logdeaths | logdeaths_post1979) zfem zdam
zminpress popmil year
```

Appendix

EXPANDING TO ESTIMATION COMMANDS NOT CURRENTLY SUPPORTED BY MULTIVRS

The architecture of MULTIVRS requires that each possible estimation command (reg, logit, poisson, etc.) be hard coded into the program. For this reason, MULTIVRS does not work with any possible regression model. The SAVEAS do file can be very useful when a needed estimation command is not supported by MULITVRS. The do file contains the entire model space, so if an unsupported model needs to be included, one can use a text editor to "find and replace" the original regression command with the new command.

This strategy was used in a recent paper by Chris Wildeman, Robert Sampson, and Garrett Baker (2023). They wanted to run both Poisson models and survival models using the same sets of controls, but their preferred survival model command (stcox) is not supported. They used the find-and-replace approach to specify the models. We refer interested readers to that paper's online appendix, which provides a step-by-step description of the process they used. (Changing the regression command from "poisson" to "stcox" is simple, but they offer code for some extra steps to efficiently extract and save the results from the newly run models.)

LIMITATIONS AND CONCLUSIONS

We believe that the MULTIVRS command is flexible enough to capture most multiverses that users would want to run, but it does have limitations. Most notable, perhaps, is that it does not allow for the use of sampling weights (see our discussion in Chapter 10 on the downsides of sampling weights and empirical criteria for adopting them). Users wishing to incorporate sampling weights (or any other modeling options that are not compatible with multivrs) can use the SAVEAS do file and the find-and-replace strategy discussed in the previous section to run the full set of models. Alternatively, it is always possible to manually code the multiverse (i.e., write one's own code to run all models and extract the model results). For an example of this, we refer readers to the replication package for the Regnerus example we presented in Chapter 11, a complex multiverse which was manually coded to test the influence of sampling weights. Finally, for R users, we point to a new tool with some similar capabilities for implementing multiverse analysis in R that has been developed by Sarma et al. (2023). We hope that in the future multiverse commands like we have presented here will become standard parts of most statistical packages.

References

Aguinis, Herman, Ryan K. Gottfredson, and Harry Joo. 2013. "Best-Practice Recommendations for Defining, Identifying, and Handling Outliers." *Organizational Research Methods* 16(2): 270–301.

Allison, Paul. 2002. *Missing Data*. Thousand Oaks, CA: SAGE Publications.

Andersen, Robert. 2008. *Modern Methods for Robust Regression*. Thousand Oaks, CA: SAGE Publications.

Angrist, Joshua D., and Jörn-Steffen Pischke. 2009. *Mostly Harmless Econometrics: An Empiricist's Companion*. Princeton, NJ: Princeton University Press.

Angrist, Joshua D., and Jörn-Steffen Pischke. 2010. "The Credibility Revolution in Empirical Economics: How Better Research Design Is Taking the Con Out of Econometrics." *Journal of Economic Perspectives* 24(2): 3–30.

Apple. 2023. Schedule 14A Proxy Statement. www.sec.gov/Archives/edgar/data/320193/000130817923000019/laap2023_def14a.htm#3209561718846054:33474679

Arceneaux, Kevin, Alan Gerber, and Donald Green. 2010. "A Cautionary Note on the Use of Matching to Estimate Causal Effects: An Empirical Example Comparing Matching Estimates to an Experimental Benchmark." *Sociological Methods and Research* 39(2): 256–282.

Ashenfelter, Orley, Colm Harmon, and Hessel Oosterbeek. 1999. "A Review of Estimates of the Schooling/Earnings Relationship, with Tests for Publication Bias." *Labour Economics* 6(4): 453–470.

Athey, Susan, and Guido Imbens. 2015. "A Measure of Robustness to Misspecification." *American Economic Review* 105(5): 476–480.

Attanasio, Orazio P., and Luigi Pistaferri. 2016. "Consumption Inequality." *Journal of Economic Perspectives* 30(2): 3–28.

Auspurg, Katrin, and Josef Brüderl. 2021. "Has the Credibility of the Social Sciences Been Credibly Destroyed? Reanalyzing the 'Many Analysts, One Data Set' Project." *Socius* 7. https://doi.org/10.1177/23780231211024421

Auspurg, Katrin, Andreas Schneck, and Thomas Hinz. 2019. "Closed Doors Everywhere? A Meta-Analysis of Field Experiments on Ethnic Discrimination in Rental Housing Markets." *Journal of Ethnic and Migration Studies* 45(1): 95–114.

Bakkensen, Laura, and William Larson. 2014. "Population Matters When Modeling Hurricane Fatalities." *Proceedings of the National Academy of Sciences* 111(50): E5331–E5332.

Bartus, Tamas. 2005. "Estimation of Marginal Effects Using Margeff." *The Stata Journal* 5(3): 309–329.

Basso, Alessandra. 2017. "The Appeal to Robustness in Measurement Practice." *Studies in History and Philosophy of Science* 65–66: 57–66.

Bateman, Ian, Daniel Kahneman, Alistair Munro, Chris Starmer, and Robert Sugden. 2005. "Testing Competing Models of Loss Aversion: An Adversarial Collaboration." *Journal of Public Economics* 89(8): 1561–1580.

Battey, H., D. R. Cox, and M. Jackson. 2019. "On the Linear in Probability Model for Binary Data." *Royal Society Open Science* 6(5): 190067.

Begley, Glenn, and Lee M. Ellis. 2012. "Drug Development: Raise Standards for Preclinical Cancer Research." *Nature* 483: 531–533.

Beheim, Bret, et al. 2021. "Treatment of Missing Data Determined Conclusions regarding Moralizing Gods." *Nature* 595: E29–E34.

Bellhouse, D. R. 1988. "A Brief History of Random Sampling Methods." *Handbook of Statistics* 6: 1–14.

Belloni, Alexandre, Victor Chernozhukov, and Christian Hansen. 2014. "Inference on Treatment Effects after Selection among High-Dimensional Controls." *Review of Economic Studies* 81(2): 608–650.

Benjamin, Daniel J. .... (with ninety-two coauthors). 2018. "Redefine Statistical Significance." *Nature Human Behavior* 2: 6–10.

Biggs, Michael, Christopher Barrie, and Kenneth T. Andrews. 2020. "Did Local Civil Rights Protest Liberalize Whites' Racial Attitudes?" *Research & Politics* 7: 3.

Blanchflower, David G., and Andrew J. Oswald. 2008. "Is Well-Being U-Shaped over the Life Cycle?" *Social Science & Medicine* 66: 1733–1749.

Bollen, Kenneth A., Paul P. Biemer, Alan F. Karr, Stephen Tueller, and Marcus E. Berzofsky. 2016. "Are Survey Weights Needed? A Review of Diagnostic Tests in Regression Analyses." *Annual Review of Statistics and Its Applications* 3: 375–392.

Borges, Jorge Luis. 1941. "El Jardin de Senderos que se Bifurcan." *El Jardin de Senderos Que Se Bifurcan*. Editorial Sur.

Bowman, Jarron. 2020. "Do the Affluent Override Average Americans? Measuring Policy Disagreement and Unequal Influence." *Social Science Quarterly* 101(3): 1018–1037.

Box, George E. P. 1976. "Science and Statistics." *Journal of the American Statistical Association* 71(356): 791–799.

Box, George E. P., and N. R. Draper. 1987. *Empirical Model-Building and Response Surfaces*. New York: John Wiley & Sons.

Brady, David, Martin Seeleib-Kaiser, and Jason Beckfield. 2005. "Economic Globalization and the Welfare State in Affluent Democracies, 1975–2001." *American Sociological Review* 70(6): 921–948.

Brand, Jennie. 2015. "The Far-Reaching Impact of Job Loss and Unemployment." *Annual Review of Sociology* 41: 1.1–1.17.

Breen, R., Karlson, K. B., and Holm, A. 2018. "Interpreting and Understanding Logits, Probits, and Other Nonlinear Probability Models." *Annual Review of Sociology* 44: 39–54.

Breznau, Nate, Eike Mark Rinke, Alexander Wuttke, and Tomasz Żółtak. 2022. "Observing Many Researchers Using the Same Data and Hypothesis Reveals a Hidden Universe of Uncertainty." *PNAS* 119(44): e2203150119.

Brodeur, Abel, Nikolai Cook, and Anthony Heyes. 2020. "A Proposed Specification Check for p-Hacking." *AEA Papers & Proceedings* 110: 66–69.

Camerer, Colin F. 2022. "The Apparent Prevalence of Outcome Variation from Hidden 'Dark Methods' Is a Challenge for Social Science." *Proceedings of the National Academy of Sciences* 119(52). https://doi.org/10.1073/pnas.2216020119

Camerer, Colin F., et al. 2018. "Evaluating the Replicability of Social Science Experiments in Nature and Science between 2010 and 2015." *Nature Human Behaviour* 2: 637–644.

Cantone, G. G., and Tomaselli, V. 2023. "Theory and Methods of the Multiverse: An Application for Panel-Based Models." *Quality and Quantity* 58: 1447–1480.

Carroll, Sean. 2019a. *Something Deeply Hidden: Quantum Worlds and the Emergence of Spacetime*. Boston, MA: Dutton.

Carroll, Sean. 2019b. "Even Physicists Don't Understand Quantum Mechanics." *New York Times*. www.nytimes.com/2019/09/07/opinion/sunday/quantum-physics.html.

Chabris, Christopher, Benjamin Hebert, Daniel Benjamin, Jonathan Beauchamp, David Cesarini, Matthijs van der Loos, Magnus Johannesson, Patrik Magnusson, Paul Lichtenstein, Craig Atwood, Jeremy Freese, Taissa Hauser, Robert M. Hauser, Nicholas Christakis, and David Laibson. 2012. "Most Genetic Associations with General Intelligence Are Probably False Positives." *Psychological Science* 23: 1314–1323.

Cheng, Simon, and Brian Powell. 2015. "Measurement, Methods, and Divergent Patterns: Reassessing the Effects of Same-Sex Parents." *Social Science Research* 52: 615–626.

Chernozhukov, Victor, Denis Chetverikov, Mert Demirer, Esther Duflo, Christian Hansen, Whitney Newey, and James Robins. 2018. "Double/Debiased Machine Learning for Treatment and Structural Parameters." *Econometrics Journal* 21(1): C1–C68.

Chetty, Raj, Nathaniel Hendren, Patrick Kline, Emmanuel Saez, and Nicholas Turner. 2014. "Is the United States Still a Land of Opportunity?" *American Economic Review* 104(5): 141–147.

Chetty, Raj, Nathaniel Hendren, Maggie R. Jones, and Sonya R. Porter. 2020. "Race and Economic Opportunity in the United States: An Intergenerational Perspective." *Quarterly Journal of Economics* 135(2): 711–783.

Cho, Adrian. 2011. "Neutrinos Travel Faster than Light, According to One Experiment." *Science*. www.science.org/content/article/neutrinos-travel-faster-light-according-one-experiment

Christensen, Bjorn, and Soren Christensen. 2014. "Are Female Hurricanes Really Deadlier than Male Hurricanes?" *PNAS* 111(34): E3497–3498.

Christensen, Garret S., and Edward Miguel. 2018. "Transparency, Reproducibility, and the Credibility of Economics Research." *Journal of Economic Literature* 56(3): 920–980.

Christensen, Garret, Jeremy Freese, and Edward Miguel. 2019. *Transparent and Reproducible Social Science: How to Do Open Science*. Oakland: University of California Press.

Ciccone, Antonio, and Marek Jarociński. 2010. "Determinants of Economic Growth: Will Data Tell?" *American Economic Journal: Macroeconomics* 2(4): 222–246.

Cinelli, Carlos, Andrew Forney, and Judea Pearl. 2022. "A Crash Course in Good and Bad Controls." *Sociological Methods & Research*. Online first.

Clark, Cory J., Thomas Costello, Gregory Mitchell, and Philip E. Tetlock. 2022. "Keep Your Enemies Close: Adversarial Collaborations Will Improve Behavioral Science." *Journal of Applied Research in Memory and Cognition* 11(1): 1–18.

Clarke, Kevin A. 2005. "The Phantom Menace: Omitted Variable Bias in Econometric Research." *Conflict Management and Peace Science* 22: 341–352.

Clarke, Kevin A. 2009. "Return of the Phantom Menace: Omitted Variable Bias in Political Research." *Conflict Management and Peace Science* 26(1): 46–66.

Coker, Beau, Cynthia Rudin, and Gary King. 2020. "A Theory of Statistical Inference for Ensuring the Robustness of Scientific Results." Working Paper.

Cook, R. Dennis. 1977. "Detection of Influential Observations in Linear Regression." *Technometrics* 19(1): 15–18.

Crede, Marcus, Andrew Gelman, and Carol Nickerson. 2016. "Questionable Association between Front Boarding and Air Rage." *Proceedings of the National Academy of Sciences* 113(47): E7348.

Dehejia, Rajeev H., and Sadek Wahba. 1999. "Causal Effects in Nonexperimental Studies: Reevaluating the Evaluation of Training Programs." *Journal of the American Statistical Association* 94(448): 1053–1062.

Desmond, Matthew, Andrew Papachristos, and David Kirk. 2016. "Police Violence and Citizen Crime Reporting in the Black Community." *American Sociological Review* 81(5): 857–876.

Desmond, Matthew, Andrew V. Papachristos, and David S. Kirk. 2020. "Evidence of the Effect of Police Violence on Citizen Crime Reporting." *American Sociological Review* 85(1): 184–190.

Dolling, Dieter, Horst Entorf, Dieter Hermann, and Thomas Rupp. 2009. "Is Deterrence Effective? Results of a Meta-Analysis of Punishment." *European Journal on Criminal Policy and Research* 15(1–2): 201–224.

Dolnick, Edward. 2011. *The Clockwork Universe: Isaac Newton, the Royal Society, and the Birth of the Modern World*. New York: Harper Perennial.

Doucouliagos, Hristos, and Martin Paldam. 2013. "Explaining Development Aid Allocation by Growth." *Journal of Entrepreneurship and Public Policy* 2(1): 21–41.

Doucouliagos, Hristos, and Tom D. Stanley. 2009. "Publication Selection Bias in Minimum-Wage Research? A Meta-Regression Analysis." *British Journal of Industrial Relations* 47(2): 406–428.

Doucouliagos, Hristos., and Tom D. Stanley. 2013. "Theory Competition and Selectivity: Are All Economic Facts Greatly Exaggerated?" *Journal of Economic Surveys* 27: 316–339.

Duhigg, Charles. 2012. "How Companies Learn Your Secrets." *New York Times.* February 16.

Durante, Kristina M., Ashley Rae, and Vladas Griskevicius. 2013. "The Fluctuating Female Vote: Politics, Religion, and the Ovulatory Cycle." *Psychological Science* 24(6): 1007–1016.

Durkheim, Emile. 1933. *The Division of Labor in Society.* New York: Macmillan.

Durlauf, Steven N., Chao Fu, and Salvador Navarro. 2012. "Assumptions Matter: Model Uncertainty and the Deterrent Effect of Capital Punishment." *American Economic Review* 102: 487–492.

Durlauf, Steven N., Chao Fu, and Salvador Navarro. 2013. "Capital Punishment and Deterrence: Understanding Disparate Results." *Journal of Quantitative Criminology* 29(1): 103–121.

Durlauf, Steven N., Paul Johnson, and Jonathan Temple. 2005. "Growth Econometrics." Pp. 555–677 in *The Handbook of Economic Growth*, edited by P. Aghion and S. Durlauf. Amsterdam: North Holland.

Efron, Bradley. 1981. "Nonparametric Estimates of Standard Error: The Jackknife, the Bootstrap and Other Methods." *Biometrika* 68: 589–599.

Efron, Bradley, and Robert Tibshirani. 1993. *An Introduction to the Bootstrap.* New York: Chapman & Hall.

Ehrlich, Isaac. 1975. "The Deterrent Effect of Capital Punishment: A Question of Life and Death." *American Economic Review* 65(3): 397–417.

Elwert, Felix, and Christopher Winship. 2014. "Endogenous Selection Bias: The Problem of Conditioning on a Collider Variable." *Annual Review of Sociology* 40: 31–53.

Engzell, Per. 2021. "What Do Books in the Home Proxy For? A Cautionary Tale." *Sociological Methods & Research* 50(4): 1487–1514.

Engzell, Per, and Carina Mood. 2023. "Understanding Patterns and Trends in Income Mobility through Multiverse Analysis." *American Sociological Review* 88(4): 600–626.

Engzell, Per, Carina Mood, and Jan Jonsson. 2020. "It's All about the Parents: Inequality Transmission across Three Generations in Sweden." *Sociological Science* 7: 242–267.

Everett, Hugh. 1957. "'Relative State' Formulation of Quantum Mechanics." *Reviews of Modern Physics* 29(3): 454–462.

Filmer, Deon, and Lant H. Pritchett. 2001. "Estimating Wealth Effects without Expenditure Data – Or Tears: An Application to Educational Enrollment in States of India." *Demography* 38(1): 115–132.

Fischer, Claude. 2009. "The 2004 GSS Finding of Shrunken Social Networks: An Artifact?" *American Sociological Review* 74(4): 657–669.

Fisher, Ronald A. 1925. *Statistical Methods for Research Workers.* Edinburgh: Oliver and Boyd.

Fisher, Ronald A. 1926. "The Arrangement of Field Experiments." *Journal of Ministry and Agriculture* XXXIII: 503–513.

Frank, Kenneth A. 2000. "Impact of a Confounding Variable on a Regression Coefficient." *Sociological Methods & Research* 29: 147–194.

Freedman, David A. 1983. "A Note on Screening Regression Equations." *The American Statistician* 37(2): 152–155.

Freeman, T., et al., 2020. "Why Do Some Countries Do Better or Worse in Life Expectancy Relative to Income? An Analysis of Brazil, Ethiopia, and the United States of America – International Journal for Equity in Health." *BioMed Central* (available at https://equityhealthj.biomedcentral.com/articles/10.1186/s12939-020-01315-z#Sec30)

Gelman, Andrew, and Jennifer Hill. 2006. *Data Analysis Using Regression and Multilevel/Hierarchical Models*. Cambridge: Cambridge University Press.

Gelman, Andrew, and Eric Loken. 2014. "The Statistical Crisis in Science." *American Scientist* 102(6): 460–465.

Gelman, Andrew and Hal Stern. 2006. "The Difference between 'Significant' and 'Not Significant' Is Not Itself Statistically Significant." *The American Statistician* 60(4): 328–331.

Gervais, Will M. and Ara Norenzayan. 2012. "Analytic Thinking Promotes Religious Disbelief." *Science* 336: 493–496.

Gilens, Martin, and Benjamin Page. 2014. "Testing Theories of American Politics: Elites, Interest Groups, and Average Citizens." *Perspectives on Politics* 12(3): 564–581.

Giolla, Erik Mac, Simon Karlsson, David Neequaye, and Magnus Bergquist. 2022. "Evaluating the Replicability of Social Priming Studies." Working Paper.

Glaeser, Edward. 2008. "Researcher Incentives and Empirical Methods." Pp. 300–319 in *Foundations of Positive and Normative Economics: A Handbook*, edited by Andrew Caplin and Andrew Schotter. Oxford: Oxford University Press.

Glenn, Norval. 2009. "Is the Apparent U-Shape of Well-Being Over the Life Course a Result of Inappropriate Use of Control Variables? A Commentary on Blanchflower and Oswald." *Social Science & Medicine* 69(4): 481–485.

Goffman, Erving. 1959. *The Presentation of Self in Everyday Life*. New York: Anchor Books.

Google. 2017. "Our Focus on Pay Equity." Retrieved March 13, 2018 www.blog.google/topics/diversity/our-focus-pay-equity/

Grant, Nico. 2022. "Google Agrees to Pay $118 Million to Settle Pay Discrimination Case." *New York Times*, June 12. www.nytimes.com/2022/06/12/business/google-discrimination-settlement-women.html

Greene, William. 2012. *Econometric Analysis* (7th ed.). Boston: Prentice Hall.

Gribbin, John. 2009. *In Search of the Multiverse*. London: Penguin.

Hall, Brian D. and Yang Liu. 2022. "A Survey of Tasks and Visualizations in Multiverse Analysis Reports." *Computer Graphics Forum* 41(1): 402–426.

Hanel, Paul H. P. and Natalia Zarzeczna. 2023. "From Multiverse Analysis to Multiverse Operationalizations: 262,143 Ways of Measuring Well-Being." *Religion, Brain, and Behavior* 13(3): 309–313.

Hansen, Bruce. 2005. "Challenges for Econometric Model Selection." *Econometric Theory* 21: 60–68.

Harder, Jenna A. 2020. "The Multiverse of Methods: Extending the Multiverse Analysis to Address Data-Collection Decisions." *Perspectives on Psychological Science* 15(5): 1158–1177.
Heckman, James. 2005. "The Scientific Model of Causality." *Sociological Methodology* 35(1): 1–97.
Heckman, James and Salvador Navarro-Lozano. 2004. "Using Matching, Instrumental Variables, and Control Functions to Estimate Economic Choice Models." *The Review of Economics and Statistics* 86(1): 30–57.
Heckman, James J., and Edward E. Leamer (eds.). 2007. *Handbook of Econometrics*. Volume 6, Part B. Amsterdam: Elsevier.
Herndon, Thomas, Michael Ash, and Robert Pollin. 2014. "Does High Public Debt Consistently Stifle Economic Growth? A Critique of Reinhart and Rogoff." *Cambridge Journal of Economics* 38(2): 257–279.
Herrala, Kaspian. 2023. "Does Industrial Development Predict Equalization in Educational Opportunity? A Multiverse Analysis." *Research in Social Stratification and Mobility* 83: 100757.
Hirschman, Daniel. 2021. "Rediscovering the 1%: Knowledge Infrastructure and the Stylized Facts of Inequality." *American Journal of Sociology* 127(3): 695–1036.
Ho, Daniel, Kosuke Imai, Gary King, and Elizabeth Stuart. 2007. "Matching as Nonparametric Preprocessing for Reducing Model Dependence in Parametric Causal Inference." *Political Analysis* 15: 199–236.
Hofman, Jake, Amit Sharma, and Duncan Watts. 2017. "Prediction and Explanation in Social Systems." *Science* 355: 486–488.
Holland, Paul W. 1986. "Statistics and Causal Inference." *Journal of the American Statistical Association* 81(396): 945–960.
Huber, Christoph, Anna Dreber, Jürgen Huber, and Felix Holzmeister. 2023. "Competition and Moral Behavior: A Meta-Analysis of Forty-Five Crowd-Sourced Experimental Designs." *PNAS* 120(3): e2215572120.
Huedo-Medina, Tania B., Julio Sánchez-Meca, Fulgencio Marin-Martinez, and Juan Botella. 2006. "Assessing Heterogeneity in Meta-Analysis: Q Statistic or I^2 Index?" *Psychological Methods* 11(2): 193–206.
Huntington-Klein, Nick, Andreu Arenas, Emily Beam, Marco Bertoni, Jeffrey R. Bloem, Pralhad Burli, Naibin Chen, Paul Grieco, Godwin Ekpe, Todd Pugatch, Martin Saavedra, and Yaniv Stopnitzky. 2021. "The Influence of Hidden Researcher Decisions in Applied Microeconomics." *Economic Inquiry* 59(3): 944–960.
Iacus, Stefano, Gary King, and Giuseppe Porro. 2012. "Causal Inference without Balance Checking: Coarsened Exact Matching." *Political Analysis* 20(1): 1–24.
Imbens, Guido. 2015. "Matching Methods in Practice: Three Examples." *Journal of Human Resources* 50: 373–419.
Ioannidis, John. 2005. "Why Most Published Research Findings Are False." *PLoS Med* 2(8): e124.
Jasso, Guillermina. 1985. "Marital Coital Frequency and the Passage of Time: Estimating the Separate Effects of Spouses' Ages and Marital Duration, Birth and Marriage Cohorts, and Period Influences." *American Sociological Review* 50(2): 224–241.

Jasso, Guillermina. 1986. "Is It Outlier Deletion or Is It Sample Truncation? Notes on Science and Sexuality (Reply to Kahn and Udry)." *American Sociological Review* 51(5): 738–742.

Jung, Kiju, Sharon Shavitt, Madhu Viswanathan, and Joseph M. Hilbe. 2014a. "Female Hurricanes Are Deadlier than Male Hurricanes." *PNAS* 111(24): 8782–8787.

Jung, Kiju, Sharon Shavitt, Madhu Viswanathan, and Joseph M. Hilbe. 2014b. "Reply to Christensen and Christensen and to Malter: Pitfalls of Erroneous Analyses of Hurricane Names." *PNAS* 111(34): E3499–3500.

Jung, Kiju, Sharon Shavitt, Madhu Viswanathan, and Joseph M. Hilbe. 2014c. "Reply to Maley: Yes, Appropriate Modeling of Hurricane Fatality Counts Confirms Female Hurricanes Are Deadlier." *PNAS* 111(37): E3835.

Kahn, Joan R. and J. Richard Udry 1986. "Marital Coital Frequency: Unnoticed Outliers and Unspecified Interactions Lead to Erroneous Conclusions." *American Sociological Review* 51(5): 734–737.

Karlson, Kristian. 2021. "Is Denmark a Much More Educationally Mobile Society than the United States? Comment on Andrade and Thomsen, 'Intergenerational Educational Mobility in Denmark and the United States' (2018)." *Sociological Science* 8: 346–358.

Karraker, Amelia, and Kenzie Latham. 2015a. "In Sickness and in Health? Physical Illness as a Risk Factor for Marital Dissolution in Later Life." *Journal of Health and Social Behavior* 56(1): 59–73.

Karraker, Amelia, and Kenzie Latham. 2015b. "Authors' Explanation of the Retraction." *Journal of Health and Social Behavior* 56(3): 417–419. https://doi.org/10.1177/0022146515595817

Kennedy, Courtney, and Hannah Hartig. 2019. "Response Rates in Telephone Surveys Have Resumed Their Decline." Pew Research Center. February 27.

King, Gary. 1991. "'Truth' Is Stranger than Prediction, More Questionable than Causal Inference." *American Journal of Political Science* 35: 1047–1053.

King, Gary, and Richard Nielsen. 2019. "Why Propensity Scores Should Not Be Used for Matching." *Political Analysis* 27(4): 435–454.

King, Gary, and Langche Zeng. 2001. "Logistic Regression in Rare Events Data." *Political Analysis* 9(2): 137–163.

King, Gary, and Langche Zeng. 2006. "The Dangers of Extreme Counterfactuals." *Political Analysis* 14: 131–159.

Kjelsrud, Anders, Andreas Kotsadam, and Ole Rogeberg. 2023. "Cooperative Property Rights and Development: Evidence from Land Reform in El Salvador: A Comment." I4R Discussion Paper Series, No. 20, Institute for Replication.

Klau, Simon, Felix D. Schönbrodt, Chirag J. Patel, John Ioannidis, Anne-Laure Boulesteix, and Sabine Hoffmann. 2023. "Comparing the Vibration of Effects Due to Model, Data Pre-Processing and Sampling Uncertainty on a Large Data Set in Personality Psychology." *Meta-Psychology* 7(6).

LaLonde, Robert. 1986. "Evaluating the Econometric Evaluations of Training Programs with Experimental Data." *American Economic Review* 76(4): 604–620.

Leahey, Erin. 2008. "Overseeing Research Practice: The Case of Data Editing." *Science, Technology, & Human Values* 33(5): 605–630.

Leahey, Erin, Barbara Entwisle, and Peter Einaudi. 2003. "Diversity in Everyday Research Practice: The Case of Data Editing." *Sociological Methods and Research* 32(1): 64–89.

Leamer, Edward E. 1983. "Let's Take the Con Out of Econometrics." *American Economic Review* 73(1): 31–43.

Leamer, Edward E. 1985. "Sensitivity Analyses Would Help." *American Economic Review* 75(3): 308–313.

Lechner, Michael. 2008. "A Note on Endogenous Control Variables in Causal Studies." *Statistics & Probability Letters* 78(2): 190–195.

Legewie, Joscha. 2019. "Retraction of the Research Article: 'Police Violence and the Health of Black Infants'." *Science Advances* 5(12): eaba5491.

Lenz, Gabriel S., and Alexander Sahn. 2021. "Achieving Statistical Significance with Control Variables and without Transparency." *Political Analysis* 29(3): 356–359.

Leonard, Megan de Linde, and Tom D. Stanley. 2020. "The Wages of Mothers' Labor: A Meta-Regression Analysis." *Journal of Marriage and Family* 82(5): 1534–1552.

Levitt, Michael, Francesco Zonta, and John P. A. Ioannidis. 2023. "Excess Death Estimates from Multiverse Analysis in 2009–2021." *European Journal of Epidemiology* 38(11): 1129–1139.

Liao, Hongjing, Yanju Li, and Gordon Brooks. 2016. "Outlier Impact and Accommodation Methods: Multiple Comparisons of Type I Error Rates." *Journal of Modern Applied Statistical Methods* 15(1): 452–471.

Liu, Yang, Alex Kale, Tim Althoff, and Jeffrey Heer. 2021. "Boba: Authoring and Visualizing Multiverse Analyses." *IEEE Transactions on Visualization and Computer Graphics* 27(2): 1753–1763.

Long, J. Scott. 1997. *Regression Models for Categorical and Limited Dependent Variables*. Thousand Oaks, CA: SAGE Publications.

Lubotsky, Darren, and Martin Wittenberg. 2006. "Interpretation of Regressions with Multiple Proxies." *The Review of Economics and Statistics* 88(3): 549–562.

Lundberg, Ian, Rebecca Johnson, and Brandon M. Stewart. 2021. "What Is Your Estimand? Defining the Target Quantity Connects Statistical Evidence to Theory." *American Sociological Review* 86(3): 532–565.

Magnus, Jan R., and Mary S. Morgan. 1997. "The Experiment in Applied Econometrics." *Journal of Applied Econometrics* 12(5): 459–661.

Maley, Steve. 2014. "Statistics Show No Evidence of Gender Bias in the Public's Hurricane Preparedness." *PNAS* 111(37): E3834.

Malter, Daniel. 2014. "Female Hurricanes Are Not Deadlier than Male Hurricanes." *PNAS* 111(34): E3496.

Marx, Karl and Friedrich Engels. 1844. "Critique of Hegel's Philosophy of Right." in *The Complete Works of Karl Marx*, Volume III, edited by Tim Newcomb (2023). Stuttgart: Newcomb Livraria Press.

Mazrekaj, Deni, Kristof De Witte, and Sofie Cabus. 2020. "School Outcomes of Children Raised by Same-Sex Parents: Evidence from Administrative Panel Data." *American Sociological Review* 85(5): 830–856.

Mazumder, Bhashkar. 2001. "Earnings Mobility in the U.S.: A New Look at Intergeneration Inequality." Federal Reserve Bank of Chicago working paper no. 2001-18.

Mazumder, Soumyajit. 2018. "The Persistent Effect of U.S. Civil Rights Protests on Political Attitudes." *American Journal of Political Science* 62: 922–935.

McCullagh, Peter, and John Nelder. 1989. *Generalized Linear Models (2nd ed.)*. Boca Raton, FL: Chapman and Hall/CRC.

McPherson, Miller, Lynn Smith-Lovin, and Matthew Brashears. 2006. "Social Isolation in America: Changes in Core Discussion Networks over Two Decades." *American Sociological Review* 71: 353–375.

McPherson, Miller, Lynn Smith-Lovin, and Matthew Brashears. 2008. "The Ties that Bind Are Fraying." *Contexts* 7(3): 32–36.

Mellers, Barbara, Ralph Hertwig, and Daniel Kahneman. 2001. "Do Frequency Representations Eliminate Conjunction Effects? An Exercise in Adversarial Collaboration." *Psychological Science* 12(4): 269–275.

Miguel, Edward. 2021. "Evidence on Research Transparency in Economics." *Journal of Economic Perspectives* 35(3): 193–214.

Miller, Michael K. 2020. "The Uses and Abuses of Matching in Political Science." Working Paper.

Mize, Trenton, Long Doan, and Scott Long. 2019. "A General Framework for Comparing Predictions and Marginal Effects across Models." *Sociological Methodology* 49(1): 152–189.

Modecki, Kathryn L., Samantha Low-Choy, Bep N. Uink, Lynette Vernon, Helen Correia, and Kylie Andrews. 2020. "Tuning Into the Real Effect of Smartphone Use on Parenting: A Multiverse Analysis." *Journal of Child Psychology and Psychiatry* 61(8): 855–865.

Molina, Mario, and Filiz Garip. 2019. "Machine Learning for Sociology." *Annual Reviews of Sociology* 45: 27–45.

Montero, Eduardo. 2022. "Cooperative Property Rights and Development: Evidence from Land Reform in El Salvador." *Journal of Political Economy* 130(1): 48–93.

Montero, Eduardo. 2023. "Erratum: Cooperative Property Rights and Development: Evidence from Land Reform in El Salvador." *Journal of Political Economy* 131(8): 2286–2287.

Montez, Jennifer Karas, Robert A. Hummer, and Mark D. Hayward. 2012. "Educational Attainment and Adult Mortality in the United States: A Systematic Analysis of Functional Form." *Demography* 49(1): 315–336.

Montgomery, Jacob M., Brendan Nyhan, and Michelle Torres. 2018. "How Conditioning on Post-treatment Variables Can Ruin Your Experiment and What to Do about It." *American Journal of Political Science* 62: 760–775.

Mood, Carina. 2010. "Logistic Regression: Why We Cannot Do What We Think We Can Do, and What We Can Do about It." *European Sociological Review* 26(1): 67–82.

Morgan, Stephen L. 2018. "Status Threat, Material Interests, and the 2016 Presidential Vote." *Socius: Sociological Research for a Dynamic World* 4: 1–17.

Morgan, Stephen L., and David Harding. 2006. "Matching Estimators of Causal Effects: Prospects and Pitfalls in Theory and Practice." *Sociological Methods and Research* 35(1): 3–60.

Morgan, Stephen L., and Christopher Winship. 2015. *Counterfactuals and Causal Inference*. Cambridge: Cambridge University Press.

Muñoz, John, and Cristobal Young. 2018a. "We Ran 9 Billion Regressions: Eliminating False Positives through Computational Model Robustness." *Sociological Methodology* 48(1): 1–33.

Muñoz, John, and Cristobal Young. 2018b. "Rejoinder: Can Models Be Weighted by Their Probability of Being True?" *Sociological Methodology* 48: 43–51.

Munnell, Alicia, Geoffery Tootell, Lynne Browne, and James McEneany. 1996. "Mortgage Lending in Boston: Interpreting HMDA Data." *American Economic Review* 86(1): 25–53.

Munsch, Christin L. 2015. "Her Support, His Support: Money, Masculinity, and Marital Infidelity." *American Sociological Review* 80(3): 469–495.

Neisser, Ulric, Gwyneth Boodoo, Thomas J. Bouchard Jr., A. Wade Boykin, Nathan Brody, Stephen J. Ceci, Diane F. Halpern, John C. Loehlin, Robert Perloff, Robert J. Sternberg, and Susana Urbina. 1996. "Intelligence: Knowns and Unknowns." *American Psychologist* 51(2): 77–101.

Neuendorf, Claudia and Malte Jansen. 2023. "Comparing Different Facets of the Social Integration of High-Achieving Students in Their Classroom: No Gender Stereotyping, but Some Nonlinear Relationships." *Journal of Educational Psychology* 115(4): 609–623.

Niedig, Harper. 2017. "Former Employees Sue Google for Gender Discrimination." *The Hill*, September 14.

O'Brien, Robert. 2018. "Comment: Some Challenges When Estimating the Impact of Model Uncertainty on Coefficient Instability." *Sociological Methodology* 48(1): 34–39.

Olsson-Collentine, Anton, Robbie C. M. van Aert, Marjan Bakker, and Jelte Wicherts. 2023. "Meta-Analyzing the Multiverse: A Peek under the Hood of Selective Reporting." *Psychological Methods*. Advance online publication. https://doi.org/10.1037/met0000559

Paik, Anthony, and Kenneth Sanchagrin. 2013. "Social Isolation in America: An Artifact." *American Sociological Review* 78(3): 339–360.

Payton, A. 2009. "The Impact of Genetic Research on Our Understanding of Normal Cognitive Ageing: 1995 to 2009." *Neuropsychology Review* 19: 451–477.

Pearl, Judea. 2011. "Understanding Bias Amplification." *American Journal of Epidemiology* 174(11): 1223–1227.

Pearl, Judea, and Dana Mackenzie. 2018. *The Book of Why: The New Science of Cause and Effect*. New York: Basic Books.

Perrin, Andrew J., Philip N. Cohen, and Neal Caren. 2013. "Are Children of Parents Who Had Same-Sex Relationships Disadvantaged? A Scientific Evaluation of the No-Differences Hypothesis." *Journal of Gay & Lesbian Mental Health* 17(3): 327–336.

Peterson, Richard R. 1996. "A Re-evaluation of the Economic Consequences of Divorce." *American Sociological Review* 61(3): 528–536.

Pew Research Center. 2018. "Wide Gender Gap, Growing Educational Divide in Voters' Party Identification." www.people-press.org/2018/03/20/1-trends-in-party-affiliation-among-demographic-groups/

Pfeffer, Fabian T., and Nora Waitkus. 2021. "The Wealth Inequality of Nations." *American Sociological Review* 86(4): 567–602.

Pinello, Daniel R. 1999. "Linking Party to Judicial Ideology in American Courts: A Meta-Analysis." *The Justice System Journal* 20(3): 219–254.

Prinz, Florian, Thomas Schlange, and Khusru Asadullah. 2011. "Believe It or Not: How Much Can We Rely on Published Data on Potential Drug Targets?" *Nature Reviews Drug Discovery* 10: 712–713.

Putnam, Robert D. 2000. *Bowling Alone: The Collapse and Revival of American Community*. New York, NY: Simon & Schuster.

Quillian, Lincoln, Devah Pager, Ole Hexel, and Arnfinn H. Midtbøen. 2017. "Meta-Analysis of Field Experiments Show No Change in Racial Discrimination in Hiring Over Time." *Proceedings of the National Academy of Sciences* 114(41): 10870–10875.

Raftery, Adrian. 1995. "Bayesian Model Selection in Social Research." *Sociological Methodology* 25: 111–165.

Reeves, Richard V., Sarah Nzau, and Ember Smith. 2020. "The Challenges Facing Black Men – and the Case for Action." Brookings. www.brookings.edu/articles/the-challenges-facing-black-men-and-the-case-for-action/

Regnerus, Mark. 2012a. "How Different Are the Adult Children of Parents Who Have Same-Sex Relationships? Findings from the New Family Structures Study." *Social Science Research* 41: 752–770.

Regnerus, Mark. 2012b. "Parental Same-Sex Relationships, Family Instability, and Subsequent Life Outcomes for Adult Children: Answering Critics of the New Family Structures Study with Additional Analyses." *Social Science Research* 41: 1367–1377.

Reinhart, Carmen M., and Kenneth S. Rogoff. 2010. "Growth in a Time of Debt." *American Economic Review* 100(2): 573–578.

Rengasamy, Manivel, Daniel Moriarity, Thomas Kraynak, Brenden Tervo-Clemmens, and Rebecca Price. 2023. "Exploring the Multiverse: The Impact of Researchers' Analytic Decisions on Relationships between Depression and Inflammatory Markers." *Neuropsychopharmacology* 48(10): 1465–1474.

Ripollone, John, Krista Huybrechts, Kenneth Rothman, Ryan Ferguson, and Jessica Franklin. 2020. "Evaluating the Utility of Coarsened Exact Matching for Pharmacoepidemiology Using Real and Simulated Claims Data." *American Journal of Epidemiology* 189(6): 613–622.

Robitzsch, Alexander. 2022. "On the Choice of the Item Response Model for Scaling PISA Data: Model Selection Based on Information Criteria and Quantifying Model Uncertainty." *Entropy* 24: 760–786.

Rohrer, Julia M. 2018. "Thinking Clearly about Correlations and Causation: Graphical Causal Models for Observational Data." *Advances in Methods and Practice in Psychological Sciences* 1(1): 27–42.

Rosenbaum, Paul R. 1984. "The Consequences of Adjustment for a Concomitant Variable That Has Been Affected by the Treatment." *Journal of the Royal Statistical Society* 147(5): 656–666.

Rosenfeld, Michael J. 2015. "Revisiting the Data from the New Family Structure Study: Taking Family Instability into Account." *Sociological Science* 2: 478–501.

Sala-i-Martin, Xavier X. 1997. "I Just Ran Four Million Regressions." National Bureau of Economic Research Working Paper 6252.

Sala-i-Martin, Xavier X., Gernot Doppelhofer, and Ronald Miller. 2004. "Determinants of Long-term Growth: A Bayesian Averaging of Classical Estimates Approach." *American Economic Review* 94: 813–835.

Santos Silva, João M. C., and Silvana Tenreyro. 2006. "The Log of Gravity." *Review of Economics and Statistics* 88(4): 641–658.

Saraceno, Joseph, Eric R. Hansen, and Sarah A. Treul. 2021. "Reevaluating the Substantive Representation of Lesbian, Gay, and Bisexual Americans: A Multiverse Analysis." *Journal of Politics* 83(4): 1837–1843.

Sarma, Abhraneel, Alex Kale, Michael Moon, Nathan Taback, Fanny Chevalier, Jessica Hullman, and Matthew Kay. 2023. "Multiverse: Multiplexing Alternative Data Analyses in R Notebooks." CHI '23: Proceedings of the 2023 CHI Conference on Human Factors in Computing Systems.

Schupbach, Jonah N. 2018. "Robustness Analysis as Explanatory Reasoning." *British Journal for the Philosophy of Science* 69(1): 275–300.

Schweinsberg, Martin, Michael Feldman, Nicola Staub, Olmo R. van den Akker, Robbie C. M. van Aert, Marcel A. L. M. van Assen, Yang Liu, Tim Althoff, Jeffrey Heer, Alex Kale, Zainab Mohamed, Hashem Amireh, Vaishali Venkatesh Prasad, Abraham Bernstein, Emily Robinson, Kaisa Snellman, S. Amy Sommer, Sarah M. G. Otner, David Robinson ... Eric Luis Uhlmann. 2021. "Same Data, Different Conclusions: Radical Dispersion in Empirical Results When Independent Analysts Operationalize and Test the Same Hypothesis." *Organizational Behavior and Human Decision Processes* 165: 228–249.

Sen, Amartya. 1999. *Development as Freedom*. New York: Alfred Knopf.

Seng, You Poh. 1951. "Historical Survey of the Development of Sampling Theories and Practice." *Journal of the Royal Statistical Society. Series A (General)* 114(2): 214–231.

Sharkey, Patrick, and Felix Elwert. 2011. "The Legacy of Disadvantage: Multigenerational Neighborhood Effects on Cognitive Ability." *American Journal of Sociology* 116(6): 1934–1981.

Sherkat, Darren E. 2012. "The Editorial Process and Politicized Scholarship: Monday Morning Editorial Quarterbacking and a Call for Scientific Vigilance." *Social Science Research* 41(6): 1346–1349.

Shmueli, Galit. 2010. "To Explain or to Predict?" *Statistical Science* 25(3): 289–310.

Silberzahn, Raphael, Eric Luis Uhlmann, David P. Martin, Paola Anselmi, Frederik Aust, Eli Awtrey, ... Brian A. Nosek. 2018. "Many Analysts, One Data Set: Making Transparent How Variations in Analytic Choices Affect Results." *Advances in Methods and Practices in Psychological Science* 1(3): 337–356.

Simmons, Joseph P., Leif D. Nelson, and Uri Simonsohn. 2011. "False-Positive Psychology: Undisclosed Flexibility in Data Collection and Analysis Allows Presenting Anything as Significant." *Psychological Science* 22(11): 1359–1366.

Simonsohn, Uri, Joseph P. Simmons, and Leif D. Nelson. 2020. "Specification Curve Analysis." *Nature Human Behavior* 4: 1208–1214.

Slez, Adam. 2018. "The Difference between Instability and Uncertainty: Comment on Young and Holsteen (2017)." *Sociological Methods and Research* 48(2): 400–430.

Solon, Gary. 1992. "Intergenerational Income Mobility in the United States." *American Economic Review* 82(3): 393–408.

Solon, Gary, Steven J. Haider, and Jeffrey M. Wooldridge. 2015. "What Are We Weighting For?" *Journal of Human Resources* 50(2): 301–316.

Stanley, Tom D., and Hristos Doucouliagos. 2012. *Meta-Regression Analysis in Economics and Business.* New York: Routledge.

Steegen, Sara, Francis Tuerlinckx, Andrew Gelman, and Wolf Vanpaemel. 2016. "Increasing Transparency through a Multiverse Analysis." *Perspectives on Psychological Science* 11(5): 702–712.

Strevens, Michael. 2020. *The Knowledge Machine: How irrationality Created Modern Science.* New York: Liveright Publishing.

Stuart, Elizabeth A. 2010. "Matching Methods for Causal Inference: A Review and a Look Forward." *Statistical Science* 25(1): 1–21.

Student. 1908. "The Probable Error of a Mean." *Biometrika* 6(1): 1–25.

Sullivan, Joe H., Merrill Warkentin, and Linda Wallace. 2021. "So Many Ways for Assessing Outliers: What Really Works and Does It Matter?" *Journal of Business Research* 132: 530–543.

Sunyer, Jordi, Elisabet Suades-González, Raquel García-Esteban, Ioar Rivas, Jesús Pujol, Mar Alvarez-Pedrerol, Joan Forns, Xavier Querol, and Xavier Basagaña. 2017. "Traffic-related Air Pollution and Attention in Primary School Children: Short-term Association." *Epidemiology* 28(2): 181–189.

Urminsky, Oleg, Christian Hansen, and Victor Chernozhukov. 2016. "Using Double-Lasso Regression for Principled Variable Selection." University of Chicago Working Paper.

van Raalte, Alyson A., and Hal Caswell. 2013. "Perturbation Analysis of Indices of Lifespan Variability." *Demography* 50(5): 1615–1640.

VanderWeele, Tyler J. 2011. "Sensitivity Analysis for Contagion Effects in Social Networks." *Sociological Methods and Research* 40: 240–255.

Veroniki, Areti Angeliki, Dan Jackson, Wolfgang Viechtbauer, Ralf Bender, Jack Bowden, Guido Knapp, Oliver Kuss, Julian P. T. Higgins, Dean Langan, and Georgia Salanti. 2016. "Methods to Estimate the between-Study Variance and Its Uncertainty in Meta-Analysis." *Research Synthesis Methods* 7(1): 55–79.

Weber, Max. 1904. *The Protestant Ethic and the Spirit of Capitalism.* New York: Scribner.

Weitzman, Lenore J. 1985. *The Divorce Revolution: The Unexpected Social and Economic Consequences for Women and Children.* New York: The Free Press.

Weitzman, Lenore J. 1996. "The Economic Consequences of Divorce Are Still Unequal: Comment on Peterson." *American Sociological Review* 61(3): 537.

Western, Bruce. 1996. "Vague Theory and Model Uncertainty in Macrosociology." *Sociological Methodology* 26: 165–192.

Western, Bruce. 2018. "Comment: Bayes, Model Uncertainty, and Learning from Data." *Sociological Methodology* 48(1): 39–43.

Whitehouse, Harvey, Pieter François, Patrick E. Savage, Thomas E. Currie, Kevin C. Feeney, Enrico Cioni, Rosalind Purcell, Robert M. Ross, Jennifer

Larson, John Baines, Barend ter Haar, Alan Covey, and Peter Turchin. 2019. "RETRACTED ARTICLE: Complex Societies Precede Moralizing Gods throughout World History." *Nature* 568: 226–229.

Wildeman, Christopher, and Kristin Turney. 2014. "Positive, Negative, or Null? The Effects of Maternal Incarceration on Children's Behavioral Problems." *Demography* 51(3): 1041–1068.

Wildeman, Christopher, Robert Sampson, and Garrett Baker. 2023. "Adult Children of the Prison Boom: Family Troubles and the Intergenerational Transmission of Criminal Justice Contact." Working Paper.

Williams, Richard. 2011. "Using the Margins Command to Estimate and Interpret Adjusted Predictions and Marginal Effects." *Stata Journal* 12(2): 308–331.

Winship, Christopher, and Larry Radbill. 1994. "Sampling Weights and Regression Analysis." *Sociological Methods & Research* 23(2): 230–257.

Winship, Christopher, and Bruce Western. 2016. "Multicollinearity and Model Misspecification." *Sociological Science* 3: 627–649.

Wooldridge, Jeffrey. 2007. "Inverse Probability Weighted Estimation for General Missing Data Problems." *Journal of Econometrics* 141(2): 1281–1301.

Wooldridge, Jeffrey. 2011. "Fractional Response Models with Endogenous Explanatory Variables and Heterogeneity." Unpublished. www.stata.com/meeting/chicago11/materials/chi11_wooldridge.pdf

Wootton, David. 2015. *The Invention of Science: A New History of the Scientific Revolution*. New York: Harper Perennial.

Wysocki, Anna C., Katherine M. Lawson, and Mijke Rhemtulla. 2022. "Statistical Control Requires Causal Justification." *Advances in Methods and Practices in Psychological Science* 5(2): 1–19.

York, Richard. 2018. "Control Variables and Causal Inference: A Question of Balance." *International Journal of Social Research Methodology* 21(6): 675–684.

Young, Cristobal. 2009. "Model Uncertainty in Sociological Research: An Application to Religion and Economic Growth." *American Sociological Review* 74: 380–397.

Young, Cristobal. 2012. "Losing a Job: The Nonpecuniary Cost of Unemployment in the United States." *Social Forces* 91(2): 609–633.

Young, Cristobal. 2018. "Model Uncertainty and the Crisis in Science." *Socius: Sociological Research for a Dynamic World* 4: 1–7.

Young, Cristobal, and Kathleen Holsteen. 2017. "Model Uncertainty and Robustness: A Computational Framework for Multimodel Analysis." *Sociological Methods and Research* 46(1): 3–40.

Young, Cristobal, and Katherine Holsteen. 2021. "MULTIVRS: Stata Module to Conduct Multiverse Analysis." Statistical Software Components S458927, Boston College Department of Economics, revised April 15, 2021.

Young, Cristobal, and Sheridan Stewart. 2021. "Functional Form Robustness: Advancements in Multiverse Analysis." Working Paper. Cornell University.

Yuling, Yao, Vehtari Aki, Simpson Daniel, and Gelman Andrew. 2018. "Using Stacking to Average Bayesian Predictive Distributions." https://projecteuclid.org/euclid.ba/1516093227.

Ziliak, Stephen T., and Deirdre N. McCloskey. 2008. *The Cult of Statistical Significance: How the Standard Error Costs Us Jobs, Justice, and Lives.* Ann Arbor: University of Michigan Press.

Zimmerman, David J. 1992. "Regression toward Mediocrity in Economic Stature." *American Economic Review* 82(3): 409–429.

Zipf, George Kingsley. 1946. "The P_1P_2/D Hypothesis: On the Intercity Movement of Persons." *American Sociological Review* 11(6): 677–686.

Zoorob, Michael. 2020. "Do Police Brutality Stories Reduce 911 Calls? Reassessing an Important Criminological Finding." *American Sociological Review* 85(1): 176–183.

Index

adversarial collaboration, 5, 7–8
air pollution and student attention span, 215–223
anomalous observations. *See* outliers and anomalous observations
Apple pay equity analysis, 102
asymmetric information, 4, 13–17, 126, 226–227
Athey and Imbens robustness measure, 117–118
auxiliary assumptions, 25–28, 154

Bayesian model averaging (BMA), 209–212, 219, 221–225
Blanchflower and Oswald, study on wellbeing, 105–106
Borges, Jorge Luis, *The Garden of Forking Paths*, 4, 32–33

capital punishment and deterrence, 29–30
censuses versus sampling, 43–45
coding errors
  in GDP growth study, 200
  in gray divorce study, 202–203
  in Latin American land reform study, 204–205
  in marital infidelity study, 201–202
  in moralizing gods study, 203
  in police violence study, 168
collider variables, 103–108
confidence intervals, 5, 46–50
  compared to modeling distributions, 63, 65, 91–92, 161, 180

confounding variables, 82, 92–94, 98–102, 109–110, 211–213
control variables
  influence analysis of, 73–74
  necessary controls, 55–58
  number of, 82, 90, 139, 142–143, 151
  order of inclusion, 74
  overuse of, 98–99, 109–111
  selection of, 111, 113
Cook's D analysis, 75, 171–172
crisis in science, 14, 18, 24, 125, 149, 160, 226
crowdsourcing studies. *See* many-analyst studies

dark matter (of research), 157, 175, 205
data processing decisions, 154–176
double lasso model selection, 214, 216–217
double lasso weights, 219, 221, 223, 225
Durante, Kristina, study on fertility and voting, 158–163

Engzell and Mood, study on social mobility, 71–72
estimand consistency, 55–58
Excel, 6, 200
experimental vs. nonexperimental data. *See* job training program effectiveness

false positives, 15–16, 44, 99, 112
fertility and voting. *See* Durante, Kristina

Freedman's screening regression, 111–112
functional form, 8, 126–127, 129–153

gay/lesbian parenting study, 177–198
Gelman, Andrew, 9, 210
Google pay equity analysis, 101–102

hurricane names, 37–42, 116

influence analysis, 8, 70–76
  empirical examples, 40, 76–92, 142, 150–153, 159–162, 189–193
influence effects, 72–76
  empirical examples, 77–81, 87–89, 150–151, 153
influence regression, 75–76
  empirical examples, 81–82, 89–90
influence weights, 219–221, 223
interviewer fatigue, 203–204
inverse probability weighting, 133
iterative model refinement. See Freedman's screening regression

Jasso, Guillermina, study on sexual frequency, 156–157, 169
job loss and wellbeing, 137–140, 150–151
job training program effectiveness, 66–69, 86–92

Leahey, Erin, 13, 154–156, 170
Leamer, Edward, 3, 29–30, 44, 57, 149
least absolute deviation (LAD) regression, 171–172
listwise deletion, 133, 193
logistic regression, 133–134

many-analyst studies, 5–8, 47–50, 127, 144–147, 156
marginal effects, 130, 135–136
marital separation study, 157–158
matching methods, 131–133
mediator variables, 100–103
meta-analysis, 5, 46–47, 74–75
meta-regression analysis, 74–75
missing data, 62, 193
model error (general concept), 5, 9, 45, 206–207
model fit, 209–219, 223. See also Bayesian model averaging (BMA)
model influence. See influence effects

model selection vs. robustness, 118–121, 219, 223–224
model space, 52–53
modeling distribution, 8–9, 51–54, 128–130
  empirical examples, 39, 62–66, 68, 137–138, 140–142, 145, 187–188
modeling standard error, 52–54, 130
  empirical examples, 62, 64, 67–68, 137, 145, 181
mortgage lending
  gender discrimination, 64–66, 76–86, 117
  race discrimination, 59–63, 76–84, 117
motivated reasoning, 24, 128, 143, 226
multiple imputation, 193
multiverse
  algorithm, 50–55
  central theorem of, 9
  control variable multiverse, 128–129, 181
  evaluating accuracy of, 147
  terminology, 4, 9–11, 31–33

outliers and anomalous observations, 156–157, 172
  examples, 40–42, 181–183, 200–201, 203–204

panel attrition, 202
peer review process, 155–156
p-hacking, 14
prediction versus inference, 119–120, 211–214
preregistration, 149–150
proportional vs. exponential model weights, 210, 219, 221, 225
proxy variables, 108–109

Regnerus, Mark, study on gay/lesbian parenting, 177–198
replication, 15–23, 176, 195, 197
researcher degrees of freedom, 24, 56, 127, 148
robust regression, 172
robustness footnotes, 5, 18
robustness ratio, 54
  empirical examples, 63–64, 188
Rosenfeld, Michael, 177–198

sample weights, 172–175, 190–192
sampling distribution, 44, 50–54

Index

saving the hypothesis, 25, 29, 155, 206
scale of coefficients, 134–136
scope conditions, methodological, 71–72, 96
sensitivity analysis, 92–94
versus influence analysis, 95–96
sign stability. *See* vote count measures
significance rate. *See* vote count measures
Silberzahn, Raphael, study on soccer penalties, 48, 127, 144–147
soccer penalties and skin tone. *See* Silberzahn, Raphael, study on soccer penalties
specification curve, 115–117
Stata, 59–62
Student t statistic, 44
subjectivity (of science), 3, 24–25, 30
super log file approach, 6–7
suppression effects, 82–84

task force approach, 7–8
total standard error, 53
empirical examples, 63–64
Trump voting patterns, 135–136, 140–143, 153

uniform model weights, 208, 219, 221

vague theory, 27–28, 56, 154
variable construction, 164–168
in study of fertility and voting, 161–162
in study of gay/lesbian parenting, 183–184
vote count measures, 54
empirical examples, 63–64, 67–68, 84, 188

wellbeing and the life cycle. *See* Blanchflower and Oswald, study on wellbeing
winsorization, 171–172
examples, 40, 192

For EU product safety concerns, contact us at Calle de José Abascal, 56–1°,
28003 Madrid, Spain or eugpsr@cambridge.org.

www.ingramcontent.com/pod-product-compliance
Lightning Source LLC
LaVergne TN
LVHW011808060526
838200LV00053B/3698